To: Debbi & Larry
who love the earth and
all God's creatures!

Love, Mom & Dad

D1560469

Asked to address a Montana booster meeting
shortly before his death in 1926, the old man was
horrified to hear himself introduced as a "pioneer."
Misty-eyed, he roared:

In my book, a pioneer is a man who comes to a virgin country, traps off all the fur, kills off all the wild meat, cuts down all the trees, grazes off all the grass, plows the roots up, and strings ten million miles of bob wire. A pioneer destroys things and calls it civilization. I wish to God that this country was just like it was when I first saw it, and that none of you folks were here at all!

Charles M. Russell

(from *Three Hundred Years of American Painting,* Time, Inc., New York)

Wolves, Bears and Bighorns

Wilderness Observations and Experiences of a Professional Outdoorsman

John S. Crawford

ALASKA NORTHWEST PUBLISHING COMPANY
Anchorage, Alaska

For my mother and father

Published November 1980
Second printing January 1981

Library of Congress Cataloging in Publication Data

Crawford, John S
  Wolves, bears, and bighorns.

  1. Crawford, John S.   2. Zoology—Northwest,
Pacific. 3. Zoology—Alaska. 4. Zoologists—
Washington (State)—Biography. 5. Authors,
American—Washington (State)—Biography.   I. Title.
QL31.C78A35   590'.92'4 [B]   80-22007
ISBN 0-88240-146-7
ISBN 0-88240-114-0 (pbk.)

Photographs by the author, except as noted
Design and Cartographics by Jon.Hersh

Alaska Northwest Publishing Company
Box 4-EEE, Anchorage, Alaska 99509

Printed in U.S.A.

Contents

v

The Lakota . . . loved the earth and all things of the earth . . .
Luther Standing Bear of the Lakota Sioux
(*The Indians,*
Time-Life Books, Alexandria, Virginia)

Have you ever stood where the silences brood,
And vast the horizons begin,
At the dawn of the day to behold far away
The goal you would strive for and win?
From "The Land of Beyond" by Robert Service
(*The Best of Robert Service,*
Dodd, Mead and Company, New York)

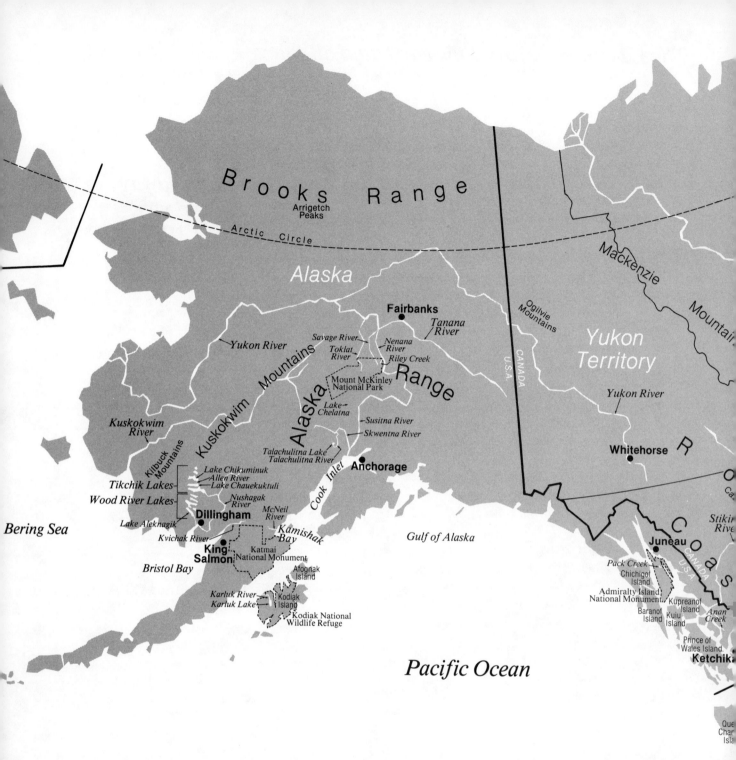

Brooks Range

Arrigetch
Peaks

Arctic Circle

Mackenzie

Alaska

Ogilvie
Mountains

Fairbanks

Tanana
River

Yukon River

Savage River

Nenana
River

Toklat
River

Riley Creek

Yukon
Territory

Kuskokwim

Mountains

Mount McKinley
National Park

Alaska

Range

U.S.A.

CANADA

Kuskokwim
River

Lake
Chelatna

Susitna River

Yukon River

Skwentna River

Whitehorse

Kilbuck
Mountains

Talachulitna Lake
Talachulitna River

R

Lake Chikuminuk

Tikchik Lakes

Allen River

Lake Chauekuktuli

Anchorage

Co

Wood River Lakes

Nushagak
River

McNeil
River

Cook Inlet

Gulf of Alaska

Stikir
Rive

Bering Sea

Lake Aleknagik

Dillingham

Kvichak River

Kamishak
Bay

CANADA
U.S.A.

Juneau

Pack Creek

as

King
Salmon

Katmai
National Monument

Chichigof
Island

Bristol Bay

Afognak
Island

Admiralty Island
National Monument

Kupreanof
Island

Baranof
Island

Kuiu
Island

Anan
Creek

Karluk River

Kodiak
Island

Karluk Lake

Kodiak National
Wildlife Refuge

Prince of
Wales Island

Ketchika

Pacific Ocean

Que
Char
Isla

Previous page — The great limestone face of Roche
Miette, famed landmark of the old Athabasca Trail,
towers over the Athabasca River valley. Photographed in
mid-April, with a band of bighorn sheep in the
foreground.

Northwest Territories

Great
Lake

Yellowknife

Great
Slave Lake

Mackenzie
River

Saskatchewan

Wood Buffalo
National Park

iard
iver

Prophet
River

Muskwa
River

Peace
River

Athabasca
River

Alberta

North Fork
Saskatchewan River

Regina

R o c k y

Missouri
River

"Big"
Smoky
River

Edmonton

South Fork
Saskatchewan River

Skeena
River

British
Columbia

Snake Indian
River

Brazeau
River

Jasper
National Park

Sunwapta
River

Banff
National Park

Whirlpool
River

Chaba
River

Banff

M
o
u
n
t
a
i
n
s

Jasper

Revelstoke
National Park

Kootenay
National Park

Revelstoke

Fraser
River

Monashee Mountains

Selkirk Mountains

CANADA
U.S.A.

Montana

Yellowstone
River

Absaroka Range

Thompson
River

Kootenay
River

i

Helena

Gallatin Range

Casper

Vancouver

Vancouver Island

Cascade Mountains

Yellowstone
National Park

Wyoming

Seattle

Washington

Wallowa
Mountains

Idaho

Olympic
National Park

Olympic
Mhs.

Columbia
River

Scale

|🏁|===|200 miles|

|===|200 kilometers|

National Parks, Monuments and Wildlife Refuges
referred to in the text are delineated by dotted lines

Portland

Oregon

Boise

Foreword:
Thoughts
on the
Way Home

December 1979—Blue River, BC

The snowflakes, sweeping toward me on the wind, are almost hypnotic in their swirling concentration. It's early afternoon, the road is getting bad, and sometimes I feel my tires — studded but well worn — start to lose traction. Two hours or so before, I crossed Yellowhead Pass over the Continental Divide and the British Columbia-Alberta boundary, then at Tete Jaune Cache Junction turned off Trans-Canada Highway 16 and down the valley of the North Thompson. Oncoming headlights crest a rise. I slow down even more to 25. **How can he see to drive that fast,** I wonder. A truck and trailer rig roars by, and my little Rambler station wagon is enveloped in a blinding, swirling whiteout. **Hell with this,** I think; **I'll just go on to Blue, and wait it out there till the plows and sand trucks go to work.**

I pull off the highway at Blue River, British Columbia, and drive to the hotel for coffee and a late lunch. I'm on my way home to the Seattle area for Christmas. For 17 years since I left government service to work for myself as a free-lance nature photo-journalist I've flown, driven or trained from somewhere in western Canada or Alaska to be home sometime during the mid-winter holidays, not always making it for Christmas. I tend to cut it close on time, working late into December, because of critical field observations that I often make in early winter — particularly predator-prey interaction between wolves and elk, moose, mule deer, and bighorn sheep. It used to be, when driving, that I always made it home in time, no matter what the weather and road conditions were. Now, if driving conditions are dangerous, I just phone home, sit tight and wait it out — a few hours or a couple of days. Several years ago I enjoyed a lovely old fashioned Christmas — straight out of a Norman Rockwell cover — in a tiny community in northern Saskatchewan.

Having experienced 11 bone fractures, severe concussions, and frostbite in three mountain accidents — one time regaining consciousness on a ledge in Southeastern Alaska, alone, with a split scalp, broken arm, and compressed vertebra, thinking it was surely my day to take the Long Journey, but managing somehow to pick my way down the last 1,500 feet of the mountain — and having been close enough to a truculent grizzly that I could, quite literally, have reached out and touched his nose, I think, perhaps, that I can draw some reasonable conclusions on comparative risk. I'm convinced that the most dangerous moments I've ever experienced have been on icy mountain highways trying to get somewhere at a specific time — not so much from the roads themselves, but from other drivers who have unrealistic ideas of their winter driving skill and of the effective traction of their tires.

In the Blue River Hotel coffee shop a recorded Christmas carol ends and a softly played tape of Anne Murray singing *Snowbird* comes on. I relax, sipping good fresh coffee, feeling the built-up tension of storm driving ebbing away. I enjoy a hot roast beef sandwich with salad, and finish lunch with a wedge of mince pie and more coffee. I think about who I've yet to get a gift for, friends still to send cards to, and suddenly recall — with a sigh — that I'm scheduled to give a couple of wildlife slide lectures in early January (I'm perplexed sometimes at the esoteric fascination some people — particularly camera club members — have for photographic equipment and exposure data — as if that was all there was to it. To some of these people, if they know what the *f*/stops and shutter speeds were, what cameras, lenses, filters and films were used, the **logistics** of a wilderness trip — how the field cameraman got into Back and Beyond, did the job, and got back out to civilization in one reasonably intact piece — are apparently of little concern.)

I look out at the falling snow and think back over nearly two decades of working for myself as a wildlife cameraman-nature writer. Has it really been worth it? From a financial point of view . . . no, hardly. There's been some degree of self-imposed hardship, and a lot of tough and dangerous work. Broken bone injuries have delayed planned projects for many months. But, too, there have been beautiful moments in my work that I hadn't counted on or even thought of.

In the late autumn-early winter of '65 I worked 10 weeks in the Canadian Rockies to film a bighorn ram duel. I wanted to photograph this sequence — which appears with the chapter *At Home with the High Ones* — with the knowledge and acceptance of the rams, and without using a telephoto lens. After selecting the specific mountain area and locating a band of bighorns that I felt offered the greatest potential for the photo sequence I was after — several competing mature rams of nearly equal horn growth and body weight, day by day I worked closer to the rams, staying from first daylight to dusk, working in every condition of winter weather from comparatively balmy temperatures just below freezing into cold well below zero, on many days not shooting a single exposure but just observing and waiting.

Over the weeks I was accepted more completely than I ever would have imagined. During the bighorn breeding season, before a serious fight gets underway, the challenging act of one ram to another — and it's as ritualistic as a pistol duel or a cavalry drill — is to stand up almost erect on the hind hoofs, cock the heavy-horned head slightly to the side and take several steps toward the intended adversary. If the challenge is accepted there is immediate head-crashing combat; if declined, the challenging ram will simply drop down on four hoofs. A dramatic and unforgettable moment came when a great ram actually challenged **me** to a duel in this manner during a momentary lull while I was photographing bighorn combat. At the time, it didn't seem strange at all, and I felt greatly flattered. The rams had apparently come to feel over the weeks of our association that I would be a worthy antagonist!

But, of course, I chickened out. Envisioning myself tumbling down the mountain slope with a concussion and a half-dozen broken ribs, I stood very still. The challenging ram dropped down on his front hoofs, and for a long moment eyed me sternly with every evidence of baleful disdain.

And there was the great, grizzled-black wolf back in the early spring of '73. While working in the Alberta Rockies out of a patrol cabin northwest of the confluence of Moosehorn Creek and the Athabasca River, I'd sighted the wolf several times from late fall through early March, but never any closer than about 200 yards. The big black was an old loner, probably with well-worn teeth, perhaps a one-time pack leader, separated from his former pack now as something of a social outcast, probably through a shift in the pack's hierarchy of dominance. He lived by trailing his former pack from kill to kill and gnawing on their meager leavings.

Then, one morning in mid-March, in the first good light after dawn, I woke, rested after a very rugged day afield, listened a moment to the soughing wind in the spruces outside, rolled out of the sleeping bag, hurriedly dressed, stepped out of the cabin. . . . and there he was — 30 yards away, lying in the snow under a spruce, and looking at me. I froze in my tracks, almost unable to believe what I was seeing. I looked at his eyes, a striking gray-amber in the grizzled black face. It was an incredibly rare, beautiful moment — in that instant he was like just a big ranch dog at home. Then he was up on his paws, a stretch, a small flurry of snow as he shook himself. Another look directly at me — a look right **through** me, and I thought there was just the suggestion of a tail wag. I almost whispered, "Here, boy!" And then he was gone in the spruces.

I blinked still sleep-heavy eyes. I must have been mistaken. Had he really been there? I walked over to the spruces. Yes, there was the packed-down impression in the snow where he had rested; there were the great tracks as fresh as my own in the light fall of new snow. And he had known, of course, that I was sleeping in the cabin — all night long man scent had drifted out the open windows. But I never saw him again.

There have been many memorable moments for me afield, and some are recorded in the stories that follow. But . . . frankly, there have been times, too, that I've questioned my motives in choosing the work I do . . . times when I've had a feeling approaching guilt — that here in a world beset with critical problems growing more critical that I'm doing pretty much what I want to do, even considering a certain degree of hardship and sacrifice. My lifestyle, I'm sure, wouldn't be too much different if I was independently wealthy.

On a mental list of persons I most admire, not many are famous, and generally people from the more visible arenas of life — politicians, entertainers, professional athletes, — while not absent, are somewhat scarce. High on that list are people who have surmounted disability . . . and those who have aided them in doing so — a prime example is former world class alpine skier Jill Kinmont whom the Seattle area was privileged to have as a teacher in its public school system. Some that I have particularly looked up to I've been fortunate enough to know personally, such as the late Justice William O. Douglas, Anchorage orthopedic surgeon Dr. William J. Mills, and former high school football coach Lou Hull. Many on my list are unknown outside their own communities; others receive fleeting recognition in news stories that, probably by most people, are promptly forgotten. . . . a young nurse who has worked five years as a burn therapist at Seattle's Harborview Medical Center . . . a teacher who is doing special work with autistic children in Chicago.

Some years ago, while reading a *Time* magazine essay *Adventure and The American Individualist* by William McWhirter in which I happened to be mentioned among other assorted odd-balls, I was struck by a quotation from historian and former Amherst College president Dr. John William Ward: "Today," he said, "the man who is the real risk taker is anonymous and nonheroic. He is the one trying to make institutions work. What we need is not to go west, but to return eastward, to create excitement and adventure in things that are no longer solitary. If a man can only find adventure by going to Alaska or running wide open across the salt flats (in a jet car) then society is in bad shape."

I couldn't agree more.

But the motivation for the work I do now is rooted in a bone-deep love for wilderness country I've had since I was a small boy — and not just for northern forests and mountains, but for every natural landscape I've ever seen — wild arroyos of eastern Oregon — where I've seen sagebrush over 12 feet high, the red rock canyons of Utah, prairie in eastern Montana, the fabled Brush Country of south Texas. Interesting terrain is part of my fascination for wilderness areas, but **only** part. Real wilderness is seldom more spectacular country than the most widely visited of our national parks. Even the awesome Arrigetch Peaks in the Brooks Range of northeastern Alaska and the Tombstone Range of the Ogilvie Rockies of Yukon Territory, Canada by no means surpass the Yosemite Valley for sheer grandeur of terrain. Indeed, much of the most visually stunning mountain scenery on the North American Continent can be viewed from the comfort of a tour bus, a railway passenger car, one's own car, or the deck of a passenger vessel.

Wilderness isn't merely tangible vegetation cover, wildlife, and terrain of a particular geological structure. Probably simply because of its isolation and remoteness, wilderness, to me, inspires a sense of mystery. A feeling that comes to you when far from the sight and sound of civilization you suddenly and completely realize that you are absolutely on your own. And you look at the majestic land beyond *not as a tourist now,* but as David Thompson, Lewis and Clark, Alexander McKenzie, and John Palliser did before you. Ahead is adventure and perhaps actual hazard. And when cresting a high ridge, fording a wilderness river or listening to some animal sound in the forest, the thought comes to you, *this is the way that it was.*

The overall theme of this book of selected articles (all of which have appeared in national magazines) is, I would like to think, the appreciation of wilderness country and the wildlife that inhabits it. Of the chapters that follow, several deal with predator-prey relationships in western Canada and Alaska. More than once I've been accused of having an emotional bias in favor of predatory animals. Well . . . perhaps I'm guilty as charged. But I think not. To me, both the northern carnivores and their ungulate prey species are beautiful and vastly interesting animals. I went afield on these predator-prey study and photo projects taking nothing for granted, determined to set aside preconceived notions, and to witness for myself the drama of predator-prey interaction. Rather than carrying a particular bias for predatory animals, I have the deepest sympathy for all wildlife and for the preservation of wilderness country. And I hope that is apparent in the chapters that follow.

Acknowledgments

I wish to thank Jane Estes of Time, Inc. for her encouragement, excellent advice and kind help with the photo projects on which I was privileged to work with her during earlier days of my career. My thanks are also due William E. Rae, former Editor-in-Chief, *Outdoor Life* magazine; and to George H. Haas, present Senior Editor, *Outdoor Life.*

The talents and energies of many people besides the author go into the production of any book, and particularly into one with substantial photo support such as *Wolves, Bears and Bighorns*, and I am grateful to the entire staff of Alaska Northwest Publishing Company. Particular thanks are due Robert A. Henning, Publisher; Barbara Olds, Executive Publisher; Dianne Hofbeck, Design Editor; Jon Hersh, Designer; Allen Janik, Superintendent of Camera Production; and Norm Bolotin, Marketing and Publicity Director, for their hard work, timely help, craftsmanship, artistic integrity, patience and friendship during a sometimes stressful period.

My deep appreciation goes to the editors of *Outdoor Life* magazine, Times Mirror Magazines, Inc., New York, for their kind cooperation in agreeing to five of my articles, previously published in *Outdoor Life*, being reprinted in *Wolves, Bears and Bighorns.*

I wish to thank Mr. John Dodd of Dodd, Mead and Company, New York, for permission to quote lines from the Robert Service poem "The Land of Beyond" from *The Best of Robert Service*, Dodd, Mead and Company, New York.

My thanks go to Time, Inc., New York, for permission to quote from the *Time* magazine essay "Adventure and The American Individualist," *Time*, November 19, 1965.

A special thanks to Historian and former Amherst College President Dr. John William Ward for permission to reprint his quotation from the *Time* magazine essay "Adventure and The American Individualist," *Time*, November 19, 1965.

Finally, my profound gratitude to literally hundreds of friends in the Pacific Northwest, western Canada and Alaska. To name everyone I would like to personally thank — and I would hate to inadvertently omit anyone — would make "Acknowledgments" the longest section of this book. I thank you all from my heart, and I would need to name practically the entire populations of such communities as Jasper, Alberta; Invermere, Campbell River, and Stewart, British Columbia; and Dillingham, Petersburg, and Juneau, Alaska. With particular warmth I remember the staffs of St. Ann's Hospital, Juneau; The Alaska Native Service Hospital, Kanakanak; Ketchikan General Hospital; and Providence Hospital, Anchorage for the T.L.C. I received there while under treatment for broken-bone injuries. And I fondly remember so many individuals living in remote isolation across a vast land. I thank you for the simple friendship of a shared pot of coffee, good stories and good laughs on a winter evening; for the sourdoughs, bacon and coffee in a spruce wood-warmed cabin on a frosty dawn; for that firm, encouraging handshake when I set off alone for three weeks in the bush; for that time you dropped in with the Super Cub — several days before pick-up time — to leave me some extra grub and make sure I was okay; for the helping hand you gave me in repairing and drying gear; for the almost unbelievable luxury of a superb home-cooked meal after eating my own cooking in the bush for weeks. And I thank you all for so many other things.

In thinking back over the kindness that has been extended to me by so many in the North Country over the years — often from people I only met once — a bit of philosophy comes to mind that, while a student at the University of Washington, for a thoughtful moment caught my attention on a church reader board — something at once so simple and profound that I've never forgotten it: *The greatest measure of a gentleman is his courtesy to those who can be of no material use to him.*

John S. Crawford

Notes on the Photography

When afield I carry three 35mm single lens reflex cameras, one tripod-mounted on a 400mm telephoto lens, another in my pack as a spare, and the third — with a normal 50mm lens — secured on my chest for quick shots of wildlife where a telephoto lens is not needed. A 135mm lens is carried in the pack for hand-held telephoto use. On some trips when carrying weight and pack space are not serious considerations, and I intend to photograph a big-scale landscape to record typical habitat, for example, of a certain species, I sometimes carry a Linhof view camera using 4x5 Commercial Ektachrome sheet film. When carrying weight and pack space **are** important considerations I take a 28mm or 35mm wide-angle lens for my Canon.

For most 35mm telephoto work I use ASA 64 Kodachrome, and for some marginal light shooting switch to High Speed Ektachrome. For most normal lens and wide-angle lens shooting with 35mm cameras I use ASA 25 Kodachrome.

Sometimes the wildlife photographer encounters a photographic challenge where he has to use a technique he's never tried before. This photo of the resting mule deer buck (which has been published several times) was taken on a misty November dusk in the British Columbia Rockies. This picture is about a two-and-a-half-second time exposure made on High Speed Ektachrome — a black and white conversion is shown here. The camera shutter speed was set on "bulb" — on which setting the shutter remains open as long as the release is held down. I got the idea — for a shot that otherwise would not have been possible — when a coyote howled. The buck turned his head toward the sound and for about six seconds was absolutely still — no soldier ever stood at attention with less movement! A moment later when the coyote howled again, camera and 400mm lens were tripod-mounted and ready.

There are a few other points I've picked up afield — as usual, learning mostly the hard way — that I do feel are worth passing on. I believe that 1/250 second should be the **slowest** shutter speed used in shooting from a helicopter or plane to completely nullify the vibration of the aircraft; I use 1/1,000 second to stop a waterfall, a leaping trout or salmon or a crashing snow avalanche. I always keep an ultra-violet filter on a lens during field use — when using this filter no correction is needed for figuring exposure — to give better definition and improve color rendition in hazy atmosphere, such as caused by the drift of forest fire smoke, and also to protect the lens itself — in effect, an insurance policy of $10.00 more or less protecting a lens that might have cost several hundred dollars.

1 Last Encounter

A ''short-yearling'' wolf pup, about 10½ to 11 months old, pauses momentarily while traversing through an aspen thicket near the upper Athabasca River, Alberta Rockies in early March.

The raven circled in the frigid early-December dawn, his wingbeats making a hissing *shhhou, shhhou* in the dense air. Then the big bird planed down to settle in a lodgepole pine, and alighting, broke loose a shimmering cascade of fresh powder snow.

The bitter, searching wind of the night had almost stilled. A great wolf stood up in the few inches of fresh snow, stretched, shook the snow from his coat, yawned—tongue curling over sharp points and ridges of canine and carnassial teeth, and looked about him at the rest of the pack still dozing in the shelter of the spruces. The wolf's black coat was grizzled with a tipping of silver over his face and shoulders. He raised his head, and his broad, black nose pad quivered as his nostrils drew in and sifted scents. Sub-zero cold inhibits scent drift, and even to his marvelous olfactory sense there was little to interest him in the now barely perceptible wind. He picked up raven

and jay, and faintly read snowshoe hare and magpie, squirrel and pine marten. The wolf padded a few yards to the river bank, raised a hind leg, and left his own scent on the roots of a windfall spruce. He looked up briefly as a gray jay fluttered from one bough to another. Behind the big wolf, one of the pups opened his eyes, withdrew his nose from the deep fur of his tail, and yawned.

The old wolf looked down the river ice. He was scarcely 75 yards above the confluence of the upper Athabasca and the Chaba River, and a half-dozen raven flight miles to the west, up the windswept valley of the Chaba, was Fortress Pass and the British Columbia-Alberta boundary. The raven croaked, dropped down from the pine, and settled himself on a leaning, fire-charred snag only a few feet above the wolf. Predator and scavenger regarded each other for a moment. The raven recognized his benefactor, but the wolf looked at the bird unknowing and uncaring that this raven was one of seventeen, plus several magpies, that had completed the final feeding on the wolves' last kill—a long-yearling cow moose—three days before. Between the gorgings of the wolf pack and the stealthy, nervous-and-watchful gulpings of coyotes, the scavenger birds had fed, and finally—after the predators had traveled on—they had probed and chiseled with their strong beaks until the last shred of flesh had been stripped from the bone.

The great silver-black wolf trotted down the river bank along the edge of the spruce and pine forest. Suddenly he stopped, the hackles of his ruff stiffening and a growl rumbling in his throat, as he caught the still-pungent scent of a week-old cougar scat buried in a few inches of snow. Then, at a rush of footfalls behind him, the old wolf whirled.

The pup that had wakened at his departure, the largest survivor of that spring's litter, had followed him. The youngster bounded up, tail wagging joyously, to sniff noses with his father. The old wolf rumbled a low growl of minor annoyance. He had wanted to sniff out the immediate surroundings alone before deciding whether the pack would remain longer in that area or move down the valley that morning. But he allowed the big, handsome pup with the smokey bluish-gray coat to come along. The pup was irrepressibly dominant among his litter mates, and—other than his huge, still-outsized paws—was already nearing adult proportion and size. He had been an apt pupil in his early hunting lessons on voles, snowshoe hares and ground squirrels, and just a few days before had been clumsily

effective in helping the adult wolves pull down the young cow moose.

The two wolves trotted out on the river ice, and in a few moments reached the meeting of the waters of the upper Athabasca and the Chaba. The bitter air was almost still. Since a light snowfall the evening before, the temperature had dropped sharply. Except for powerful runs of the swiftest current, the braided channel of the Chaba was covered with ice. The few, narrowing runs of open water were choked with swiftly floating fragments of drift ice that produced a constant rushing hiss as they rubbed together. Nearly two decades before, a lightning-strike forest fire had swept the slopes to the west bordering the Chaba Valley. Young spruce and lodgepole pine now grew among the charred and weathered snags—many still precariously standing, more of them lying in criss-crossed, snow-covered profusion on the ground, "shintangle" to men of the mountains.

The old wolf's gray-amber eyes looked with searching indifference at the awesomely spectacular limestone peaks that towered above the valley. Then the wind stirred in a frigid breeze from the west. The pack leader stopped. He had caught a scent drift from directly up-river. His silver-black head moved slowly from side to side. Even in the bitter air the heavy, musky-rank scent came on the wind with compelling clarity. The nostrils in the broad black nose pad quivered. The pup, also eagerly sniffing, whined with excitement. The old wolf raised his snout, and partially opened his jaws in a low, throaty moan.

In a few moments his light-gray mate of

Above — The confluence of the upper Athabasca with the Chaba River, about six miles east of Fortress Pass and the British Columbia-Alberta boundary, in early December.

Right — A huge, heavy-racked bull elk in superb condition, photographed in early December in the upper Athabasca Valley, Alberta Rockies. For the opportunistic wolves the risks in attacking a mature bull in his excellent condition are much too great. The formidable physical equipment of such bulls, coupled with their usual aggressively confident demeanor, make them invulnerable to wolf predation except in very special situations of weather, terrain, snow and vegetation cover.

five years and the other six wolves of the pack—two of the litter of the year before, and four other pups of that spring—joined them in a nose-sniffing, tail-wagging, shoulder-pawing greeting. The pups ranged in coloration from almost as light as the mother to one pup darker than the pack leader. The wolves sat on their haunches and howled in chorus. The wild singing rose, merged with yapping and barking, deepened to throaty moaning, rose again chord on chord, echoing back from the great brooding peaks.

The hunting pack trotted behind the silver-black leader, following the scent drift from the west. They moved swiftly and easily on the river ice, on the wind-slab crust of old snow, over windswept gravel bars between the branches of the braided channel, and—a half-mile up the Chaba—over a great sheet of glass-smooth ice where flooding water, forced out of the channel by ice jams, had frozen and glaciered over several acres. Above the traveling wolves, a half-dozen flapping ravens circled and planed.

A great bull elk was bedded down near the edge of the spruce and willow cover a few yards from the river bank on the north side of the Chaba Valley. The early winter snow-pack was yet light, and he was still finding good feed on the burn. Resting now and chewing his cud, his breath was rising in frosty plumes. Seven cows that winter were carrying calves that he had sired, but near the first of October he had been badly beaten in combat by a bull just as big and two years younger, and during the battle his remaining harem of eleven cows had been dispersed and stolen by still other bulls.

Gored, bleeding, his ribs raked by his antagonist's antler tines, his skidding hoofs carving the torn meadow turf, he had finally broken away, turned and fled.

For days his wounds had festered painfully, and after his defeat he had slowly drifted up the valley of the upper Athabasca, once taking to a deep, swift channel when wolves scented his injuries, stalked and closed on him. During the following weeks his incredible vitality had prevailed, but while he healed and regained body weight and strength, only the fortuitous circumstance that there was other prey just as vulnerable and more accessible had saved him from death by wolf predation. Now, in early winter, his injuries had healed and he had regained his strength, but a measure of what men call confidence was gone.

Now, from his vantage point near the edge of the timber, he saw the silhouettes of the approaching wolves 200 yards downriver. His ears turned forward instantly, and for a few moments he stopped chewing his cud. But there was no feeling akin to what men know as apprehension. Watching intently, he remained lying down as the wolves came trotting up-river, watching them now with a cautious alertness—much as a man driving an automobile does when he approaches a railway crossing.

As the bull watched, the wolves moved from a brisk trot to an easy lope on the wind-scoured bars of the river. Much keener sighted than the bull, they had already picked out his antlers and the broken outline of the dark neck and tawny body in the spruce-willow cover.

The bull had dealt with wolves in many previous encounters during his life. In immaturity he had enjoyed the protection of others as a gregarious herd animal. Once, late in his second spring, he had grazed away from the herd, had been surprised by the sudden downwind appearance of wolves, and only the sharp squealing barks of several old cows had warned him in time. He had made his belated escape by racing to a small lake at the head of the muskeg meadow. After that near miss, he had been more watchful and cautious. That season he had become as swift afoot as he would ever be, but each following year as he neared full maturity he had grown heavier and stronger. One early September, the second year that he had been a successful herd bull, he had once again been approached by wolves. Then at the peak of his aggressive vitality, great neck swollen at the beginning of the rutting season, massive, heavy-corded muscles rippling and bunching under his hide, he hadn't merely stood his ground; he had walked in slow menace toward the wolves, head lowered, encountered a small tree in his way, and, as his great six-tined antlers slashed the boughs from the young spruce, the wolves had turned and trotted away.

Now the bull saw the silver-black pack leader stop on the ice below a swift channel of open water almost directly across from him. The other eight wolves trotted up in single file, and pausing, closely bunched, they all looked at the bull. The pack leader padded out on the channel ice and eased into a trot with the others following. They crossed the ice a few yards below the open run, then a drift area where windblown early-season snow had been caught at the bend of a dry channel branch. A tough crust

had formed by thawing and sharp refreezing. The wolves—with greater paw surface than large dogs of comparable weight, tracking in the few inches of new powder, crossed the drifts without breaking the crust. For a few moments they again paused together, tail-wagging and nose-sniffing; then, spreading out, they trotted toward the bedded bull. The elk stood up.

There was nothing that the bull did immediately that indicated to the pack leader that he could be vulnerable to attack without too great a risk, and noting the motion of the bull rising, he rumbled a warning growl to the pups. The ease and swiftness of the bull's movements already suggested to the old wolf a vital and dangerous defensive capability. But it was a routine hunting tactic. The bull was a lone ungulate. The wolves were hungry and hunting. The elk would be tested.

The bull's defeat during the rutting season had altered his reaction patterns to danger stimuli. He felt an impulse now to run for the open channel, but hesitated, watching the pack leader and the gray female as they turned slightly on the bull's up-river side, trotted through the edge of the willows, bounded lightly up on the bank, and began to circle behind the elk in the scattered spruce-willow cover. Quickly the bull turned his head to check the other wolves. With the pack moving in a closing stalk, the silver-black leader again growled a warning to the pups. But the big blue-gray pup, his nose full of the musky-rank scent of the bull, was too excited for caution. As the bull looked back at the pack leader trotting behind him, the pup suddenly sprang in bounding leaps in on the elk's flank.

The bull's peripheral vision caught the movement. He pivoted in a blur of speed. His great antlers scythed in an arrow-swift arc, impaled the pup on two tines, and hurled him 30 feet into a spruce. The pup dropped limply through the boughs to fall on his side in the snow, coughing as blood welled from a punctured lung into his throat.

The bull, not knowing he had mortally injured the attacking pup, whirled instantly to watch the other wolves, now in a still and silent circle around him. But one rush by one wolf, a rash and fatal mistake by a bumbling youngster, had established the bull's dangerous capability, and the silver-black started to call the pack away. The bull had now only to stand his ground.

A few months before, prior to his rutting season defeat, he would have. And here, when the pack was moving in a closing stalk, the bull had not acted on his initial impulse—to run for the still open river channel. But now, a few seconds after his goring of the pup, the bull suddenly broke for the river.

He hooked with a lightning antler thrust at a second-year pup directly in his path. As the wolf dodged away, the bull crashed through the edge of the spruce willow cover and leaped out over the bank. His flight triggered instant pursuit. The bull galloped at his greatest speed over the gravel bar flat. On the windswept bar, almost barren of snow, the bull began to pull away from the pack—with the spring pups falling several yards behind the four older wolves. But then the bull hit the drifts in the dry channel, 60 yards from open water. He didn't flounder, but he slowed. And life and death in nature often hinges on mischance and split seconds.

Immediately breaking through, at times nearly belly-and-brisket deep in the drifts, the bull began to drive his way through in powerful heaving lunges. But the pack leader and the gray female, racing in great bounds, caught up. The silver-black sprang at the bull's upper ham. His teeth cut through the hide, hung on, closed, and tore away over a pound of muscle from high on the bull's rump. The bull swerved just as the female bounded in on his flank, almost missing with her bite, shearing hide, fat, blood vessels and muscle not quite deep enough to eviscerate. Again the silver-black leaped. His jaws chopped at the elk's rump and hung on. The pack leader was still clinging, fangs biting deep into the muscle tissue of the bull's upper ham, when the two second year pups attacked, tearing at flanks and rump. The spring pups bounded up, running the hard crust alongside.

Breaking the crust in a blood-stained trail across the snow, the bull powered through 15 yards of drifts, and heaved himself out on the bank, dragging the weight of three clinging wolves. The bull staggered as the wolves bit through flesh and dropped off, but he immediately picked up speed on again almost bare gravel.

For a few yards the bull ran at full stride; then he staggered and came to a stop so abruptly that the nearest pursuing wolves overran him. They charged past, braked with stiffened front legs, turned quickly, then circled back in an easy trot, holding off, no longer attacking, the silver-black growling to warn the pups away.

Massive damage had been inflicted by the wolves on the muscle structure of the elk's hind legs. The stress of maximum effort had increased the injury by tearing still more muscle fibers, and the bull was no longer able to run. Trotting around the bull, knowing that the end was near and that there was no need for further risk, the wolves circled, waiting.

Frosty vapor rose from the bull's gasping breaths, *huhhh! huhhh! huhhh!* Fifty feet away was the open river channel filled with swiftly floating fragments of drift ice. The bull turned in an awkward, hobbling circle, head down, facing the wolves. The wolves now sat on their haunches or lay down. They had only to wait. Several ravens glided down to land on the bar, then walked and hopped a few feet from the bull— sometimes directly under his belly, pecking at the blood-soaked snow.

The gray female looked at each of the pups. She looked across the 120 yards to where the chase had started. She made a low whimper, *eeough! eeough! eeough!* Then she trotted across the drifted channel and the gravel bar flat.

A raven flew off as the gray female approached. The blue-gray pup had died in a few seconds after being struck by the bull's antler tines. Blood from his open jaws had frozen in the snow. Moments before the largest and most promising of her spring litter, he was now only carrion in an unforgiving wilderness, and already ravens had pecked out his eyes. The she-wolf briefly sniffed the carcass, then trotted slowly back across the gravel bar flat to lie down again beside the silver-black male, nose on forepaws, to wait.

Blood was dripping from multiple injuries on the bull's flanks, legs and belly, freezing in crimson icicles from the hair of his torn hide. His body was calling on its ultimate reserves, and he was no longer aware of pain. Now, in the desperate last moments of his life, the feral rage returned that he had known when he was locked in combat with the powerful challenger that had finally defeated him, and through eyes bulging from anger and effort he had seen lesser bulls disperse and steal his cows.

Surrounded by the pack on the gravel bar, the bull's ravaged body haltingly turned, and with antlers lowered he lunged awkwardly toward the nearest resting wolf—a second year pup. Then the gray female sprang in a blur of bounding speed. With a deep slashing bite, at the juncture of the bull's flank and belly a few inches ahead of a hind leg, she opened the elk's visceral cavity. Simultaneously there was massive blood loss and a billowing cloud of steam in the frigid air as the bull's entrails pushed out and slid to the gravel. The entire pack closed as the bull's legs buckled and he collapsed on his steaming viscera.

—From experiences during eight winters of wolf research.

Below — A young male wolf near the confluence of the Chaba and upper Athabasca Rivers, Alberta, Canada.

Below — After a rare windless night in early December, this line of fresh wolf tracks was photographed along the north bank of the Chaba River in the Alberta Rockies.
Right — This photograph shows where the wolf veered abruptly out on the river ice to sniff my own tracks (made early the previous day), then turned and trotted back to his original line of travel.

The photographs which follow on pages 10 through 13 depict a grim drama of death in the wild — of both prey and predator — which I witnessed on a bitterly cold late November morning on the Sunwapta River of the Alberta Rockies. Some biologists who have studied predator-prey interaction between the great cats of East Africa and various species of antelope have theorized that the prey animal goes into shock in the killing stage of attack. This, I believe, is a plausible theory, well supported by field observations, and equally valid concerning wolf predation on North American ungulates. The cow moose, in her death, helped support a chain of life in a sometimes cruelly harsh winter ecology of northern wilderness. Her carcass was utilized to the last shred of flesh by wolves, coyotes and smaller carnivores such as the marten, as well as by scavenger birds.

The text accompanying the photographs on pages 10 through 13 describes them in sequence.

The first sunlight of a sub-zero late November morning falls on an injured cow moose that has just lain down after climbing out of a frigid channel of the Sunwapta River. In the bitter cold only the rushing current velocity has kept the channel open. Attacked by wolves, the cow had sought refuge in the river. In the first moments of the attack she had killed one of the younger wolves with a lightning fast rib-crushing hoof blow. She had lifted a clinging 100-pound-plus wolf and swung him off the ground with his teeth buried in her nose. Then, her nose torn, bleeding from multiple gashes and tears in her shoulders, flanks and rump, her near-final energy reserves drained by standing in bone-chilling water, she lies down, her life already past the point of no return.

From a stand of pines on the east bank of the Sunwapta, I look at her across the river. I think, she'll never get up again. But the cow raises her head. There are no wolves yet in sight, and there has been no sound of them perceptible to human ears, but she senses their approach. With a fortitude that is awesome, that perhaps goes beyond our comprehension of courage in human terms, the cow somehow manages to rise to her feet, and she turns to face the mountain slope behind her.

Through the spruce and pine cover on the steep slope six wolves trot down to the river. They pause at a point 250 yards downstream from the cow — superbly conditioned, beautifully deep-furred animals in full winter pelage — and bunch together touching noses and wagging their tails. Two wolves trot toward the cow while the rest of the pack remains downriver, one wolf out of sight in the pines. The two wolves trotting upstream, the dominant male and female of the pack, actually approach within a few feet of the cow, but do not attack again. The wolves slowly circle the cow a few feet away; then, incredibly, while they lick up her blood from the snow, the moose walks stiffly over to some willows and actually takes a few bites of browse!

Moments later, in one of the strangest predator-prey encounters I've ever witnessed one of the wolves walks up and looks at the cow, face to face, less than three feet away from her. A fabled predator and his doomed, incredibly courageous prey communicate a message between them — a mystery of death in the wild that, perhaps, no man can fathom. The wolf makes no attempt to attack, nor the moose to defend. For long seconds they stand 30 inches apart and look at each other. The wolf turns away and, with his mate, trots slowly downstream to the waiting pack, as one of the yearling pups leaves his scent on a young spruce (left).

The moose lies down again, this time never to get up.

For long periods the cow makes no movement. A raven wings down to land on the moose's back and pecks at a bleeding gash. There is a muscular shiver, and the raven hops off. After a while the moose's head drops slowly to the snow. For a long time there is no movement whatever, then a slight flick of an ear. The cow lies motionless. Another raven circles briefly, and drops down on the cow's head. The cow doesn't move. The raven perches between the cow's ears, reaches down with its great beak, and pecks out one of the eyes.

At that instant I turn my binoculars 250 yards downriver to where the wolves are resting and waiting. They know. Nose-touching and shoulder-pawing, they stand and bunch together, wagging their tails. Moments later they file up the mountain slope behind them *(right)*, not to return to feed until evening *(below)*.

Early the following morning, after the pack has gorged and retired to rest, a pair of coyotes *(top of opposite page)* stealthily approach the kill. At the moose carcass they are nervous and watchful, but they feed voraciously, tearing off flesh in gulping mouthfuls until they see one of the wolves coming, running heavily with a meat-filled stomach. The coyotes each take a last big bite and run. At the carcass the wolf feeds briefly again before returning to rest.

One-hundred-plus pounds of wolf pushed these tracks into the snow; days later the tracks remain, but above the surrounding surface as lashing winds sculpted away the unpacked snow around them.

Two wolves of a very dark color phase photographed in early December feeding on the carcass of a moose calf on the west bank of the Sunwapta River, Alberta Rockies. In this area of the northern Rockies dark color phases (typically black with a silvery or yellowish tipping over the face and shoulders) occur with near equal frequency to the light grayish and grayish-brown phases.

Right — A bugling bull elk photographed in late September on Wellbourne Muskeg, upper Snake Indian Valley, Alberta Rockies. This is a herd bull answering the bugle of a challenger during the breeding season.

Center right — This wolf pack, photographed in the upper Athabasca Valley, Alberta Rockies in early December, has been scent-trailing a moose through open spruce forest and muskeg. The pack has just sighted the moose ahead.

Below — Wolf predation on a mature and, apparently, physically sound bull elk, such as the one in the upper right photograph. This photograph was taken in early December near the confluence of Ranger Creek and the upper Athabasca River, Alberta Rockies. In this case the wolves were literally driven off the kill — only moments after the bull had been brought down. It can be seen that massive damage was done to the muscle structure of both upper hind legs. It is important to note that this is not hamstringing — the severing of the Achilles' tendon. I have not seen hamstringing on any kill I've examined of any prey species, nor have I met any knowledgeable Canadian or Alaskan outdoorsman who claims that he has. I don't believe that wolves use hamstringing as a deliberate tactic to disable and bring down prey. To hamstring an elk or moose, a wolf would have to make himself extremely vulnerable to the prey animal's rear hoofs, and an elk or moose can kick at least as hard and accurately as a mule. The idea of wolves hamstringing to disable and bring down prey appears to be just another popular wildlife myth that has carried over the years.

This bull elk kill was of particular interest to me because all indications pointed to the conclusion that this bull was a physically sound animal. I believe that psychological factors may have made this bull vulnerable at that particular time.

Five hundred yards from an open channel in the Athabasca River, this bull was jumped from his bed by six wolves. At the onset of the chase, the bull leaped a large fallen spruce. To clear the boughs the bull had to reach a height of about six and a half feet. Over 27 feet

of horizontal distance was covered by the bull in that leap, hardly indicating a disabled animal. One hundred and fifty yards further in the chase the bull was pulled down, but with almost incredible effort struggled again to his feet and continued his desperate race for the river, but was put down for good by a slashing bite low on the flank that gutted him.

It should be emphasized that this is a classic case of the typical tissue damage done by wolves to bring down a large ungulate such as a moose or an elk — massive destruction of muscle tissue in the upper rear legs, and slashing bites low on the flanks resulting in evisceration. In contrast to the long ordeal of the cow moose (pictured on pages 10 through 14) this bull elk was killed in a matter of seconds from the time he was jumped to when he was pulled down.

Below right — Remains of the bull elk carcass photographed five days after the kill was made. At this point it was already near 100% utilization — by wolves, coyotes, and scavenger birds, and by the time the ravens and magpies had finished, every fiber of flesh had been stripped from the bone.

15

Thinning spruce forest merging into tundra with tusking
peaks of the Alaska Range on the horizon, classic wolf,
moose and caribou country of Alaska's subarctic interior
photographed after a late September snowfall.

In the opening vignette of a master predator taking prey, all animal action and descriptions of weather and terrain of an actual locale are entirely factual, and are drawn from my eight winters of wolf research in the Canadian Rockies. Working in every condition of winter weather, I've seen some very surprising and— what seemed at first—rather appalling things. Sometimes I got lucky, and circumstances of light, weather, terrain, and equipment condition were such that I was able to record some of these happenings on film, and at other times—all too often—I couldn't. Trying for the most unusual of wildlife pictures is like going after that big and elusive trout we all seek—I've lost better than I've taken.

It is beyond dispute that wolves primarily take the sick and injured, the aged and immature, and those animals that have severe infestations of parasites. But from observations I've made during recent years, I believe that wolves have the strength, stamina, speed and killing equipment to bring down the fit and strong, and that at times they do. However, attacking a fit and powerful ungulate—such as a prime moose of either sex—presents a considerably greater hazard factor that wolves, under most conditions, are unwilling to accept.

Further north in the great tundra regions, escape speed and endurance against wolf pursuit, rather than making a fighting stand, is the primary defense of the Barren Ground caribou against wolf predation. A healthy caribou, even a few-weeks-old calf, can outrun a healthy wolf. The general belief that the wolf preys only on the ''unfit'' holds more truth on the rolling barrens of the Far North than it does in my project area in the Canadian Rockies.

In my major wolf research area in the northern Rocky Mountains of British Columbia and western Alberta—which included the river valleys of the Big Smoky, Jackpine, upper Athabasca, Wildhay, Snake Indian, Brazeau, Chaba, Restless, Medicine Tent, Rocky, upper Fraser, and Sulphur—defensive aggressiveness against the testing rushes of wolves is the major survival factor for moose and elk against wolf attack. In that country elk, moose and mule deer are the big game ungulates that wolves most frequently prey on—to a considerably lesser extent whitetail deer (in this area whitetail numbers are well below the mule deer population), mountain caribou, and bighorn sheep are also taken. There are good numbers of Rocky Mountain goats in that region—particularly in Jasper National Park itself—but wolf

Wolf tracks on a stream bar beside my size 11-EE mountain boot. Taken in early October in the Cassiar Mountains of the Stikine Plateau, northern British Columbia.

predation on them is quite limited. Goats spend little time in terrain where they could be vulnerable—such as when they descend to lower elevations to visit mineral licks. And in predator confrontations there is no cooler, tougher, or more courageous animal than the mountain goat.

In the examination of wolf kills—which I find both by direct tracking of wolves in snow, and watching for the converging flight of ravens and magpies (of course, with kills older than a week or so it's largely just by chancing upon them in the bush)—there's often so little left in the way of remains that it's impossible to determine why that particular animal was vulnerable—injury prior to wolf attack, disease, heavy parasite infestation, etc.

But I have seen fresh wolf kills on adult elk and moose, both bulls and cows, where all the evidence—actual observation of the predation or checking the track patterns in the snow as to whether the prey animal runs or makes a stand, examination of the ungulate's flesh and/or bone marrow condition, and—in a couple of cases where I just walked up and spooked the wolves off of still-steaming kills only moments old—examination of the organs for parasites—pointed to the conclusion that the prey animals had been in good condition and had not had disabling injuries prior to the wolf attack.

In one case that I found particularly interesting, the prey animal was a bull elk that in running from a pack of six wolves leaped a large fallen spruce. To

Above and below — Traveling wolves, photographed in late November, near the upper Athabasca River, Alberta Rockies.

Right — The remains of a Rocky Mountain bighorn ram killed by wolves on bighorn winter range overlooking the upper Athabasca Valley, Alberta Rockies, in early April. This case is a classic example of an animal predisposed to wolf predation due to a prior injury. I observed this ram two days before he was killed, and quickly noted that he had a badly sprained left rear leg — probably the result of a fall. In that area I would have been surprised if the ram had survived as long as two weeks following the injury.

Below — A dark color-phase wolf feeding on an elk killed on a marshy lake shore in the British Columbia Rockies, in late April.

Upper left — A big calf elk, photographed in late October, nursing from his mother. Taken near Nez Perce Creek, Wyoming.

Center left — A young bull moose, whose energy and body fat reserves have been badly depleted by a severe winter, photographed in late March in the upper Athabasca Valley, Alberta Rockies.

Left — Rocky Mountain mule deer *(doe, left; buck, right)* in the upper Athabasca Valley, Alberta Rockies, in late December. Deer defenses against predation are primarily alertness and speed. This buck and doe are in excellent physical condition.

clear the boughs the bull had to reach a height of about six and a half feet. The horizontal distance of the bull's leap was so impressive that I measured it.

From where the bull took off on one side of the spruce to where the hoof tracks were imprinted on the other was a bit over 27 feet, hardly indicating a disabled animal. The bull was pulled down, but with almost incredible effort struggled again to his feet, momentarily threw off his attackers, and continued his life or death race toward an open channel in the upper Athabasca River. But he didn't make it. He was put down for good by a slashing bite low on the flank that gutted him.

One can only speculate on why this bull ran, rather than standing his ground. As he had the energy to make such a spectacular escape attempt, it would seem that if he'd just held his ground with an aggressive stand the wolves would have left him alone after a few testing rushes. This and other cases I've observed of moose and elk being killed by wolves have led me to believe that—lacking a more precise term—"psychological" factors definitely can make an adult physically sound ungulate vulnerable **at a particular time** to wolf predation.

Several old-timers—retired wardens and veteran outfitters and trappers in the western Canadian and Alaskan bush—have expressed to me their opinion that five or six healthy, fully-adult wolves could bring down the biggest and strongest of bull moose and bull elk if they wanted to. They're probably right. But the fact is, however, that in most packs—usually numbering less than 10 wolves, and containing the dominant male wolf, his mate, their pups of the year, often several individuals of the previous year's litter, and sometimes an older relative or two

in the pack's family tree—there just aren't that many wolves with the speed, strength and seasoned expertise to be effective hunters of healthy adult big game animals. Indeed, hunting accidents appear to be a major mortality factor during the first two years of the wolf's life.

Wolves are highly intelligent opportunists in their predation. They know well the hazard of clubbing, shearing, rib-crushing hoofs and the lethal hooking sweeps of antlers, and if there's an easy, safe meal in the area—in the form of abundant small game, or an immature, weakened, or injured big game animal—they will find it and take it.

———————————

Of points I wanted to bring out in the opening vignette of this article, two are basic truths that I've been often reminded of during years of field work on predatory animals. One is that the element of pure chance—a fascinating variable in the process of natural selection—is itself a highly important factor in predation. Secondly, that just because one animal kills and eats another doesn't necessarily make him a villain. The bull elk, the wolves, and even the ravens and magpies were all just doing the best they could, with the equipment they were given to work with, to survive in a sometimes bitterly harsh wilderness environment. I've come away from these long seasons in the northern bush with an ever-increasing admiration for the fortitude—that perhaps goes beyond what we think of as courage—of both the hunted and the hunters. During the long winters of predatory animal study in Alaska, northern Saskatchewan, and the Rockies of British Columbia and Alberta, it's been brought home to me time and again that the wilderness plays no favorites.

2 Blackie
and the Silver Horde

A black bear climbs back up a rugged slope over jumbled slabs of rock and over and under windfall trees, to eat his salmon catch in the seclusion of the forest. Photographed near Anan Creek, about 30 miles south of Wrangell in Southeastern Alaska, in early August.

"Blackie and the Silver Horde" is from *OUTDOOR LIFE*, April 1969 Times Mirror Magazines, Inc. 380 Madison Avenue New York, N.Y. 10017 looked up at the face of the mountain. Through the shifting overcast I could see that the snowline had dropped a good 1,000 feet since the previous afternoon. I continued hiking over barnacled stones, between jumbled masses of driftwood, and through rank sea grass until the tidal flat met the forest at the head of the saltwater arm.

On that chill, rainy day in mid-October 1958, I was working alone, one of a three-man U.S. Fish & Wildlife Service survey crew camped on Three-Mile-Arm of Kuiu Island, Southeastern Alaska. The two other guys, Dick Myren and Dick Williamson, had run a skiff 10 miles around the point from our camp to check a stream flowing into Sumner Strait. Our job was to gather data on salmon spawning and, in the streams of that vicinity, to get as accurate an estimate as possible of the numbers of salmon by species, which included the humpback (or pink), chum (dog), and coho (silver).

I stepped into the forest. Your eyes adjust quickly to the gloom there, and, until you use a camera's exposure meter, it is difficult to realize how much the light is excluded by the trees. This was the rain forest of Southeastern Alaska—ancient Sitka spruce and hemlocks hanging with moss, rotting windfalls caught in the branches of strong and living trees, moss and seedlings growing from the trunks of dead giants, ferns, berry brush, devil's club with its tiny wicked thorns. It is a forest that has a character of its own, as somberly distinctive as the jungles of the Amazon.

I hiked up the small stream, wearing hip-length fishing boots, frequently fording from one side to another for better observation. Hundreds of humpback salmon were digging and spawning, and I noted that a fresh run of humpies had moved in since the last survey.

About one and a quarter miles above the tide flat, I reached a deep tea-colored pool below a tangle of down timber. The water poured over the trunk of a windfall spruce that formed a low dam. Seventeen coho salmon were finning near the bottom or gliding slowly about the pool. Some were fresh-run and silvery, but most were in their red-sided spawning coloration. One big, hook-snouted male looked like he would go 18 pounds. Cutthroat trout and Dolly Varden chars up to about three pounds, already fattened on salmon eggs and waiting for more, flanked the salmon.

For several minutes I watched the pool, figuring that there might be several more salmon under tree roots or the undercut bank. Then I recorded my count in a waterproof field notebook, and started to climb over the windfalls. This movement startled the salmon, and they slashed across the pool in powerful darting runs. They didn't break the surface; they stayed deep, but I could actually hear the sound of their rushes—it was a muted rumble, like far-distant thunder.

A few minutes later, further upstream, a black bear sow splashed across the creek with her two cubs, climbed over a windfall, and stood watching me a few seconds. Then she huffed at her cubs, and the family vanished into the rain forest.

I'd seen this sow and her cubs several times before. From our observations, at least 14 blacks were fishing this stream. Bears and salmon form one of the classic predator-prey relationships in nature, and on almost every survey we saw bears. There had been no hostilities, however, and both we and the bears were becoming pretty casual about our meetings. Two .30-'06 Springfields, government property, were included in our equipment, as were our personal firearms, but I rarely bothered to carry a rifle. That day, I was packing only a .22 Ruger handgun in a belt holster, figuring that I might take a grouse for supper. The bears had been no trouble to us, and we interfered with them as little as possible.

My survey ended at one of the largest and strongest beaver dams I've ever seen. The dam backed up the stream to form a sizable lake. The dam's height, though an impassable barrier to the chum and humpback salmon, would be no problem to the cohos. But the lake and the feeder stream above it lacked the gravel bottom necessary for salmon spawning, and, though I didn't take it for granted, I doubted whether even the cohos came up this far.

I recorded the time, took air and water tempera-

A black bear pads its way down the steep, tilted rock slabs on the rugged slope overlooking the falls on Anan Creek. Note the immensely powerful shoulders and forelegs.

23

A salmon leaps in a tremendous effort to clear the falls on Anan Creek while many others can be seen struggling in the current below. The salmon that got over this falls — and many did — did not make it by leaping but by remaining submerged, and, with a great tail-lashing effort in power swimming, driving their way up the face of the rock.

tures, and wrote down this information along with notes on wind, precipitation and cloud cover. Counts for each stream section of the three species of salmon present—both living and dead fish (separate counts were made of salmon that had died following spawning and those that had been killed by bears)—were totaled and recorded. Then I climbed up on the beaver dam and watched the lake for about fifteen minutes. The muskeg water was black with depth. Mist partially shrouded the great cedars—some of them centuries old—that towered from massive, arching roots on the near shore. A few yards from the bank, a big trout leaped, smacking the water solidly on his descent and sending heavy ripples rolling toward shore.

During my brief period of observation, no other fish broke water, no fin or heavy swirl indicated the presence of salmon. This lack of visible salmon was not conclusive; it was merely another negative indication supported by previous surveys.

I decided that there was still time enough—before the fading light would force me to head for camp—to take a short hike above the lake to see if any deer (Sitka blacktails) were feeding on the meadow. Also, there was some chance of seeing a wolf. Plenty of sign was evident, and during several evenings we'd heard howling.

As I started across on the dam toward shore, there was a sudden harsh cry. A heron rose from the shallows in front of the cedars and flew off, its weird, grating call coming back almost eerily through the mist.

Ashore, I pushed through brush and timber, turning away from the lake to avoid a swamp at its head, and hiked to the lower edge of the meadow, which I carefully glassed with 7x50 binoculars. Nothing in sight.

The rolling sweep of meadow—short heather, grass and moss, with small ponds in the lower areas and a few dwarfed brushy-limbed lodgepole pines on the knolls—was a striking contrast to the great forest behind me. I walked in a light rain toward the upper meadow, and in places the ground shivered and sank underfoot, like a tough hide of turf over quicksand. I stopped for a few minutes to watch and listen. There was a wildness about this country that almost defined the word.

Crisp in the stillness, a dead branch cracked to my left. Forty yards away, on a slight rise near the edge of the forest, a black bear was digging under a rotten log. The downed snag certainly wasn't big enough to have hidden him from my glassing, and I realized that he must have ghosted out of the timber while I stood watching the upper meadow.

His coat was a beautiful blue-black, and he was a bigger bear than any other I'd seen on recent stream surveys in the area. What he was so intently after under the log, I couldn't tell. Probably grubs or ants.

Then I heard a faint cracking of brush from the forest behind the bear. He raised his head from the log and stood looking over his shoulder, listening. Then he began moving his head slowly from side to side as he sniffed the breeze. Apparently undisturbed, he turned his head back, and, for the first time, he saw me.

For several seconds he was completely still.

Through my binoculars the bear's image filled most of the field of view. I could see his eyes and the bits of bark and duff that clung to his muzzle and face. He looked so perplexed that I almost laughed. Again his head began to move from side to side, nose quivering, trying to pick up my scent.

Well, he's spooked now, I thought. He'll be hitting the woods fast.

But, to my considerable surprise, the bear began walking toward me. He moved slowly, watching me, but with his head turned—rather oddly, I thought—halfway to the side. The black stopped at another downed snag, probed under it with his nose, but kept looking my way. He raised his head, eyes on me, nose quivering. A slight crosswind had come up, and it rippled through that glossy blue-black pelt. I stood watching, fascinated by his behavior. I hadn't seen this bear before, and wondered if he'd just traveled into the watershed of this stream from another area of Kuiu Island.

Then I thought, maybe this bear has never before seen a man or caught human scent.

What the color of objects means to a bear, if anything, is open to speculation. Some zoologists maintain that bears don't react to color at all. But, just for the record, I was wearing a hip-length rain parka and fishing boots, both of an olive color, over my bush clothing.

I thought, if he's never before seen a man, just what does he think I am?

In the next moment, though fully realizing the chance I was taking, I decided to play out my hand with this bear.

Here was a big prime black facing what could well be his first encounter with man on an island where he had no natural danger to fear except unlikely attack or harassment by wolves—which his size and present physical condition would largely preclude. I believed, however, that he would spook before he got much closer and that I could scare him at any time by yelling at him. And I wanted to see whether I could learn anything new about bear behavior by just standing still and watching. I was very curious to see this black's reaction, based solely on sight and scent, to a man who was neither moving nor making a sound.

Again he started walking my way. When a bit less than 15 yards separated us, he hesitated. Then he continued toward me, to all appearances baffled and curious. Now he was moving a step at a time, tentatively, hesitatingly, his nose quivering. His glossy coat reflected his superb condition. He was built like a tank.

I was increasingly surprised that he didn't spook. He paused again, barely 20 feet from me. When he'd been 40 yards away and had first noticed me, he'd been both funny and interesting. Now, at 20 feet, he was just interesting. I'd recognized from the outset the possibility of his attacking, but I still considered it extremely remote.

Blackie moved a step closer.

I ought to holler at him right now, I thought.

But I wanted the bear to make up his mind without my yelling at him—if that could be brought about within the bounds of reasonable safety. I was just as curious about him as he was about me.

Another step. Each step by the bear now seemed to be a decision made.

With calculated slowness I pulled the .22 handgun from the holster and thumbed off the safety. I'd practiced a great deal with the pistol, had become fairly handy with it, and had shot close groups using the National Rifle Association pistol target at prescribed ranges. But a .22 in this situation would be a desperation measure only to be used if the bear actually attacked.

The bear edged a couple of steps still nearer and then stopped, frozen in place, one paw extended. He was now closer, I realized, than I ever should have let him get. I'd let my curiosity get the better of me, just as the blackie had his. I'd have bet 50 bucks with anybody, even after the bear started toward me, that he would spook before he got within 20 yards.

The edge of a granite boulder stuck up through the turf near the bear's front paw. Afterward I measured the distance from me to that spot and found that the blackie stood there a shade over 11 feet away.

Now only his head moved, very slowly, and his nose quivered. Seconds passed, and the tension mounted in both of us. In the absolute concentration of that moment I couldn't tell whether either the bear or I were yet really afraid. But neither of us was backed against a wall. We both had our alternatives.

I thought, If he starts another step toward me, I'll holler at him. If that doesn't turn him, he's had it. If it comes to that, though, we've probably both had it.

I looked into those small, dull eyes, which still

Overleaf — This photograph was taken from the canyon rim, looking down on an almost incredible concentration of pink and chum salmon below the falls on Anan Creek in early August.

25

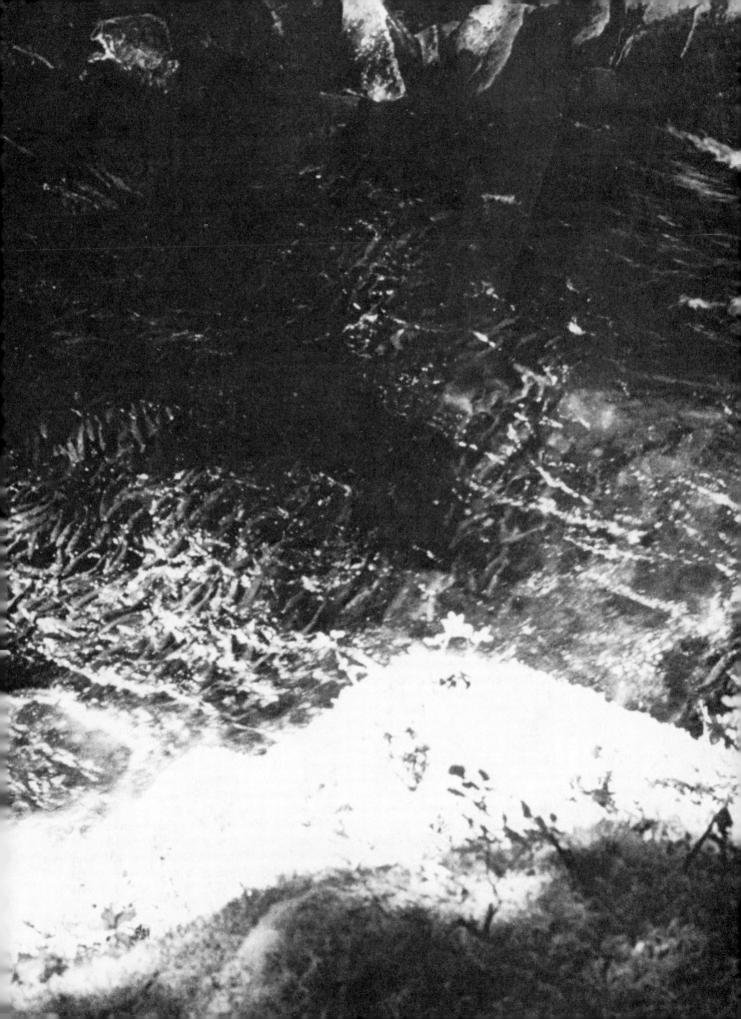

seemed only puzzled. Then there was a sudden change of expression. I believe I saw in that bear's eyes the moment when curiosity became primal fear.

He pivoted, still watching me over his shoulder. His breath exploded in a huffing grunt, *Huaaahhhh!* Then he was on his way.

Within a few yards he was in a full run, big rump bouncing, accelerating with every long paw-reaching stride. By the time he reached the edge of the meadow he was hitting a pace that I've never seen a bear exceed. He tore through a blueberry thicket at the edge of the forest and crashed up the timbered slope beyond. Moments later, there was only wild stillness.

My firsthand experience with the black bear of Southeastern Alaska began when I worked as a seasonal employee for the U.S. Fish & Wildlife Service to pay my way as a student at the University of Washington. Since then I've been fortunate in being able to observe the blackie in wilderness habitat each year for periods of a few days to several months, both while working with the Fish & Wildlife Service and while doing picture projects on my own.

Some of my best days afield have been spent seeking and observing the picturesque wily black, and I know that people who have seen him only as a mooching bum in Yellowstone Park have no idea of what a fascinating, challenging animal he can be when he's making an honest living in wilderness habitat.

However, the black **is** an opportunist wherever you find him. It's a fact that he will turn down neither easy grub nor cushy winter lodging.

At Jasper, Alberta, black bears—sometimes as many as eight—for many years wintered under a Canadian National Railway equipment warehouse, sleeping against the steam pipes beneath the building. During the occasional warm days, such as midwinter chinooks, these bears would crawl sleepily out onto the snow and bask in the sunshine. As their lethargy wore off they would play a bit, wrestling and cuffing one another around; then, when the air chilled off later in the day, they would retire again to their steam-heated quarters. Their soft touch ended with the dismantling of the warehouse.

The wilderness black is intelligent—perhaps more so than any other North American big game species—tough, and courageous. The general rule that the black gives ground to the grizzly is not without its exceptions.

One evening in late August of '67, while I was

A very large adult black bear which I confronted at close range in early May on an avalanche fan in the British Columbia Selkirk Range.

working on a grizzly study and photo project in British Columbia's Monashee Mountains, I saw a black bear sow with cubs chase off a young grizzly male that, by conservative estimate, outweighed her by 150 pounds. Enough similar cases have been reported to me by western-Canadian wardens and guides to indicate that my own observation was not particularly unusual.

Though the black bear in Alaska is well distributed over the interior from the Cook Inlet area north to the limit of spruce growth in the arctic, his greatest abundance is on the islands south of Frederick Sound, adjacent to the Southeastern Alaska Panhandle. These islands make up the best black bear country I've ever worked in, and very likely the best in North America. While working on salmon migration route and racial identification studies for the Fish & Wildlife Service, I visited all the major Southeastern Alaska islands, north and south of Frederick Sound.

There is an interesting point of wildlife ecology about these islands that has always intrigued me and for which I've never heard or read an explanation that I felt was entirely valid. Along the mainland Panhandle, wolves, black bears, and Alaska brown bears share the same range. However, on the islands that are Alaska brown habitat (Chichagof, Baranof, and Admiralty), neither the black bear nor the wolf occurs. Both wolves and black bears—but no Alaska browns—are found on Prince of Wales, Kupreanof, Kuiu, Etolin, Wrangell, Zarembo, Revillagigedo, and several smaller islands.

The cinnamon color phase of the black bear—quite common in the Rocky Mountain and Pacific Coast States, British Columbia and Alberta—is something of a rarity in Alaska. The only cinnamon black I can recall seeing in Alaska was fishing on a mainland stream about 30 miles south of the town of Wrangell.

The black bear, no less than the grizzly, is unpredictable, as my experience with the big bear on the meadow above Three-Mile-Arm would suggest. Another curious close-quarter encounter that impressed me happened one late August afternoon on the Cleveland Peninsula of the Southeastern Alaska mainland. Ashore from our research vessel base, the

62-foot diesel yacht *Heron,* a four-man Fish & Wild-life Service crew was surveying an excellent salmon spawning stream, two guys working each side. I was hiking the right-hand side 50 yards upstream from John Murphy, with project leader Carl Elling and Bob Ekwall observing from the opposite bank.

Sunlight broke through the wind-driven clouds. The good rain-washed scent of spruce-hemlock forest, at times covered by the fetid smell of dead salmon, carried on the downstream breeze. I put on polaroid sunglasses to better see salmon through the reflection and shadow of the water. Stopping on a gravel bar at the foot of a long, deep pool, I looked ahead at the largest school of pink salmon that we'd yet seen in the creek.

I studied the massed horde of salmon, and because of cloud reflection, the angle of the sun's rays, and sometimes wind-ruffling of the surface I found I could see the fish more clearly by looking down-stream. So I backed in slow cautious steps up the bar, trying not to spook the salmon, mentally gridding or dividing the school into sections. With far too many salmon to actually count, I could only try for the best estimate. Among the hundreds of schooled salmon, I spotted several that had been trap-captured in salt water, tagged by our crew (on Sumner Strait, using half-inch plastic discs applied just under the front portion of the dorsal fin) and released. Better stop now, and get this stuff down, I thought.

I turned and looked at the big windfall a dozen yards or so upstream near the head of the pool. An ancient Sitka spruce lay across the bar and nearly spanned the stream. I'll tally up again there, I thought. I dropped to one knee on the gravel, and, facing downstream, wrote and sketched for a few minutes recording my observations in a survey note-book. Then crouching almost motionless on the bar, I watched the salmon a minute or so longer before making a few additions and revisions on my notes.

The wind-driven overcast closed, and the light dropped like the falling of dusk. I took off the sunglasses, and pocketed them with the ball-point and notebook. I looked up at the darkening sky. A pair of ravens passed just overhead, the strokes of their great black wings hissing in the moist air. It's going to rain again anytime, I thought.

I stood up, and continued the slow, cautious back-ward steps up the gravel bar, intently watching the salmon, hearing but not registering the soft back-ground sounds of the stream, crying gulls and the occasional croaking of ravens. Must be about up to the windfall now, I thought. With my left hand I reached for the notebook and ball-point tucked in my shirt. Still watching the salmon, pulling the notebook from its pocket, I started to reach back with my free right hand for the expected spruce boughs, then looked over my shoulder.

I felt my pulse leap.

It was a shock that was almost physical—like touching an electric stock fence.

Instead of touching a spruce bough my reaching hand had almost grasped a handful of black fur. My stern end had come within four feet of bumping into the same anatomy on a bear! The blackie was facing at a diagonal upstream, his head buried to the ears in the water, as he, too, studied the salmon.

Quite likely without taking a breath, I tiptoed back five yards, and pulled a small movie camera from its case. The bear raised his head, water pouring from his face, looked straight back into the pool, and pushed his head in again.

I still couldn't believe it. But there he was. A wet, black 275-pound fact. How? I wondered. He must have come downstream and downwind on me, and this, of course, prevented him from getting my scent. But how could he have gotten there without seeing me? And how could he have done it without me hearing him? This baffled me then, but I've found from considerable further observation that bears—when they want to—can move as quietly as drifting smoke. And as I thought it over afterward, weighing the various probabilities of the strange encounter, it did add up. I had backed slowly and quietly up the gravel bar concentrating completely on the great school of salmon. The windfall spruce had screened me from the bear's sight on his approach from upstream. Almost certainly, the bear had either climbed over the spruce from the gravel bar on the upstream side or—as he was thoroughly wet—he may have waded into the creek above the tree and swum under it. I thought of the time I'd spent taking notes—my crouched, at-times-motionless silhouette, clad in olive-green rain gear, may not have caught his attention at all, or perhaps he was so interested in the salmon that he didn't even look my way.

But now on the gravel bar, at the same time recovering my composure and pulling the cap off the movie camera lens, I saw the bear again raise his head from the water. He cleared the water from his nose with an explosive *snoouuufff!* and shook his head in a mist of spray. Then he turned his head, slowly, looking slightly back over his shoulder, and, incredibly, for the first time he saw me.

For a long moment he stood looking at me, the most disbelieving bear I've ever met, as still as if he was painted against a classic forest and stream background of Southeastern Alaska. Then the bear's paws thrust backward, throwing gravel like a skidding car. He launched himself into the water in a wild shower of spray, dove under the spruce, and surfaced on the far side. Only then did the other guys on the crew finally see him. The blackie surged through the deep water, galloped in a spray-flying dash through the shallows, charged across the bar, faster with every rump-bouncing, paw-reaching stride, and

was gone in the rain forest before I could expose more than a couple of feet of film.

I've met a good many other bears on somewhat intimate terms over the years—blacks, Alaska brown bears, and the interior grizzly in mountain and tundra habitat—but I can't recall another situation from my own experience where more happened that fast.

Of bear study and photo trips that I've done on my own as a free-lancer, one I recall as a particular favorite was a late July-early August trip on the Southeastern Alaska mainland to Anan Creek, a rugged and beautiful stream that flows into Bradfield Canal, some 30 miles south of Wrangell and the mouth of the Stikine River.

The logistics of the trip were simplified when Skip McKibben, Alaska Department of Fish & Game officer, kindly offered me a lift in his patrol skiff on his way to move a stream guard.

The sky was clear when we arrived after a swift and scenic run from Wrangell, and the morning radio forecast from Juneau had indicated that the good weather was likely to hold for several more days. For this reason, along with my eagerness to get started with my field work, I decided not to take the time to put up my mountain tent that first morning, but quickly made a tree cache for my provisions. This I did only as a routine precaution. Because of the abundance of their natural food, I wasn't very concerned about possible trouble from bears. With the grub tarp-wrapped and hung between two trees about 20 feet above the ground, I secured the remainder of my equipment and clothing in a big Trapper Nelson pack, hung the pack on a spruce trunk, and headed out with my day-pack and camera gear.

In the first five minutes of hiking I sighted two black bears, both of which were a bit spooky and hit the woods before I could stalk close enough for good photos. But what at first most surprised and impressed me were the bald eagles and ravens. Though scavenger birds and birds of prey are observed on all salmon spawning streams, never before had I seen them in numbers like this.

But as I hiked further up Anan Creek, my surprise about the abundance of the big birds quickly ended. Senses and instinct had guided them well. Below the first major waterfall I reached upstream I stood on a high moss-covered bank and looked down on an almost incredible concentration of pink and chum salmon. From bank to bank, fins and tails were breaking the surface as far as I could see downstream. It was the largest salmon run, for that size of stream, that I'd ever witnessed.

Anticipating the arrival of one or more bears any moment, I quickly set up my tripod-mounted telephoto lens and reflex camera in a good natural blind. The camera gear ready, I looked back down at the salmon, marveling at their numbers.

In this return to their native stream, the salmon had beaten long odds. Bears fishing for salmon make up one of the more visible—and therefore, to us, more dramatic—predator-prey relationships in the ecology of the Pacific salmon. But compared to what the salmon face from the egg stage on throughout their lives, the impact of bear predation on salmon in their spawning streams is relatively minor. In fresh water trout and chars take a huge toll of eggs, fry, and smolt. Young salmon after the outmigration to sea are eaten by a host of predators including larger salmon. The more mature salmon are preyed on by seals, killer whales, sea lions, and—further north in Cook Inlet, the Gulf of Alaska, Bristol Bay and the Bering Sea—the white Beluga whale.

In the rugged terrain of Southeastern Alaska, salmon are often blocked by impassable waterfalls less than a mile or so from salt water. I've observed salmon, halted below falls that were obviously impossible for them to surmount, battering themselves against the rocks in exhausting efforts to get upstream. Watching, I could only wonder if they would finally give up and spawn below or kill themselves trying to get further upstream.

I've seen many salmon pushing upstream with flesh torn away by seal bites, others raked to the backbone by eagle claws. If a primitive instinct could be called courage there is no living thing that has more of it than the salmon.

The salmon's homing instinct is believed to be guided in part by a wonderful olfactory sense by which the salmon tastes or scents the water of his native stream many miles at sea in the outpourings of great rivers such as the Yukon, Nushagak, Kvichak, Skeena, Fraser, and Columbia.

Now as I watched the struggling hordes of pinks and chums below the falls on Anan Creek, every salmon that I saw actually jump fell well short of the crest and was swept back down. But salmon **were** getting upstream, and later that day I saw many above the falls. The salmon that I did see make it remained submerged and with a tremendous tail-lashing swimming effort powered their way up over the face of the rock.

These first big falls on Anan Creek tax the energy of the salmon, and may approach the limit of what pink and chum salmon can ascend. The pink, chum, and sockeye salmon are not capable of the beautiful arcing leaps of the king (chinook, tyee) and coho (silver), to both of which these falls on Anan would be no problem. And none of the Pacific salmon can match the steelhead trout in surmounting rapids and falls—the steelhead being, pound for pound, the strongest swimmer of all Pacific Coast anadromous fish. (The Atlantic salmon, *Salmo salar,* is, like the steelhead, actually another big ocean-going trout. It has a life history very similar to that of the steelhead, and is also comparable in its ability to leap falls and to swim effectively against very swift current velocities.)

Below the falls on Anan, ravens and gulls perched on the rocks, feeding on torn pieces of salmon dropped by the bears. It was obvious that a bear—or bears—had left the stream just before my arrival. At frequent intervals, between shooting pictures of salmon struggling against the falls, I scanned the steep, heavily-timbered opposite slope looking for bears. I didn't have long to wait.

Hardly 15 minutes after I got there, I looked up to see a black bear sitting on his haunches under a windfall hemlock on the rugged slope above and across from me. I put the binoculars on him—a big bear in excellent condition, his coat a glossy, bluish-black. Seconds after I spotted him, the bear stood up on his hind paws, his head moving slowly from side to side as he sniffed the air currents; then he dropped to all fours and started down, climbing over or crawling under the windfall trees, descending the steep pitch with superb balance, padding with long, reaching steps down over the mossy slabs of granite. Sitting up on the slope, he had looked ponderous and rather comical, but now his hefty bulk seemed to flow in its easy grace and controlled power. A few yards from the stream he stopped, almost seeming to stand on his head on a steeply inclined slab-like boulder.

I looked at him through the 9x50 glasses, giving me a field-filling head and shoulder portrait. I wondered, at that moment, if shifting air currents had brought him my scent. He was cautious; his eyes and quivering, wind-sniffing nose signaled wariness and apprehension.

Then, though still seeming edgy, he stepped down halfway into the stream, and stood intently watching the water, his hind paws yet up on the rock, and the turbulent current foaming and swirling around his forelegs. I waited, set to react, watching through the camera viewfinder.

Seconds later the bear pushed from the rock with a sudden, powerful thrust of his hind legs; his head plunged into the foam and rose with a struggling, bleeding salmon trapped in his jaws. He turned, heaved himself up on the bank, shook his coat in a misty shower of spray, then climbed with impressive ease up the rugged slope to eat his catch in the forest.

In about 20 minutes he was back, and within the hour there was further camera action with two other bears. During my five-day stay on Anan Creek I came to recognize as individuals 11 bears—all blacks, though coastal grizzlies may well have been fishing further upstream—and undoubtedly other bears were nocturnal and very early morning fishermen that I didn't see.

Like all other bears that I've seen catch fish, these blackies without an exception did so with their jaws, not by throwing salmon out on the bank with paw swats. The concentration of salmon below the falls was so great that the only real effort the bears had to make was in their travel to and from the stream— likely a minimal distance according to the degree of each bear's feeling of security or insecurity within the hierarchy of dominance of the bears fishing that section of stream.

Most of the bears ate their salmon within a few yards of the stream, but others such as the first bear that I saw catch a salmon there, carried their catches up the slope to eat them in the seclusion of the forest.

The night following my arrival at Anan Creek, the sky, as the Juneau radio forecast had predicted, was holding clear. Returning to my campsite just before dusk, I built a small cooking fire, and prepared a quick, simple but tasty supper of Swiss vegetable soup, Thuringer sausage broiled with cheese on an alder twig, coffee, and pilot bread crackers with butter and jam.

It had been a long day, and a few minutes after finishing supper my head began to nod as I sat by the warmth of the campfire. I splashed cold water on my face to clear my head for the few chores I had to do before hitting the sack. Not yet needing the flashlight, I spread a canvas ground cloth on the mossy forest floor, blew up an air mattress, and rolled out a light down sleeping bag. With that great salmon run in the stream, I wasn't worried about a prowling bear sniffing out my high hanging grub cache.

A breeze came up off the bay, carrying that wild, lovely mingling of scents of salt air and spruce-

Black bear cubs sent up a tree by their mother at the approach of potential danger. Photographed in June in the Selkirk Mountains of British Columbia.

hemlock forest. Listening to the soughing of the boughs, the lapping of waves on the rocks just below me, and the subtle, unidentified night sounds of the forest I dropped off to sleep. A few hours before dawn I awoke, momentarily with that always strange feeling of not knowing where I was. Then, remembering, I raised up on one elbow to look around. The light wind had stopped, and a chill sea fog had come in. Snug in the down bag, I fell quickly back to sleep.

Waking again soon after daybreak, I could see that the fog was already thinning and that it was going to be another beautiful day. But then with sudden anger I noticed something that wasn't. Ravens roosting overnight in the spruce boughs above me had splattered my sleeping bag and ground cloth. A painstaking and time-consuming washing and drying job would be the first chore of the morning. My irritation ebbed, however, as I considered my relative good fortune in that, despite several near misses, I hadn't been hit on the head. Clear weather or not, that tent goes up today, I thought.

Though not getting away as early as usual, I covered more ground that day than on any other during the trip. Returning down the creek that evening, with tough miles behind me and some promising film exposed, I really felt on top. But a half-mile or so upstream from camp I heard a very displeased bear. The angry, huffing *huuaaahhh!* startled me to an abrupt halt. Close. Much too close. But just where it came from I couldn't tell.

In one hand I was carrying a tripod-mounted reflex camera and telephoto lens. A .30-'06 rifle was slung on my shoulder. I stood very still, listening and watching. There was no sound now but the soft crying of distant gulls, the murmur of the creek, and the sighing rustle of the downstream wind through boughs. Then I stepped a few yards away from the stream and into the forest, moving very slowly and as quietly as I could. And then I saw the bear.

A black sow was about 25 yards from me and 20 feet or so up a hemlock. I don't know if she actually saw me then, but an instant after I saw her she started down fast, flaking off bark with her claws. Her two spring cubs were above her, and following their mother's stern order they were now climbing like squirrels.

Left — Anan Creek, on the Southeastern Alaska mainland, photographed in early August during a very heavy run of pink (humpback) and chum (dog) salmon. Anan Creek flows into salt water near the head of Brad-field Canal, about 30 miles south of Wrangell and the mouth of the Stikine River.

A blackie plunges into the foam *(right)*, missing a salmon on his first try. He resumes his fishing and a few moments later, again plunges his head under the foam and comes up with a struggling, bleeding fresh-run pink salmon clamped in his jaws *(below)*.

Right — The blackie stops his fishing for a few moments and appears apprehensive, perhaps after catching man scent on the shifting air currents of the canyon, although I don't believe that at that time this bear had seen me.

Above — Another salmon-hungry black bear, on his way to the stream to fish, eyes me warily from the cover of the rain forest greenery.

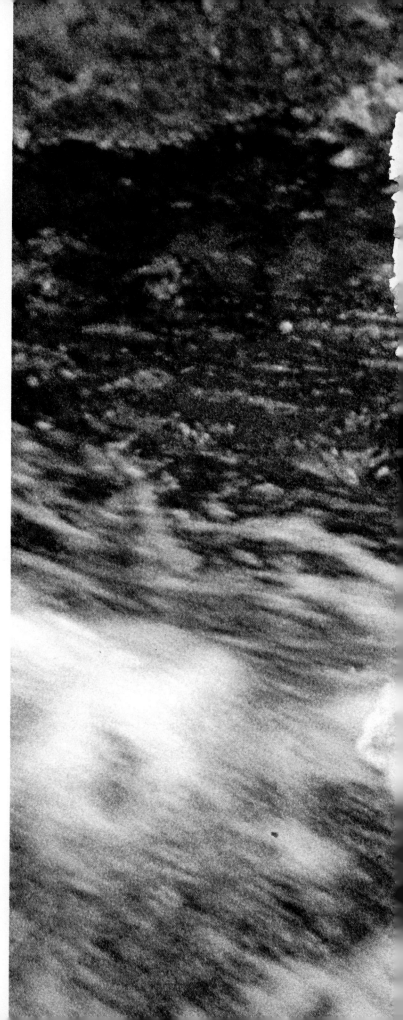

Another pair of black bear cubs sent up a tree by their mother at some sign of danger. Photographed in June in British Columbia's Selkirk Mountains.

The sow had my scent, was reacting defensively to it, and here, I figured, was a bear that was going to need some room. Moving back quietly, I hiked through the timber and out over to the trail about 50 yards upstream. Standing on a bend of the creek, I had a much better overall view now of the immediate area. I quickly spotted the cubs again, so high up in the hemlock they were swaying its crown. From that point I could only see about the upper third of the tree, but guessed that the sow was on the ground near its base.

Probably another 30 seconds passed as I watched. Then I heard a short, huffing grunt— apparently the sow telling the cubs that the coast was clear and it was okay to come down. Immediately they started a scrambling descent. Moments later I watched the bear family ford the creek and disappear in the forest.

I hiked downstream again for camp. The rifle, still hanging by its sling from my shoulder, hadn't been moved. Certainly not expecting to use it, I'd brought it along on that trip against the rather remote chance of running into a belligerent rogue—a bear injured by bullet wounds months or years before that had recovered, and had psychologically associated the scent of man with the lingering pain that he had endured. Those are bears that have been known to **come looking** for trouble (read the experience of hunting guide Jim Stanton in "The Brown Bears of Pack Creek," Chapter Six). But in the situation of meeting this sow bear as I hiked downstream on Anan Creek, it was a very clear case of the bear having the right of way.

If I had forced the issue by continuing downstream at that time under those circumstances, the fault for the almost certain trouble would have been **mine**, not the bear's.

Bears that have recovered from bullet wounds, and bears that have become spoiled national park bums have to be considered in categories apart from normal bears making an honest living in wilderness habitat. Generally, I've found that getting along with wilderness bears is only a matter of staying alert, keeping cool, and using some common sense.

38

3 Trails
of the
High Country
Coyote

Observations ⟍ of the coyote and his
co-predators in their mountain habitat.

Hungry but very nervous coyotes feed off a wolf-killed
elk (concealed from view) on a meadow in the Alberta
Rockies in early January.

**"Trails of the High
Country Coyote"** is from
ALASKA® magazine, May-June 1976
Alaska Northwest Publishing Company
Box 4-EEE, Anchorage, Alaska 99509

The deep cold of midwinter had settled over the northern Rockies. My descent down the timbered slope was steepening now and, remembering the patches of hard ice a few days before, I picked my way carefully in the few inches of new snow. But suddenly, even with this concentration, one of my pacs lost its hold, and I grabbed at a spruce bough as I started to slip. It snapped off, as brittle and fragile as an icicle, but it was just enough to help me regain balance and save a fall. What damned insanity this is, I thought.

But even while conceding the near truth of that thinking, I grinned behind the protective woolen face mask. This was my job, and I really wouldn't want to

40

do anything else. I stopped a moment on the slope to adjust the fit of the mask. It was humidly warm on the inside and frosted stiff on the outside. I use it in sub-zero cold, particularly if there's any wind, to shield an old frostbite injury I picked up a dozen winters ago in Western Alaska. I'd worked in colder weather than it was that day in the Rockies (late January '68), and would again. In this work, if you let weather—any weather—hold you back, you've lost the ball game.

The angle of the steep slope eased off, and I detoured north a quarter-mile around a bad stretch of "shintangle"—the downed snags of an old burn, then turned due east again through the spruce and lodgepole pine forest toward the canyon of the Snake Indian River.

Three hours away from my winter camp in the wilderness backcountry of Jasper National Park in the Alberta Rockies, I reached the west side of the canyon. Below me the river—rushing and wild, spring through autumn—was flowing subdued under ice and, with the dropping of the frigid morning wind, I could hear the occasional rumbling of its buckling stresses as more ice built up. Across the river the canyon wall rose sheer, then beautiful, open parklike country sloped back from the rim with scattered spruce, poplar and pine. Beneath the light snow on the wind-scoured slopes were dormant mountain grasses, kinnikinnick, and a form of ground-hugging mountain juniper.

I heard a fluttering in the pine boughs beside me. A whiskeyjack (gray or Canada jay) settled in a branch within arm's length, and looked me over with his black beady eyes. His feathers were greatly fluffed out, providing trapped air insulation against the bitter cold. "How're you gettin' along, little guy?" I said through the woolen mask.

I looked back across the canyon, and just then I spotted the rams. Seven bighorns lay bedded in the snow a few feet below a ledgy outcropping of reddish limestone. I uncased 9x50 binoculars.

Three of the rams were watching me, four were looking away, and all were calmly chewing their cuds, at ease and conserving precious energy on a savagely cold day. All but two were a deep chocolate brown that under an overcast sky would have appeared almost black. One ram was a light yellowish-brown, and the biggest of all was reddish-colored with an admixture of silvery-gray, much like the color of a strawberry roan horse. He was an old-timer, and one of two rams in the bunch that I felt sure

would measure 40 inches or better around the outside curve of their horns. Fresh chips had been knocked out of his great horns, and he had a skinned patch a couple of inches above his nose that, through the glasses, looked like it had just healed. As he turned his head, I could see that he had a very pronounced Roman-nosed profile, and undoubtedly he'd sustained an upper jaw fracture more than once in his adventurous life. In the now-still air the rams' breath was rising in frosty plumes.

One of the dark rams stood up, grazed briefly on the wind-exposed grass, presently returned to his bedding spot, scraped it several times with a front hoof, made a complete turn around and lay down again.

These slopes overlooking the east side of the Snake Indian canyon, where scouring winds sweep away the snow to drift it deeply further on against rocky shoulders or copses of spruce, are favored winter range for bighorn sheep. From November through May I've often seen ewes, lambs and younger rams as well as the mature rams I was watching now. As I moved the glasses up the slope and north along the ridge checking for other sheep, I picked up a coyote just dropping over the crest.

The coyote lost elevation quickly, and 100 feet or so above the canyon rim he turned downriver traversing the open slope, stopping often to sniff at animal trails in the snow, and once raising a hind leg to leave his scent on the wind-exposed roots of a dead juniper. He appeared to be in excellent condition, with a beautifully deep-furred late January coat. The coyote trotted up on a shoulder of the slope and, cresting, sighted the rams.

For a few moments he stood very still, then his head moved slowly from side to side, his nose sifting the frigid currents of air. I swung the glasses back on the rams. They were all looking at the coyote.

I pulled the protective cover off the tripod-mounted 400mm lens and reflex camera, set up the tripod in the snow, and focused on the coyote through the ground glass viewfinder of the camera. The lens barrel rotated quickly and smoothly, winterized by the removal of the normal temperature lubricant and the substitution of powdered graphite.

The coyote trotted down off the rise. Panning the camera with the tripod head, I "tracked" the coyote, keeping him framed in the viewfinder. Twice I triggered the shutter release. Must be getting close to those rams, I thought.

Then, too excited by the possibility of getting a

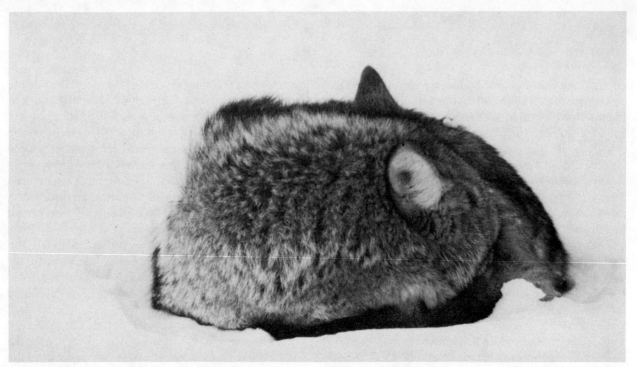

The sequence of photos from page 40 to page 45 was taken on a frozen mountain lake in the Alberta Rockies. The coyote was resting on the lake ice after feeding on the remnants of a wolf-killed moose. The coyote was aware of my approach but did not spook until I was within good telephoto range.

Above, his nose and the pads of all four feet are tucked into the luxurious denseness of his tail fur.

Opposite, and on page 40, he raises his head, decides that the intruder is getting too close, rises in a great stretch, *page 44,* yawns, *page 45,* and then stands looking in every direction and sniffing the wind currents, probably apprehensive about the wolves whose moose meat he has been stealing between feedings of the larger predators, and trots away across the lake ice into the forest.

dramatic picture sequence, I literally and figuratively "blew it." Tracking the coyote through the waist-level viewfinder, I carelessly exhaled a breath at the wrong time and it froze in a hard, translucent glaze over the ground glass finder of the camera. It's a delicate removal job, without scratching the glass, and there wouldn't be time for it. I swore softly, and grabbed up the binoculars. The trotting coyote was traversing the slope at the same elevation as the rams, and he was barely 40 yards from them. But not a ram had yet bothered to stand up; they hadn't even interrupted their cud-chewing.

About 50 feet from the rams, the coyote turned slightly up the slope, trotted on a few more yards, crested the ledgy outcropping of limestone, stopped abruptly, and stood there looking down at the bighorns, a short five yards from the nearest ram.

The coyote stood motionless. The bighorns looked up at him. Still not a one had risen, but now they'd stopped chewing their cuds. A sudden frigid draft of wind rippled the coyote's heavy coat; otherwise, for a few moments, the entire tableau had been motionless. Through the 9x50 glasses, rams and coyote against the picturesque background were like figures

in a Charlie Russell painting. What the hell's that coyote up to? I wondered.

Then I saw the ram closest to the coyote shift his weight, about to rise. That old boy's going to run him over the ridge, I thought.

But the ram settled back in his bed, and a moment later the coyote turned on the ledge, leaped down, and trotted away in a climbing traverse—as graceful as fog rising off a marsh. He paused a few times to sniff at tracks and check the scents in the wind, then trotted on again until he crested the ridge and vanished.

It's tough to guess what a coyote will do next. But there's one thing you can usually count on. He'll surprise you.

A few autumns ago on the north slope of the Alaska Range, I was eating lunch one chill November day on the bank of the Nenana River, a major confluent of the Yukon River system. The day was overcast and, at the time, almost windless. Sitting on a fallen cottonwood, warmly outfitted in a down jacket and thermal pacs, I'd been enjoying the sandwiches, hot coffee, and the almost spooky solitude for about 20 minutes.

There was at the time a good population of snow-shoe hares in the area, and that morning I'd jumped a dozen or so out of their forms. In that locality, near the northeast boundary of Mount McKinley National Park, it was good country for lynx, coyote, red fox, wolf and wolverine.

Finishing lunch and putting my day pack back together, I decided I'd work downriver for the rest of the day, checking for predator sign, and seeing what I might call up. Pulling one of my homemade calls from the pocket of a wool shirt, I noticed that some lint had caught in it. I probed it out with a broken tip of willow twig and, to check its tone before heading downriver, I blew a soft, squealing cry from it. Not bad, I thought.

I picked up my pack, shrugged into the straps, and started to stand up. Then, just perceptibly—from two directions, I heard soft, swift footfalls in the snow. I dropped back down and sat absolutely still on the log. A red fox blurred through the willows. Seeing me, he stopped abruptly; a front paw held up, his motion arrested in midstride. I remained dead still. A couple of seconds later a running coyote angled in from downstream and behind me, and stopped just as suddenly less than five yards from the fox. Both predators were so close that I couldn't have focused on them with the 400mm lens.

They studied me carefully for a long moment, unspooked; looked at each other with what seemed at the time rather surprising equanimity—neither curled a lip nor showed a fang—then back at me.

Hoping not to spook them, I reached in a smooth, deliberate motion for the normal lens "grab shot" camera hanging on my chest.

But fox and coyote turned from each other and trotted swiftly away in opposite directions, both apparently coming to the conclusion that I was the disappointing source of the harelike sound.

In early April of '73, on a cold, cloudy morning that hinted of new snow, I was watching a coyote crossing a still-frozen marshland in Alberta's upper Athabasca Valley where, three days before, the Canada geese had returned. The coyote had appeared suddenly from the snowy spruce and willow cover just east of the marsh, and with artfully feigned disregard he approached the honkers, stopping frequently to sniff among the tussocks of grass and twice to leave his scent on a willow clump and the shattered base of a windfall spruce. As he trotted closer, the geese reproached him with a loud and resentful *eeronk! eeronk!*

The geese—rather surprisingly to me—did not take flight as the coyote trotted within a dozen yards of them. But the angry honking became louder and more agitated. On the coyote's part, though, it was an Academy Award performance in indifference. There he was, moving within a few yards of the finest eating that a coyote could dream of, and yet as I watched him, at no time did he seem to look directly at a goose.

Once, for several long moments the coyote stopped, and with head raised looked off across the valley at the great brooding mountains as if admiring the scenery.

I wondered. Tomorrow, the next day, or next week? I noted the coyote's fine condition and excellent winter fur. He certainly hadn't gotten very hungry that winter. I watched him until he disappeared in the heavy cover across the marsh. He was a coyote that could afford to wait and play the main chance. And he's sure working on a goose dinner, I thought.

In his ability to adjust to new and changing habitat, the coyote excels all other native wildlife species on this continent. Since the time he was first seen by white explorers, the coyote made his most extensive—and dramatically swift—push into new country three-quarters of a century ago. The records of fur buyers and traders, and the observations by pioneer North Country bushmen, verify that the

coyote was not in northern British Columbia, Yukon Territory and Alaska until the turn of the century or a few years later. The reports of old-timers pretty well substantiate that the coyote extended his range northward during the 1898 Klondike gold rush by following the stampeders north and feeding on the carcasses of horses and mules that died along the trail.

In my home state of Washington, the coyote has moved into the extreme western area, establishing himself in the rain forest and high meadows of the Olympic Range, partially filling an ecological niche left by the killing off, decades ago, of the Olympic gray wolf—a magnificent animal that was as particularly adapted to the dense forest and steep mountains as the famed Roosevelt elk that he preyed on.

The coyote makes his living the only way he can—by his remarkably developed sense organs, his intelli-

gence, and his teeth, plus his incredible patience, speed, stealth and stamina. Early outdoor writers, even men of the stature of Dr. William Hornaday and Theodore Roosevelt, were contemptuous of the coyote and frequently used such adjectives as "slinking" and "cowardly" to describe him. It baffles me that men who otherwise seemed such skilled and accurate observers of nature could be, in my opinion, so far off the mark in their appraisal of coyotes.

While working at summer vacation ranch jobs as a kid, in the high, semiarid wheat and cattle country of the Rattlesnake and Horse Heaven Hills of east-central Washington, I saw coyotes, fighting as individuals, give away up to 10 or 12 pounds to ranch dogs and still whip them.

The coyote is a small predator-scavenger, smart enough to know his limitations, and smart enough

not to go against long odds. But for his size he's no more a coward than the moose and grizzly are.

During an eight-winter study of the hunting behavior of wolves in the Canadian Rockies, I had some interesting opportunities to watch coyotes feeding on the carcasses of wolf-killed elk and moose—while the heavily fed big predators were resting a hundred yards or so away. These kills were found both by direct tracking of the wolves in snow and, more often, by watching the sky for the converging flight patterns of ravens and magpies.

One coyote, a young male, especially impressed me with his deft and daring larceny on the carcass of a wolf-killed bull elk near the confluence of Ranger Creek and the upper Athabasca River in the Alberta Rockies. I witnessed this incident late one afternoon in the early winter of '72. A pack of six wolves had downed and fed heavily on the bull. They'd just left

the kill, trotting slowly away to curl up and rest in a stand of young spruce. Later I paced off the distance from the elk carcass to their resting site, and found it to be a bit over 85 yards. This was rather surprising to me, as it seems reasonable that the wolves would always choose a resting site handier to the kill so they could more easily protect it from scavengers. But that's their secret, and I can only speculate on it. I've seen wolves bed down right beside a kill after feeding, and on other occasions move to a resting site as far as a quarter-mile away. Likely it depends a great deal on how good recent hunting has been. Here, apparently, there was just something about the cover of the dense Christmas-treelike spruce stand that appealed to them. Also, the wolves here knew I was watching them and, while they had been hungry enough to feed under my discreet observation, probably in this situation they felt more at ease resting some distance from the kill.

As I watched the ravens and magpies wing down and settle on the elk, a coyote appeared out of the spruce-poplar forest upriver from the kill and the resting wolves. He trotted out onto the glade where the carcass lay, stood still a few moments testing the wind; then, acutely alert, looking cautiously around him, he trotted up to the kill and began voraciously feeding. The ravens and magpies scattered momentarily, then settled back down around the coyote.

It was getting dusky now, with a light snow falling, but visibility was still good.

Both on edge and ravenously hungry, the coyote ate in gulping mouthfuls, sometimes grabbing a piece of tough connective tissue around a joint, bracing his paws, tugging, shaking his head as powerful jaws and sharp carnassial teeth severed the flesh. But almost with every bite the coyote looked around to check his surroundings. About a dozen ravens and magpies were on the kill with him. Coyotes will often rush and snap at scavenger birds when they are feeding together on a carcass, but here he ignored them. He was too apprehensive about the wolves to bother about the presence of his fellow freeloaders.

The coyote knew where the wolves were resting, and most of his attention was directed that way—though his view was partially screened by timber. But he was watching all around, too, obviously expecting that the wolves might circle and return from any side.

I made a slight adjustment in the focus of the binoculars, and quickly brushed the accumulated snow off them with a bandana.

Suddenly two big grays broke cover. As careful as the coyote had been, there may have been an unfavorable wind shift for him as it seemed that he was momentarily caught off guard. The wolves came in a bounding rush, and they meant business. But the coyote took off, flat-out, racing through the poplars, almost immediately opening ground on the meat-sluggish wolves, and was well away when the chase went out of my sight in the timber.

In a few moments the two wolves came trotting back, breath smoking in the cold, tongues lolling. It had been a brisk run on a full belly. Stopping at the kill, they fed again briefly before trotting back into the spruce to let their heavy meal digest further.

They could hardly have settled themselves in the snow before the coyote was back on the kill. The rush came sooner this time, but again the coyote easily outran the two big grays.

Within five minutes the coyote returned. There seemed to be a perceptible change in his attitude now. No less alert, but seemingly less nervous, he tore into his feeding with voracious relish. He'd taken the measure of the wolves in speed.

Four times, before it was too dark for further observation, I saw the wolves chase the coyote off the kill, only to have him soon return. Evidently he had the discretion not to take on **too** full a belly, as I saw him again the following day.

The coyote is essentially a small game hunter, and particularly for rodents. Many times I've watched them stalking meadow mice and ground squirrels; one of my favorite localities for this is a brushy meadow area bordering the Kootenay River a few miles from Canal Flats, British Columbia. The coyote's patience, grace, agility and speed would do credit to a superbly trained bird dog. He may stand motionless for long moments like a pointer or setter, then suddenly pounce in an arcing, jackknifing leap, trapping the mouse under his front paws.

Most of the areas where I observe coyotes rodent-stalking are in remote country, but one of the best spots in the Rocky Mountain West is easily accessible, and I'd recommend it to anyone interested in watching coyotes hunt. It's a great willow-thicketed meadow in Yellowstone National Park, and you see it on your right just as you crest out after climbing the switchbacks when driving south from Mammoth Hot Springs, Wyoming.

In the northern Rockies, the coyote feeds mainly on ground squirrels, meadow voles and other rodents, the snowshoe hare, berries and a variety of other vegetation, with higher ranging coyotes—to timberline and above—taking marmots, conies and pikas whenever opportunity arises. Grouse, ptarmigan and other birds are choice coyote fare, but are taken much less frequently.

The flesh of deer, elk, mountain sheep and other big game ungulates is eaten largely as carrion—particularly as winterkill in the early spring, robbing wolf kills, and on animals that have been killed or badly injured on highways and railroads. It's a curious situation about cougar kills and coyotes. The coyote of the northern Rockies, as we've just seen, sometimes helps himself on fresh wolf kills, and in other ways lives by the calculated risk; but evidently he has a hearty respect for the silent stalking and lethal, catapulting rush of the cougar. I've watched cougar kills on deer and elk for several days, and I've yet to see an attempt by a coyote to feed on a cougar's kill, even in several cases where I saw coyotes in the near vicinity, and was sure that they'd winded the kills.

Beavers out of the water on their logging operations are highly vulnerable, and I've seen remains of several kills in the Canadian Rockies where beavers had been caught and eaten—in two cases definitely by coyotes; in the others, on the evidence available, there was no sure way of identifying the predator.

Old-timers in the northern Rockies and Monashee Mountains of British Columbia have told me of individual coyotes that had learned the difficult and dangerous technique of killing porcupines—which seems almost instinctive to the lightning fast and lethal fisher, a large, dark-coated member of the weasel family that sometimes approaches a weight of 18 or 20 pounds.

The coyote circles the porcupine, feinting in swift rushes, deftly avoiding the slaps of the quill-loaded tail, steadily wearing the porky down; and, finally, when the porcupine tires, darts in, and one paw thrust with quick, lethal precision flips the porcupine on his back; then the coyote attacks the unprotected belly. This takes judgment and well-honed skill, and only older coyotes, seasoned and accomplished hunters of other small game would have much chance of getting away with it. A bumbling pup would likely be so badly quilled that he'd probably never again attempt a porcupine—if he survived, which sometimes even fishers don't.

On the Alaska Railroad between Anchorage and Fairbanks, and in western Canadian areas adjoining railroads, carrion resulting from train kills provides windfall food for the coyote and other predators.

Moose, elk, mule deer, caribou and even mountain sheep are killed by trains during the winter and early spring, and occasionally predators themselves are hit when crossing the track to feed on casualties. Coyotes, wolves, lynx, wolverines, foxes, grizzlies, black bears and cougars all feed on the railway kills.

The still widely held belief of old cat hunters and stockmen that the cougar won't eat carrion just doesn't hold up. I've observed cougars feeding on train-killed elk, moose and bighorn sheep near Tete Jaune Cache, British Columbia, and Henry House and Brule Tunnel, Alberta—all on the Canadian National Railway.

Year after year, for a variety of reasons such as heavy snow depth in late winter and spring, proximity of mineral licks and/or favored feeding areas, the same points along the Canadian National line are bad spots for the killing of certain species of wildlife. On the C.N.R., moose casualties occur with particular frequency near Red Pass Junction and in the Grantbrook and Fitzwilliam sections, all in the British Columbia Rockies. The often extreme snow depth prompts the moose to take to the track, the only easy going there is.

Traditionally unfortunate places for the killing of bighorn sheep are Windy Point and Brule Tunnel, both in Jasper National Park in the Alberta Rockies. Elk are killed more randomly, but most often along the Snaring and Devona sections of the C.N.R. through the Alberta Rockies. There's usually little that the locomotive engineer can do to avoid these collisions, other than using the whistle and, at night, momentarily turning off the headlight. The brilliant light tends to dazzle and confuse the animal, and turning it off for a few seconds will often allow the elk or moose to step off the track.

But nothing really can be done as far as reducing speed to avoid hitting an animal. Even by "pulling air"—emergency braking—there is usually no way that a stop can be made in time, and with the tonnage behind the locomotive it makes little difference to the elk or moose if he's hit at 45 mph or 12. The animals apparently have little concept of the speed and enormous mass of the trains; and, curiously, some animals, frustrated by the deep snow and reluctant to leave the easy going of the rail bed, may run ahead of the train for several hundred yards, then, instead of stepping off the track, will stop and turn back toward the whistling, onrushing locomotive in belligerent challenge. Bull moose particularly, and, on more rare occasions, also bull elk and bighorn rams have ac-

A mountain coyote photographed in late September in the Kootenay Rockies of British Columbia. I called this coyote simulating the cry of a small injured animal by using a heavy rubber band tautly stretched between two small pieces of cedar shingle wood. The coyote is essentially a hunter of small prey such as hares, mice and ground squirrels. The coyote can usually take larger animals such as deer and mountain sheep only when they are very young, injured or diseased, or when there is deep snow with a heavy crust, or in other special conditions of weather, cover and terrain.

tually charged locomotives on the C.N.R. main line through the Rockies (bighorns periodically descend from the windswept benches of their winter range to lick salt brine lost from refrigerator cars on the track). The railroad engineers that I know are, to a man, conscientious and do everything feasible to avoid these collisions.

The railroads are a definite and not insignificant factor in the wildlife ecology of large areas of western Canada and Alaska. One may deplore the loss of large ungulate wildlife as train casualties (unlike the natural selection operating in predation, railway kills of wildlife appear to be quite random as to the age, sex and physical condition of the animals), but there is another way of looking at it. The railroad kills are totally utilized by predators. The train casualties found by wolves are that many head of large ungulates the wolves won't need to pull down themselves. The predators, no less than their prey species, are beautiful and wonderfully interesting animals; and during winters when the snowshoe hare is near the low of its cycle, and other small game is scarce, railway kills become, in some areas, a major factor for the survival of the smaller predators such as the lynx, coyote, fox and fisher.

Though the coyote in mountain habitat is a generally larger form than the coyote found in prairie, desert and foothill country, he's not the true predator on the adults of large ungulates that the wolf and cougar are. Only in exceptional circumstances is the coyote capable of taking mature big game, such as when the animal is already severely injured from another source—a badly placed hunter's bullet, a broken leg from a fall, a disabling injury suffered in combat—or an animal weakened by old age, heavy parasite infestation, starvation during a severe winter, or a combination of these factors (quite often the case). Winter-weakened deer in deep snow become vulnerable to coyote predation.

In my wolf-study area in the Canadian Rockies there are occasional winters of exceptionally deep snow. The typical pattern of thawing and refreezing during late winter and early spring produces a hard, very abrasive crust that is brutal for the heavy, sharp-hoofed deer, elk and moose. Such conditions heavily favor the predators. While the ungulates break through, the crust will often support the predators, with their paws—particularly the wide-padded paws of the cougar—helping greatly in weight distribution. There are times in such snow conditions—and on already weakened big game animals—that the coyote becomes an effective hunter of large ungulates.

But if there is a mild winter of light snow, and a minimal die-off of ungulates in the spring, coupled with low hare and rodent populations, then the coyote is in big trouble, and some of them will face starvation.

It's still a common misconception that predators are the primary factor in limiting populations of big game. Actually, prey populations from small rodents to elk and moose **control predator numbers** to a greater extent than any predator controls prey. We need to keep in mind that there are fluctuations in all wildlife populations—primarily based on the abundance or scarcity of food—whether there is predation or not.

In the North Country the most dramatic example of this is the snowshoe or varying hare—observed particularly in connection with my wolf work in Alaska and northern Saskatchewan—which in a cycle of about 7 to 10 years goes from an almost incredible abundance to a scarcity that almost seems to border on extinction. The Canada lynx—the hare's major predator—doesn't control hare numbers, not even with all the voracious help of the coyote, red fox, wolf, fisher, wolverine, owl, golden eagle and gyrfalcon. But when the hare population ultimately peaks and, soon after, crashes, lynx numbers will drop drastically within a year.

The lynx, of all the northern predators, is most keyed to the rise and fall of the hare population, but the coyote and the other predators painfully feel the loss of this food source and, while the more adaptable of each species will adjust and survive, their numbers will drop, both directly through starvation and indirectly through the resulting birth of smaller litters.

In the northern Rockies, far more big game ungulates become food for the coyote through winterkills than from any other circumstance. So-called winterkill usually occurs in the early spring—in my project area mostly in April.

A deer, elk or moose can starve through a severe winter of extreme low temperature and deep snow, and still be alive when green feed is again available in the spring. But when the body and bone marrow fat is mostly absorbed, the animal reaches a point of no return; he is irretrievably headed over the Big Divide no matter how balmy the early spring turns out to be or how succulent the new feed is. These are the big game animals that the coyote mostly feeds on, but this can hardly be called predation.

In May and June there is limited predation by coyotes on the fawns, calves and lambs of the deer, elk, moose and bighorn sheep. Moose and elk cows, and mule deer and whitetail does are dangerously defensive against predation attempts on their young. Some females with young—particularly cow moose—seem at times actually **too** aggressive for the effective protection of their offspring. On my project work in the Canadian Rockies several years ago in June, I saw a big muley doe leave her fawn and chase a coyote. She wasn't content to merely drive him away from the immediate area; she seemed determined to overtake and kill him. She was away from her fawn long enough that if two coyotes had been hunting together, as is often the case, the waiting partner coyote would have had more than ample time to kill the fawn.

In the DeSmet Range of the Alberta Rockies and in the Ashnola-Similkameen country of the British Columbia Cascade Range I've watched thwarted stalking attempts by coyotes against bighorn ewes with lambs. When Dall and bighorn ewes and Rocky Mountain goat nannies near their time to give birth they go into some of the ruggedest country of their ranges, and while all—particularly the mountain nanny—are courageous and effective defensive fighters, they depend more on this precipitous terrain for the protection of their newborn.

In major elk calving areas—such as the Kicking Horse River country in the British Columbia Rockies, the meadows bordering the Snake Indian River between Willow Creek and Deer Creek in the Alberta Rockies, and in southern Montana on the great sweep of open, grassy slopes above Hellroaring Creek in the Absaroka Range—the cows must be on guard against grizzlies and black bears as well as coyotes and other predators.

One of the more curious examples I've witnessed of aggressive action by big game animals against coyotes was about the first of May in the Gallatin Range of Wyoming. Twenty-seven head of elk—cows and yearlings with a few younger bulls among them—took after a coyote in a galloping stampede across a big meadow. They chased him for a good 200 yards before the coyote raced into heavy timber. It could be that the elk just felt frisky on new spring grass and wanted a run, or perhaps with the near approach of calving time the old cows were becoming edgy at seeing coyotes.

In his role as a predator-scavenger, the high country coyote is controversial, but few outdoorsmen would disagree that as a wilderness songster the coyote is unexcelled—even by his big cousin, the wolf. The most unforgettable coyote vocalizing I've ever heard was one evening in late February on the ice of the upper Athabasca River.

There were 11 coyotes, all within 200 yards of one another—the largest number of adult coyotes I've seen together anywhere. It was during the coyote breeding season, and there was the added attraction of the carcasses of a cow elk and calf—train casualties on the Canadian National Railway. It was nearing dusk when I first saw them. As I glassed them on the ice, they began the concert, all 11 taking part, and they came closer to singing through their entire vocal repertoire than any coyotes I've heard yet.

It was a memorable performance that should have been tape-recorded. I rate it with the greatest experiences in listening that I've enjoyed in the bush—comparable to: the day when I was trout fishing from a raft on a high lake in the Canadian Rockies and got caught in a brief but torrential rain squall, and as the storm blew on through to the east, out of the rising, enveloping mist drifted the weird, wild crying of a loon; hearing the challenge bugling of a bull elk one frosty autumn dawn on the Kicking Horse River in the British Columbia Rockies; listening to the throaty moaning of a great silver-black wolf calling to his pack on the Chaba River near Fortress Pass and the British Columbia-Alberta boundary; and in subarctic Alaska several autumns ago, catching the mystic, fluting music of the sandhill cranes as massing in a huge flight they circled for altitude, climbing to clear a high pass in the Alaska Range on their return journey south.

4 Getting Along with Grizzlies

A male grizzly photographed in early October on the upper Savage River, sub-arctic Alaska.

"Getting Along with Grizzlies"
is from *OUTDOOR LIFE*,
November-December 1969
Times Mirror Magazines, Inc.
380 Madison Avenue
New York, N.Y. 10017

In late afternoon I turned around on the old trail, climbed back toward the Continental Divide, and reached the small lake in the pass a half-hour after sunset. In the fading light, with the alpenglow still tinging the snowy summits with rose-gold, I gathered armloads of firewood from windfalls of timberline fir. I built the campfire so the heat would reflect back from a huge boulder. Then, soaked from sweat and from bucking deep snow-drifts, I sat down beside it to dry out.

As I rested by the fire I heard the crashing descent of a dislodged stone. I uncased binoculars and glassed the near slope. A mountain goat nanny and two kids were making a steep traverse. For several minutes I watched them, then followed the flight of a golden eagle, remembering the eagle of two weeks before in the Selkirk Range that in a few moments of insolent sport had made four wind-hissing passes inches above the paw reach of a grizzly.

Finally I set the binoculars on my pack and looked at the lake and surrounding peaks. "If there's a more beautiful place in North America," I thought aloud, "I've never been there."

My siwash camp in Athabasca Pass, a wild and remote area of Jasper National Park, was almost exactly on the Continental Divide and the British Columbia-Alberta boundary. I was on one of many exploratory surveys of mountain-grizzly habitat made during a 1966-68 grizzly study and photo project. This period I devoted especially to the observation of the interior grizzly of northern mountain and tundra regions; but I've had the good fortune of making many other grizzly behavior observations during field projects on other wildlife species—including wolves, mountain sheep, mountain goats, moose, and the northern red fox.

Athabasca Pass was first crossed by white men in the winter of 1811 on an expedition led by the Scottish explorer David Thompson. During the ensuing years the pass was used by trappers and fur traders of the Hudson's Bay and Northwest fur companies on the long trek from Fort Edmonton across the Rockies to the Columbia River. Today, Thompson would find this pass area changed by nothing but the elements. From old reports and information veteran Jasper wardens could give me, I believed my chances to observe the mountain grizzly would be as good

here as anywhere in that region of the northern Rockies.

I hadn't planned on a siwash (northern bush slang for an unplanned bivouac, without tent or sleeping bag, and with only what shelter you can improvise on the spot; to most northern woodsmen "siwashing" means simply sitting out the night by a campfire) for the night when early that morning I left my mountain tent camp near Scott Glacier in the Whirlpool Valley. But I had a vast area of wilderness country to look over in a relatively short time—I'd be heading out in a few days to check the upper Snake Indian and Moosehorn valleys to the northeast—and I decided early in the afternoon not to return that night to my Scott Glacier camp, but to push on across the Divide into British Columbia, then make a siwash camp in Athabasca Pass.

So I crossed and recrossed the Whirlpool, using the old fording sites of the mountain men, followed the trail that now wasn't as clear as the moose trails that joined it, turned northwest where the clear fork met the roaring, milky, glacier-fed river. I followed the clear fork through beautiful Caine Meadows, then up its open, climbing valley, bounded by towering lime-stone peaks, to the pass. Studying the country, searching always for grizzly sign, I pushed over the Divide and about five miles down into British Columbia, then hiked back up to siwash on the boundary.

Beside the fire I dried my sweat-soaked shirt, set a can of coffee water on a stone to heat, cut a willow branch, and spitted cheese and slices of hard wine-cured sausage for broiling. On day trips away from camp in tough mountain country I travel light, but I always anticipate the possibility of a siwash and carry the essentials for survival and reasonable comfort, including extra grub, coffee and/or tea, waterproof matches, a couple of pairs of wool socks, rain parka, heavy sweater, light tarp, flashlight, compass, and topographic map of the area.

It had been a clear, warm day in the third week of June 1967, but as the sliced meat hissed on the spit, the wind freshened and clouds began to roll in from the west. I'd been in the bush in this watershed for a week and had no idea what the weather might be building up to.

I was shortly to find out. Rain started just after

This ash-blond grizzly of Alaska's subarctic interior was photographed in the third week of October — rather late for grizzlies still to be active on the north slope of the Alaska Range (but not particularly unusual). Autumn temperatures had been normal for the area, but there had been very little snowfall.

10:30, built to a wind-lashed downpour in a few minutes, and then, rather suddenly, moved east.

I built up the fire and then dozed off, wrapped in my tarp and leaning back against the boulder. But less than an hour later another front blew in with rain, lightning, and driving hail. Deafening volleys of thunder rolled, then echoed crashing and rumbling back from the peaks. A lull followed, and the only sound was the soft patter of rain on the lake. Then, moments later, I heard a heavy splashing. It was continuous, and I quickly realized that it was moving closer.

"Now what the hell's that?" I wondered aloud.

I was reaching under the flap of my pack for the flashlight when a great flash of sheet lightning illuminated the pass as if it was mid-day. Fifty yards out from me I saw a bull moose splashing shoreward. I could hear his progress in the darkness until he climbed out and was gone.

This squall, and two others after midnight, moved east into Alberta, down the valley of the Whirlpool to its confluence with the great Athabasca River. The wind had stopped, but the temperature was dropping fast. I fed my campfire with broken branches of dead fir that had seasoned for decades. The sky cleared, showing the great white wash of the Milky Way across a depthless black. I catnapped, waiting for daybreak.

At first dawn, when I could just see to travel, I drowned the embers of the campfire, made up my pack, and headed east across the cold-hardened snow of the pass.

Hours later, down in the Whirlpool Valley but still several miles from my tent camp, I lay down on a gravel bar and slept in the warm sunshine.

I awoke to the gurgling rush of the river, raised up on one elbow, and looked around. A small bird, a water ouzel or "dipper," flew past me downstream, skimming so low that he was almost hitting the wave crests. I looked at the sun, guessed at the time, and checked it against my watch. I'd slept nearly three hours. I brushed off a few ants and got to my feet, feeling totally revived and ravenously hungry. I'd snacked during the long night and had eaten a cold breakfast just below the snow of the pass, and now the only thing edible left in the pack was instant coffee. I poured some into my hand and swallowed it with a couple of handfuls of the cold water. It was delicious.

Then, looking upstream, I saw bear sign I hadn't noticed on the way down—a big pile of droppings 20 yards up the bar. Both black and grizzly bears ranged this region of the northern Rockies. I walked up to check the sign and found two clear paw prints in the wet sand at the river's edge: a small grizzly, likely a third-summer cub just sent away by his mother to face the world on his own. The tracks were only hours old. I looked up-river, felt the light wind on my face, blowing downstream. I hadn't been very alert when I got there in the early morning, and I might have missed this sign then. But I wondered. It was entirely possible that the bear had stopped and crossed the river there while I was asleep.

I put my pack on, and headed downstream for camp. I'd learned a lot about that country and was planning to return in a few weeks when the berries would be ripening. The trip hadn't been easy, but it was all part of grizzly hunting with a camera.

During the April-through-November seasons of 1966-68 I worked on this grizzly project in the mountain ranges of Montana, Alberta, British Columbia, Yukon Territory and Alaska. There were times that I put in weeks of hard hiking and climbing without sighting a bear. But on other trips I found all the grizzlies I wanted . . . and one or two more.

The decisive experience that whetted my interest in the grizzly—an interest that has developed over the years into a profound respect and sympathy for the great bears—happened when I was a university student working for the U.S. Fish & Wildlife Service.

At the time I was one of a two-man biological survey crew, and my partner Gene Hull and I, both students at the University of Washington, were gathering data on sockeye salmon spawning in the tributary-lake systems of Alaska's Susitna River drainage. We were presently camped at Judd Lake of the Talachulitna system. From this camp we were scheduled to run surveys on two lakes and their outlet streams and feeders.

On that mid-September day, our plan was to survey the main feeder stream above the upper lake, Talachulitna, to the head of salmon migration. Beaver dams were the problem. Four large dams completely blocked the migration of the late-running salmon. Earlier runs had made it during high water. We would have to make a break in the center of each dam, enough to let a head of water through that would allow the salmon access upstream. The beavers, of course, would complete repairs within 24 hours, but by then the fish would have made it through to their spawning areas.

The first dam was the largest and toughest.

Working on top, Gene and I pulled out alder limbs until we'd opened a good break and a strong head of water was racing through. Curiously, the salmon were not spooked by our activity. In a dramatic display of the urgency of their instinct to reach the spawning grounds, they actually started up the chute of water while we were still tugging at the branches, with some of the fish even brushing against our hands. Within a few minutes the entire school was over the barrier.

But working on the dams had extended our survey time by two and a half to three and a half hours over what it would have been for just the basic work of counting — where feasible — and estimating the numbers of salmon, section by section upstream as far as the salmon went, and taking samples of scales from spawned-out salmon for racial identification studies. By the time we'd hiked to the upper limit of salmon migration, we knew that over three miles of the trip back would have to be made in darkness. Supper was still a long way off, and we were already hungry enough to eat our boots.

We decided to stop for 15 minutes at Talachulitna Lake, brew tea, and have a bite to take the edge off our hunger. While I measured and recorded air and water temperatures, Gene got his handy little Primus stove going. Then, with a squaw-wood fire for warmth, we rested and waited for the tea.

It was just after sunset, and we looked around at the silent subarctic forest—frosted aspen and cottonwood red-gold among the dark spruces. From across the water, where a light mist was rising, came the laughing, spooky call of a loon.

We'd be leaving Alaska in two weeks to start the fall quarter at the university. We were looking forward to it . . . mostly; but the Susitna country had gotten in our blood, and the prospect of pulling out wasn't an entirely happy one. We looked at the lake, the forested foothills, and the peaks of the Alaska Range that loomed beyond, and we didn't say much.

I checked the tea water. Not quite ready.

"What do you want for chow tonight?" I asked.

It was my turn to cook. Our bush meals were inventive, though not always quite successful. But we had the appetite and digestion of wolverines, and all culinary efforts were appreciated.

Gene thought for a moment. "Why not make one of your hunter's pies?" he suggested.

I nodded, mentally reviewing the provisions left in our camp cache. We had the stuff, all right.

The water on the Primus stove began to boil. We

54

drank tea from battered enamel cups and ate some pilot bread crackers with jam.

I thought about the hike back to camp, remembering the terrain and the river from other surveys that season and the year before. I was concerned about one stretch about halfway back to Judd Lake where the slopes closed in and formed a brushy, rugged canyon. It would be tough traveling at night, and almost certainly bears would be down there fishing. But we would have moonlight, and above and below the canyon the going wouldn't be bad.

After a few minutes we drowned the fire, picked up the rifle and packs, and headed down. We hadn't covered 300 yards when we heard violent splashing and huffing snorts as a bear was spooked away from his fishing.

"Hope they're all that easy," I said to Gene.

Twilight was going fast, but we made good time on the upper reaches of the river. I had 9x50 binoculars with exceptionally good optics for night use, and we glassed at every bend of the river. Grizzlies feed at all hours, and when salmon are available they often fish at night.

We'd seen plenty of bear activity while pushing upstream that morning. Salmon jaws, heads, and strips of milt glands lay scattered on the gravel bars and back in the alder and willow thickets. Wind shifts alternated the good scent of the autumn forest with the heavy, fetid smell of rotting salmon. Grass along the banks was flattened by bears traveling to and from favorite fishing spots.

Then it was full night. The three-quarter moon was helping us, but the slopes were closing in, and the going was rougher. We stayed as much as possible on the gravel bars and in the water, only taking to the brush and rock ledges of the bank when we hit a deep pool or unusually tough current.

We'd reached the end of the canyon where the terrain started opening up again when we sighted two bears ahead on a gravel bar. In the moonlight the bears looked big to the naked eye, but with the binoculars we could see that they were only second-autumn cubs. Where, we wondered, was the old lady?

A light wind was blowing upstream, so the cubs couldn't smell us. We stood still, watching and waiting for the sow to appear. Then Gene whispered, "There she is! Right against the bank! Just downstream from the cubs, on the left. Must've just walked out of the brush."

The sow was facing downstream a little over 75 yards away. Her straw-gold coat contrasted with the dark brush, but as she stepped forward she blended perfectly with the dead grass on the bank. She half-turned, moving her head and forequarters in profile to us. I examined her with the binoculars, then handed them to Gene. He whistled softly. Through the glasses, the sow's big rump looked a couple of ax handles wide.

We'd seen this bear several times before. She was big—a prime, fully matured sow with a beautiful fall coat. Once we'd seen her in good sunlight at the head of Talachulitna Lake. She had stood up on her hind paws, hearing us but not yet getting our scent because of wind direction, and as her great head moved slowly from side to side, seeking our scent, the breeze had rippled her striking blond coat like a wheat field in the wind.

But now she was a problem.

Waiting for her to fill up on salmon and leave might mean waiting most of the night. With the terrain and light as they were we would have trouble climbing the slope on either side of the river and trying to get downstream from her. She had to be spooked out of there. But a confident, dominant sow grizzly on her favorite fishing area just might not spook. We quietly talked it over and one by one discarded possibilities.

Yelling at a feeding grizzly is like what football coaches say about a pass: several things can happen, and only one of them is good. But here, we decided, trying to spook the sow was our best bet.

I opened the bolt of the .30-'06 government Springfield and chambered a 220 grain Core-Lokt round. The soft, oily *snick* of the closing bolt was just audible over the sound of the river. Just then we heard heavy splashing downstream. I raised the glasses. The old lady had nailed a salmon.

I looked around at Gene. He was grinning, eager to go. A couple of years back he'd been an all-conference quarterback at Seattle's Roosevelt High School. He was also a daring and talented mountain climber, and wasn't one to lose his nerve.

"Well, let's get 'em out of there," I said. But I wasn't all that confident.

Then we were on our way, yelling like cowboys rounding up range cattle. But we'd gone only about 20 yards when a commotion ahead halted us. Quickly silent again ourselves, we heard crashing brush, rolling rock, and blasts of laboring breath. It sounded like we'd done the job. We hollered again and then stood waiting. We heard no sound except the soft rustle of cottonwood leaves and the gurgle of the water swirling into a deep eddy across from us.

We waited two or three minutes more, then continued cautiously downstream. But we'd gone only a few steps when we heard two deep, breathy coughs.

We stopped in our tracks. Almost instantly, crashing brush and huffing breath merged in a rush of violent sound that came as swiftly as a wild horse until it seemed to be on top of us. Then, just as suddenly, there was silence again, except for the river and the rustling leaves. But we could see the shadowy outline of the grizzly on a brushy ledge. She wasn't 10 yards from us.

Willows rustled as her big head moved from side to side. Then it came—the most impressive sound I've heard in North America. It started low as a strange groaning growl that made my scalp crawl, then built into an almost explosive huff like an old-time locomotive releasing steam pressure: *whuuuaaaahhhh! whuuuaaaahhhh!*

I waited, rifle raised. There wasn't time to doubt whether I could get a sight picture—if I had to—with the open iron sights in the near darkness at point-blank range. There wasn't time, actually, for conscious fear. There was only our absolute concentration on those moments.

Seconds passed. I wouldn't try to guess how many. But suddenly the sow whirled on the ledge, lunged away, and powered up the steep slope in the darkness, the sound of her panting huffs and brush-crashing flight gradually fading.

The tension was gone. I turned, laughing, and punched Gene on the shoulder. "Put 'er there, Buddy!" I said.

Gene and I shook hands happily and pushed on for camp. Nearing Judd Lake the country became more open, the going easier, and we picked up the pace, thinking about supper. But even as hungry as we were we stopped a few moments to view a stunning display of northern lights—a great lavender-pink band, bordered by yellow flame-like light, across the northern horizon. It capped off a memorable day.

During those tense moments of hesitation on the ledge, the grizzly had become apprehensive and had lost the impulse to attack. We were young and cocky and believed at the time that we could take care of ourselves no matter how the situation might develop. We were perhaps too self-confident to visualize what a grim show it would have been had the sow actually attacked.

I'd seen quite a few grizzlies before, but it was on that salmon survey trip that I really began to appreciate the grizzly as one of the world's most kingly animals and the very symbol of the vanishing wilderness of western North America.

During the years I spent on my grizzly study-photo project, I worked in interior ranges of western Canada and Alaska, well away from salmon spawning rivers. I chose these areas because I wanted to learn as much as possible about grizzlies of high mountain and tundra habitat. I was well aware that finding the bears in such country would be much more difficult than in coastal British Columbia, Southeastern Alaska and on the Alaska Peninsula. In even the most remote and primitive mountain grizzly country—ranges such as the Ogilvie Rockies and the Cassiars—the grizzly population is much less dense than it is in prime coastal areas where heavy salmon runs occur. It must be remembered, however, that bears converge on the spawning streams from many miles away, and grizzlies observed along a good stretch of river by no means indicate a year-round population for that locality.

For "shooting" wildlife, good camera range is necessarily much closer than the usual rifle range. On this project, at least four out of five grizzlies that I was able to approach within reasonable rifle range spooked before I could get within good camera range.

I haven't carried a rifle or handgun on a bear-filming trip since 1962. But I definitely would again if I had reason to believe, after consulting wardens and guides, that a grizzly that had suffered bullet wounds and recovered was ranging an area I wanted to work. Such a bear will sometimes go out of his way to look for trouble (see the reference to guide Jim Stanton in "The Brown Bears of Pack Creek," Chapter Six).

During my grizzly study project my proximity to the bears provoked seven of them to charge, but I managed to get through all encounters unharmed.

Bear behavior, and that of grizzlies in particular, is commonly described as unpredictable. But in certain classic man-meets-bear situations the bear's reactions are about as predictable as any animal reaction can be. Frankly, I don't believe that it is morally justifiable for an armed man, for the sake of photographs, to provoke a grizzly into an attack with the self-protective idea: "I'll shoot him if he gets tough." We haven't got many grizzlies left, and no pictures are worth a grizzly's life.

I like the bear to be aware of me and to accept my presence when I'm stalking for pictures. Every grizzly approach is a different situation, even with the same bear on the same day. I work in slowly, carefully watching the bear's reaction when he first learns I'm around. A bear that you can approach with reasonable safety on one day can be quite dangerous the next. For they have day by day variations in disposition; bears, probably no less so than humans, have their good days and their bad days. When I get close enough for good photos, I often keep talking to the grizzly in low tones, perhaps more for my own psychological benefit than for his. Talking seems to take some of the tension out of the situation for both the bear and myself.

But at times, however, I've used wind, terrain and cover, as a rifle hunter would, to stalk within good camera range of a grizzly without the bear knowing it. An example is a stalk I made in late April of '67 (pictured on the next page) when I tracked a sow grizzly on an avalanche fan in the British Columbia Selkirk Range. I was climbing into a stiff breeze and following her trail, which was less than an hour old, when I spotted her curled up like a big furry mound on the snow. I moved off the avalanche fan into cover across the slide from the sow, continued climbing until I figured I was just below her elevation, and then crossed the snow toward her.

With the sow unaware of me, I got two shots of her from about 40 yards before her cub, a hefty yearling that was playing at the edge of the timber just above her, spotted me. He made a *woof,* reared up on his hind paws, and his animated reaction alerted the sow. But with rather surprising deliberation she just sat up, turned her head toward me, and stared for a long moment. Then she stood up and, without making a sound, walked slowly away into timber bordering the avalanche fan.

I've had other encounters in which bears knew about—but hardly accepted—my presence. One such incident took place on a late September afternoon on the north slope of the Alaska Range. While glassing the country up the East Fork River (a confluent of the Toklat), I spotted a sow grizzly and her two second autumn cubs digging for peavine roots, a spring staple for grizzlies in northern mountain and tundra regions, and an important food item in the fall, especially when the berry crop has been light.

They were beautiful specimens in superb condition for their winter sleep. The sow was the color of ripe wheat, one cub was dark brown with silver tipping, and the other had a striking ash-blond back, a light brown face, and nearly black lower legs and paws.

The East Fork is a classic example of a braided stream channel. I stalked upwind, moving through low arctic willow, then out onto open gravel, crossing the wide river bed where the stream flow was split by broad gravel bars into several easily forded channels. A strong, chill wind was gusting down from the glaciers. I headed slightly upstream, moving when the bears were absorbed in their digging and eating, standing still when they looked my way. I took my first picture when I was about 120 yards away, then worked gradually closer.

The bears moved up and down the bank, digging and feeding. Several times the dark cub stood up on his hind paws and moved his head slowly back and forth as he tried to pick up my scent. So far, his only reaction was curiosity. I was still downwind, and the grizzlies couldn't get my scent, but I was shooting partially into the sun and decided to move upstream for a better light angle.

As I stepped closer, the sow, who hadn't seen me yet, stopped digging, raised her head, and for several seconds looked away, motionless, as if listening intently to some suspicious sound. Then she turned my way and again froze as she saw me. Seconds later, her head began to move slowly from side to side as she tried to pick up my scent.

As I watched the sow through the viewfinder of the camera, she stopped her wind-sniffing, moved one front paw forward, and once more, for a few moments, became as still as a museum mount. And then she charged.

I saw her in the ground-glass, front paws reaching, powering back, moving faster with each stride, rump bouncing, heavy autumn fat shaking under her hide. In the intensity of the moment, my only thought, half-aloud, was "I've set her off . . . I could be in for it!"

At 20 yards plus, the sow pulled up abruptly. She stood in the willows at the edge of the bank, staring at me, her hump and back hair standing up straight. I took two quick head-on exposures and then one profile shot as she turned away. She hadn't made a sound.

The bristling she-bear stalked slowly away, pausing frequently, looking back over her shoulder, finally moving on to within a few yards of where she'd been feeding. Then all three grizzlies padded along the bank 50 yards upstream, and continued their digging.

Looking back on it, I think I should have just let it go at that.

But I waited about 10 minutes and then followed the bears, hoping that the sow might get accustomed to my being around and that I'd have a chance for a good photo sequence of this family.

The sow stopped her digging and feeding to watch me. Suddenly she half-stood, made several coughing huffs, dropped down, slammed her front paws on the tundra turf, and rushed at me. She stopped just at the edge of the bank, shoulder and back hair bristling, and stared balefully at me as I stood behind my tripod on the gravel bar, then again she turned slowly away.

The sow headed further downstream with the cubs. I waited another 15 minutes. I should have known better, but I wanted more pictures. This time the sow

In this early May sequence photographed in the British Columbia Selkirk Range, I stalked a very large sow grizzly by tracking in snow on a mountain slope. Constantly searching ahead and above, I spotted her through binoculars as she rested on an avalanche fan. Making a climbing upwind approach, I moved into excellent camera range without the grizzly being aware of it. The bear appeared to be a big furry mound on the snow. But then her single second-year cub, playing in the willows and alder just above the sow (out of the frame), spotted me and the cub's animated reaction alerted the mother. Fortunately, the sow just rose from the snow, eyed me for a few moments, then walked away up the slope through the brush with her cub — without a huff, grunt or growl, or any outward sign of hostility. However, such a grizzly approach can involve considerable risk and is definitely not recommended.

charged sooner and closer, stopping with hair bristling and saliva dripping from her jaws, formidably on edge. I realized, belatedly, that I'd pushed a grizzly to the brink of actual attack. I didn't take pictures now, but stood still, talking softly to the bear, more than glad just to wait her out.

When she turned away from me to rejoin her cubs I was very willing to call it a day with that grizzly.

I'd had some tense moments with the old lady, but nothing like the awful, doomed feeling—which I know too well—that you get when you lose your footing on an exposed mountain pitch. A number of things might or might not happen when a grizzly heads your way, but there's nothing unpredictable about the law of gravity.

When you sight a grizzly some distance away and, unarmed, decide to stalk within good picture range, half subconsciously you go through a process of mental conditioning—"psyching yourself up." You rather expect the rushes—bluffing or otherwise—of the bear defending territory or, perhaps, the carcass of a moose or caribou. With experience, you learn to remain cool-headed during such encounters. This mental armor is lacking, however, when—because of circumstances of wind, terrain and cover—you confront at close quarters, to your mutual surprise, a bear you didn't know was around. A charge by a bear in such a situation is a traumatic experience whether you are physically injured or not.

Approaching for pictures a sow grizzly with first-year cubs, **if it's to be done at all,** should be done with extreme caution, with the full realization that you're dealing with a much more dangerous animal than a male bear or a sow with older cubs or without cubs. If a sow with young cubs is approached, it should be done in full view, and vocally letting the sow know of your presence **well before** you are in picture range (of course, assuming the use of a telephoto lens). If, at her first sighting of you, the sow exhibits overt signs of hostility and/or alarm the stalk should be halted immediately. If not, you can probably get away with a prudent closer approach of a few yards. But no entirely safe generalization can be made regarding grizzlies. There **may be no warning** before a charge and actual attack.

Confidence devoid of cockiness, and a deep basic respect and fondness for grizzlies are, I feel, prerequisites for successfully working with grizzlies within good camera range in reasonable safety. It's well to remember that, in a real sense, you're a stranger and a trespasser in the bears' country.

Approaching a feeding grizzly can be a hazardous business anytime, but more so when he or she is on a carcass than when the same bear is eating roots, berries or other vegetation. Some years ago Charlie Ott, the noted photographer of Alaska-Yukon wildlife, wrote to me about a curious drama that he, Bill Nancarrow, and nature artist Bill Berry had observed off and on during a two-week period that spring near Mount McKinley National Park. They used a spotting scope from Nancarrow's cabin at Deneki Lakes, a few miles east of the park.

An estimated 27 head of Stone's caribou (estimate made from later examination of skeletal remains) had been buried in an April avalanche while crossing a steep slope on Mount Carlo of the Alaska Range. Eventually eight grizzlies were drawn to the scene, their wonderfully keen noses telling them that a stock of good grub was in cold storage there.

One old boar hit a bonanza. But, like men who have gained affluence, he found that it didn't entirely solve life's problems. Not content with feeding on just one carcass until it was cleaned up, he exhumed five in less than 20 minutes of digging. During this time he was constantly harassed by a pair of golden eagles and a horde of magpies and ravens. He would look up from his gorging on one caribou and see birds feeding on another carcass a few yards away. Then, in lunging charges, he would strike at the birds with lashing paw swats. But he never connected. The birds would fly to his other carcasses, including the one he'd just vacated, and continue feeding.

The sight of these freeloaders dining on his meat was intolerable to the bear, and he worked himself into a saliva-dripping rage charging from one carcass to another. For man and other earthbound animals that would have been a mean bear to approach!

While the old boar's furiously possessive reaction may seem extreme even for a grizzly, he was protecting a rare windfall. Grizzlies make far fewer kills on big game animals than is generally believed. Even marmots and ground squirrels, which grizzlies love to eat and for which they pay a high price in time and energy spent digging, are far from regular fare in their diet. Actually, of necessity, grizzlies of interior ranges and northern tundra areas feed largely on vegetation—a great variety of roots, berries, grasses, sedges, and other plant life.

Big game animals are too swift and wary or, particularly in the case of moose, too tough and courageous to be taken often by grizzlies. Incredible as it may seem, there are at least two authentic cases, from the Alberta Rockies, of mountain goats killing grizzlies. In one case the grizzly carcass with the lethal horn wounds and the dead goat with a broken back were found only a few yards apart.

However, when conditions for surprise attack are favorable the grizzly can close and kill with astonishing speed. A Yellowstone Park ranger told me of witnessing a grizzly kill a cow elk in the Madison River. A band of elk was starting to ford the river when the bear made a lightning rush from cover. So swift and startling was the attack that the elk were taken completely by surprise, and for a few seconds milled in panic. The grizzly selected the handiest victim and made the kill by striking the cow with a front paw—one incredibly fast and powerful blow to the head. The skull was more than crushed. As the ranger described it, "It was almost an explosion of brains, blood, and bone fragments."

But, generally, the grizzly's feeding on large ungulates is done on winterkills, carcasses stolen from wolves or recovered from avalanche fans, or, in the Far North very young caribou calves. The tough and belligerent cow moose is so formidable a defender that not many moose calves fall prey to grizzlies.

In the Rocky Mountains, grizzlies prey on young elk calves. A classic example of this predation is found on the great sweep of open grassy slopes above Hellroaring Creek in the Absaroka Range near the Montana-Wyoming boundary, the ancestral calving ground of the north Yellowstone elk herd.

While generally the grizzly of interior mountain and tundra regions doesn't get to eat a lot of meat, he would still be a part-time vegetarian even if unlimited meat fare was easily available. I've seen Admiralty Island brownies up on the alpine meadows feeding on vegetation when the spawning streams in the valleys were filled with salmon. The bears had been feeding heavily on salmon and would be doing so again in a few days. But they need and like this variety in their diet.

The mountain grizzly works hard for his living, and only a few exceptional specimens approach the average size of the Alaska brown or the British Columbia coastal grizzly. The weight of some zoo specimens and garbage-fed national park bears is not an accurate index of the weight of bears in primitive habitat. A weight of 600 pounds would be about average for a mature mountain grizzly male in the autumn.

A grizzly that may well grow to be the largest ever held in captivity—with the exception of Alaska browns—is Al Oeming's Swan Hills grizzly, Big Dan. The young grizzly, one of the attractions at Oeming's famous Alberta Game Farm a few miles northeast of Edmonton, weighed 1,050 pounds as a mere five-year-old (as of mid-August 1968). Oeming expects Dan to scale 1,500 pounds or more at maturity (about 10 years old). He believes that the grizzlies of western Alberta's Swan Hills are the last survivors of the plains grizzlies that once roamed the North American prairie and preyed on the bison herds.

If a grizzly dens up in poor flesh (generally caused by the loss or partial loss of an important food item such as a berry crop failure or a small return of spawning salmon) he's likely to emerge many weeks before he normally would to search for food. I've seen Alaska Peninsula brown bears out in mid-February when the previous fall had produced a very poor salmon run.

The grizzly's winter sleep is an interesting and controversial aspect of his natural history. Neither the grizzly nor the black bear truly hibernate, and both species can be quickly awakened. An animal that does hibernate is the hoary marmot, the "whistler" familiar to everyone who has spent time in northern bighorn, Dall, or Rocky Mountain goat country. A hibernating marmot's body temperature and metabolism rate drop greatly, producing a sleep that is deep and death-like.

The length of the grizzly's sleep varies greatly over his range and depends on the severity of the climate and the resultant availability of food. Old records indicate that the now-extinct California grizzly, with the exception of sows about to give birth, was active every month of the year in the southern and coastal portions of its range.

Even in much colder areas, grizzlies will not den up while food remains plentiful. For example, in 1961 grizzlies were active in the North Thompson River country west of Yellowhead Pass, British Columbia, in mid-December. At the time there was deep snow and sub-zero cold. But moose entrails left from a very successful hunter take and the carcasses of moose killed on the Canadian National Railway provided an abundant food supply.

On the arctic slope and in the bitterly cold subarctic interior of Alaska, Yukon Territory, and Northwest Territories grizzlies den in October and come out in April or early May. The latest I've seen fresh bear sign on the north slope of the Alaska Range (in this case, tracks in new snow) was on October 24.

In the North Country and in colder areas of the Rockies grizzlies carry brush and grass into their dens for added warmth. In the warmer, wetter ranges west of the British Columbia Rockies the grizzly's winter sleep is shorter and he makes less elaborate preparations for it. He sometimes won't dig a den but will simply crawl under a projecting ledge or a tangle of windfall trees where an insulating blanket of snow will cover him.

A curious variation of this behavior was related to me by Noel Gardner, avalanche expert and ski mountaineer, who for many years directed avalanche research for the Canadian government in the Selkirk Mountains near Rogers Pass, British Columbia. The Selkirk Range generally does not have severe winter temperatures, but it does have one of the greatest yearly snowfalls of any mountain range in North America.

While traversing on skis just below Rogers Peak late one winter, Noel descended to investigate a thin column of steam rising from a snow-covered mound on the abandoned grade of the Canadian Pacific Railway. The mound turned out to be a sleeping grizzly. Evidently, the drowsy bear had just lain down on the grade—after emerging sometime in late winter from another, probably more conventional sleeping site and not bothering to return to it—and just let the snow cover him up. Noel kept an eye on the bear during the following weeks and noted the fresh tracks of his departure in early April.

Sows with cubs, or about to give birth, go into their winter sleep earlier than boars. One to three cubs (apparently on rare occasions, four) are born in the den in January and February. I've never seen an interior grizzly sow with four cubs, but I have seen an Alaska brown bear sow, in the Karluk Lake area of Kodiak Island, with four yearlings, all of them probably—but not necessarily—her own.

The maternal instinct of the grizzly sow is so strong that she will sometimes adopt an orphaned cub. In the Selkirk Range I watched a grizzly sow caring for both a yearling and a tiny spring cub (the female grizzly has a breeding interval of at least two years and probably three). Jim Stanton, the noted British Columbia guide, told me that he has observed this remarkable grizzly behavior in the Klinaklini River country above Knight Inlet, British Columbia.

I've heard and read too much long-winded argument on whether the mountain grizzly or his coastal and island cousin, the Alaska brown (which, of course, is a grizzly himself) is the more dangerous to stalk. I don't think there is any inherent difference in temperament between the brownie and the interior grizzly, as there is between the grizzly and the black bear. Every bear must be considered individually, and circumstances at the time of the encounter, such as wind, terrain, and cover, and what the bear is doing, are just as important as his general disposition.

Taking these factors into account, I believe that stalking grizzlies on the British Columbia coast or in Southeastern Alaska is generally more dangerous than on the meadows and slides of interior ranges or on the northern tundra. But only because of the country itself. In the coastal forests you can get into more situations where, because of heavier cover, erratic wind shifts, and the sound-muffling effect of swift water, you can step within a few yards of a bear before either of you knows the other is around.

All factors considered, as dangerous a bear as I've ever worked with was a young Shiras brown-grizzly sow on Admiralty Island, Alaska. She had a single spring cub, probably her first. Old North Country woodsmen agree that you'll never find a more protective, aggressive sow than one with her first cub (experiences I had with that bear are narrated in the story "The Brown Bears of Pack Creek," Chapter Six).

My own wilderness experiences with grizzlies and those of old friends have prompted me to give some serious thought on just what you should do to protect yourself when you're unarmed and facing a close quarter charge by a grizzly.

Old-time rangers, wardens and guides of the Alaskan and western Canadian bush have told me that if you're caught in that kind of a show and it seems that the bear is actually going to close on you, the best maneuver is to get as quickly as possible to the ground, draw your body into a tight ball, knees up against the chest, and fingers interlaced over the back of the neck, thereby giving some protection to the most vulnerable areas of your body, and play dead. Against the rush of a surprised, suddenly aroused bear such as a feeding grizzly disturbed at close range on a carcass or a sow with cubs met on a trail—I believe this tactic is your best defense. Those bears won't be bluffing.

But in my work I've waited out many rushes by brownies and mountain grizzlies just by standing still. With few exceptions, however, these bears had known for some time that I was around. A bear charging in this situation is most often challenging or bluffing, and here I believe strongly that your best bet is to stand still. The bear will usually pull up short, and the time he takes to reconsider the situation is very much in your favor.

Running from a bear is a panic reaction that can in itself cause an attack when that wasn't the bear's original intent. And the indolent actions of grizzlies when they are taking it easy belie the speed they can turn on when they want to.

Some years ago, on the Cascade Valley fire road north of Banff, Alberta, three national park wardens in a pickup truck were pursued by a sow grizzly. She was approaching the road with her two young cubs when the wardens edged by in the pickup. Angered by the noise and closeness of the truck, the sow charged after it. The speedometer showed that she attained a speed of just over 40 mph before losing ground and breaking off the chase.

Numerous men have escaped grizzly attacks by climbing trees. But a tree can be doubtful protection against an aroused grizzly. Though an adult grizzly can't climb a bare tree trunk (young cubs can), which a black bear with his short, curved claws can do so efficiently, the grizzly can and sometimes does use boughs, much as a man does, like ladder rungs. At Pack Creek on Admiralty Island I once saw a three-year-old brownie take to a big, brushy hemlock with surprising agility when a huge, grumbling boar approached.

The following experiences of three friends of mine point up the variability of grizzly reaction in close-quarter encounters with humans. I think a valuable insight into grizzly nature may be gained by examining these cases. Each of these men showed plenty of courage and good sense, and I believe that each did the right thing in the particular circumstances he faced.

*N*oel Gardner, *famed avalanche research director, now retired and, at the time of this writing, living on his ranch on the Castle River near Pincher Creek, Alberta:*

At the time, August 10, 1962, Noel headed a year-round avalanche research program in the British Columbia Selkirks. Accompanied that morning by his German shepherd dog Smokey, Noel left the Fidelity Peak research station shortly before 8:00 A.M. and headed out on a routine hike to check weather instruments. Just minutes away from the station, Noel heard huffing breaths and heavy, bounding steps.

Through the partly screening fir trees he saw a grizzly running up the slope, **upwind,** directly toward him.

A good climbing tree was handy, and Noel swung up and climbed to a height that he felt was well above the grizzly's reach. Smokey stayed near his master, did not draw the bear's charge, and didn't attack the grizzly until it was within a few yards of the tree. But in a headlong rush the grizzly, believed to be a sow, at first almost ignored the defending dog and, using boughs, pulled herself up in the tree after Noel, leaving claw marks 18 feet above the ground. Then, reaching Noel as he tried to move higher, the grizzly, with a tearing bite, ripped a long strip of muscle from the back of his thigh. In the violent excitement of the encounter Noel wasn't even aware that he was injured, and he hung on with his left arm and dealt the sow a terrific hammerlike blow with the heel of his right fist flush on her nose.

"I felt that impact clear up to my shoulder," Noel told me.

Stunned by the blow, the sow lost her hold and fell ponderously down through the boughs to where the furious Smokey was waiting. Deftly eluding wind-whistling paw swats, the big shepherd darted and feinted, shot in with lightning nips, then springing away—evading the lashing, ripping-clawed counter swats. Finally, Smokey's heroic defensive effort drove the grizzly away.

Realizing now that he was injured, Gardner knew he could pass out from shock and blood loss and that the grizzly might return. He tied himself into the tree with his belt and ordered Smokey back to the station. The big German shepherd raced away, and soon returned with members of the avalanche research crew. Noel was driven to Revelstoke for emergency medical treatment and hospitalization. He believes that his dog's courageous fight against the grizzly probably saved his life.

Noel offers a possible explanation for the grizzly's behavior. This bear seemed to have the same coloration and markings as a sow whose cub had been killed by an overdose of a tranquilizing drug when it was captured for examination by wardens and biologists in the nearby Ross Peak area. If this was the

A powerful young grizzly male digging for roots of the peavine, a spring and autumn staple for grizzlies of Alaska's subarctic interior, Yukon Territory, and the Mackenzie Mountains of Northwest Territories. This photograph was taken in late September on the north slope of the Alaska Range.

same sow, she might well have associated man scent with the loss of her cub, and this association could explain her enraged upwind charge—from a considerable distance—against Gardner.

Mike McGraw of Penticton, British Columbia, retired trail foreman of Canada's Glacier and Revelstoke National Parks in the British Columbia Selkirk Range (also an ex-professional boxer and former fight manager, Mike will be remembered under his ring name by old-time boxing fans as the tough, classy middleweight contender Frankie Jerome):

In June of 1966, Mike and his assistant Frank Foster were cutting out windfalls from the Grizzly Creek Trail (aptly named), which leaves the Beaver River at its confluence with Grizzly Creek and threads its way up to a primitive, majestically beautiful alpine area, the Bald Ridge country above the headwaters of Copperstain Creek.

About 7:30 in the morning, Mike and Frank were slogging their way up the trail, which was muddy and puddled from recent heavy rains. Both men were carrying heavy packs, and both were unarmed. Suddenly they heard a commotion of cracking twigs, grunts, huffs, and the frantic clucking of a grouse hen in the timber just ahead. Mike and Frank stopped abruptly. Then things happened fast.

A fool hen, or spruce grouse, flew just over their heads and landed in a bough a few feet behind and above them. The grouse had barely touched its perch when a big dark-coated grizzly broke from the timber on a bounding run straight toward them.

Even as close as the bear was, he didn't at first see the motionless men. But a breeze must have stirred, for he got a sudden draft of man scent, and he reacted as if he had run into a wall. His front legs stiffened; mud splattered and flew as his paws pushed out to brake. Then the grizzly's eyes focused on the silent, motionless figures against the spruce trees. The nostrils of his wide black nose quivered and flared.

"What the hell do we do now, Mike?" Frank whispered.

"Nothin'," Mike answered softly. "Next move's up to that guy."

What had happened was obvious. The grouse was a hen with chicks. Attempting to lure the bear away from her hidden brood, she had gone into the characteristic broken-wing act, drawn him into a chase, and all but brought him into Mike and Frank's lap.

"Look at his hair, Mike!" Frank whispered.

The hair on the grizzly's shoulders and back had risen and was standing up as straight and stiff as bristles on a wire brush. Long seconds of pure tension passed. Then Mike took a calculated risk. He was carrying a machete in his right hand, and he rapped it sharply, several times, against a spruce trunk. That broke the spell.

With a soft, breathy *woof,* the bear turned and walked slowly, sullenly away, hesitating, looking back over his shoulder, then finally moving on into the forest. As soon as he was out of sight in the brush and timber he broke into a gallop, and a few moments later was out of earshot. Mike and Frank looked at each other, then up at the clucking grouse still in the spruce above them. They grinned and shrugged. After letting their nerves unwind a bit, they headed on up again toward the Copperstain.

*I*an Stirling, formerly of Kimberly, British Columbia, now at the University of Canterbury, Christchurch, New Zealand, where at the time of this writing he is completing work for his Ph.D. thesis on the Weddell seals of McMurdo Sound, Antarctica (this article originally appeared in 1969; more recently Ian Stirling has been engaged in polar bear research with the Canadian Wildlife Service):

In mid-June of 1960 Ian, then an undergraduate at the University of British Columbia, was working for the Warden Service in Kootenay National Park. On this day he and another seasonal crewman were clearing windfall trees from a trail that leads into the basin at the foot of 10,125-ft. Mount Verendrye of the Kootenay Rockies. About noon they had reached the 7,000-ft. level in the big avalanche-raked basin, and were near the base of the peak itself.

As Ian related, "The call of nature came, so I put pack, ax, and saw on the trail and went up behind the roots of a fallen spruce that was about three feet thick at the base of the trunk. My partner, Frank Arnold, had gone up the trail a few hundred feet to the next rib of spruce trees. Suddenly I heard the noise of something coming up the trail, and by looking through the roots I could see that it was a grizzly."

Later observation supported the men's initial belief that the grizzly was a sow, but apparently she wasn't traveling with a cub. Ian had seen many wilderness bears before, and he wasn't worried about this one. He just remained still, waiting to see how the bear would react when she discovered their presence.

In the meantime, Frank Arnold had also spotted the approaching grizzly, and called out a warning to Ian—whom he couldn't see at the time, then climbed up on a stump.

Ian, from behind the screening roots, watched the grizzly coming on, slowly, attentively, closer and closer. The bear veered from the trail, and, still slowly, walked directly to the roots at the base of the fallen spruce, only a few feet from where Ian was watching. Probably at this time the grizzly actually saw Ian, for she started around the roots toward him.

Ian hopped over the log, and the sow came after him, though not in a charging rush; she still seemed unhurried. But three times she followed him around the roots and over the trunk. Then, on the third crossing, Ian rolled over the log in such a way that he was, for the moment, out of the bear's sight.

Something then distracted the grizzly, probably a quick wind shift. She stood up on her hind paws, looked around, sniffing, and apparently caught the scent of Frank Arnold. She ran up the trail to the stump, made a huffing *woof!* at Frank, then stood there watching him.

Ian decided then that his best bet would be to try crossing the slide to the rib of large spruce trees and climb one. But, as he described it, "When I was in the middle of the slide, the bear looked over her shoulder, let out a noise that I can still only describe as a roar—I've never heard a bear make a noise like it before or since—and tore after me, leaping over the fallen log as if it wasn't there. I knew I didn't have a chance of getting to the spruces, so I just threw myself headfirst into a thick patch of alders, lay on my stomach, hooked a couple of solid alders inside my elbows, interlocked my fingers over my neck, crossed my ankles, and lay as still as I could.

"What I'd decided—in a cool way, though I was terrified and thought my time had come—was to lie as still as possible to avoid attracting the bear's attention through movement, and hope for the best. But actually what I expected was an immediate mauling. I braced myself, every muscle taut, for that first smash or bite in the hope that the bear would stop there and leave me alone."

In an instant the grizzly was standing over Ian. He felt the sow's nose touch his left knee as she sniffed him. But after a couple of minutes she backed away 15 or 20 feet. Ian couldn't see her, as he remained absolutely motionless on his stomach, but he could hear

Above — A majestic alpine basin high in the Palliser Range of the Alberta Rockies — classic high country grizzly habitat. Photographed in early July.

Right — A young adult male grizzly in superb condition, feeding on autumn-frosted blueberries in the Alaska Range. The bear made a series of bluffing rushes at me — the first from over 150 yards away, and for several minutes was so close to me I could not focus the tele-photo lens on the bear — at times he was less than 20 feet away! Curiously, he then seemed to ignore me and continued munching on the frosted blueberries until I stepped backward into camera range. The bear then made yet another huffing rush. I spent a fascinating but sometimes rather unnerving 20 minutes with the bear.

Below — Two young grizzlies (third-spring cubs, and brother and sister of the same litter) patrol an avalanche fan in the British Columbia Selkirk Mountains in late April.

Bottom — Bear, deer and moose tracks at the edge of the Whirlpool River in the Alberta Rockies. The very definite pad marks of the bear tracks are obvious in the soft earth. The larger of the cloven-hoofed prints are those of moose; the smaller are those of deer.

Right — A male grizzly bear is dramatically skylined on a rocky ridge in the Alaska Range.

Looking east into the Alberta Rockies, down the valley of the Whirlpool River from a point just east of the summit of Athabasca Pass, the Continental Divide and the British Columbia-Alberta boundary. In my grizzly field work I made a siwash camp at the summit of the pass. Athabasca Pass was first crossed by white men during the winter of 1811 by an expedition led by the Scottish explorer David Thompson. The pass was then used for many years by trappers and fur traders of the Northwest Company and the Hudson's Bay Company on the long trek from Fort Edmonton up the Athabasca Valley and across the Rockies to the Columbia River.

Right — This male grizzly, in excellent condition for winter denning, is feeding on autumn-frosted blueberries in the Alaska Range in early October.
Below — An old grizzly female and cub photographed on the Toklat River, Mount McKinley National Park in early September. The bear had been digging roots of the peavine.

High in the British Columbia Selkirk Range in early May, this grizzly warns me with a rumbling growl. I had trailed the grizzly across an avalanche fan into timber. What appears to be a slight green haze is caused by out-of-focus cedar boughs in front of the lens.

A grizzly sow and a third-year cub photographed in the third week of September feeding on peavine roots on the East Fork of the Toklat River, Mount McKinley National Park. The sow is on the left, the cub on the right. The sow became angry when I stepped a few yards upstream for a better camera angle, charged and there was a tense situation for a few moments *(right)* before she turned away.

A mated grizzly boar *(head to the right)* and sow *(head to the left)* rest and play in the cold water of the Beaver River in the British Columbia Selkirk Mountains in early July. The elaborate courtship of mated grizzlies lasts for weeks. Hearing the huffing and splashing, I cautiously approached through jungle-like cover to record as risky a bear picture as I have ever taken.

her breathing as she stood there, apparently watching him.

For five or six minutes that seemed like an eternity, Ian listened to the sow's breathing. Then finally he heard her walking slowly away. But knowing that she could still be watching him from a distance and that the slightest movement could bring her back, he didn't dare try to look for about half an hour. Then he began to check the surrounding area, moving his head a fraction of an inch, then lying still, then moving it again, and so on until he had carefully looked all around him and had seen nothing.

"My body went limp and shook," Ian told me. "I tried to stand up to find Frank, but my knees were too rubbery, so I sat down and relaxed awhile. When I got to the trail, about 50 yards away, Frank greeted me cheerfully with, 'Hey, did you see that bear?'"

On an October afternoon several autumns ago, I hiked up a beautiful tributary of the upper Columbia River in southeastern British Columbia's Kootenay Rockies. The country appeared to be a total wilderness, with sweeping stands of virgin timber. From old

habit I studied the stream's gravel and gradient. In its lower and middle reaches much of the stream was ideal for salmon spawning and had, in fact, formerly supported excellent runs of salmon and steelhead. But the last runs of anadromous fish that were able to return to the upper Columbia passed the nearly completed Grand Coulee Dam in 1938.

With the loss of the salmon, which had been one of the staple foods of grizzlies in the upper Columbia and Kootenay watersheds, the ecology of the region changed and the country could no longer support its former grizzly population.

Dams are but one of the many not-readily-apparent ways in which man has adversely altered the habitat of the mountain grizzly. Sometimes our actions and projects have been justifiable for our own best interests; sometimes they haven't. Legal hunting, or more exactly, hunting under the terms of **fair chase** as defined by the Boone & Crockett Club, has not been a significant factor in the decline of the grizzly.

Today, oil and mineral exploration, the Trans Alaska Pipeline, military outposts such as the DEW Line stations, and even substantial settlements are penetrating some of the most remote and primitive grizzly habitat. Grizzly trails and man trails will be crossing more often. If the grizzly is to survive as more than a national-park remnant, we must learn to do a far better job of getting along with him. No animal is more worthy of respect—and preservation—than this magnificent loner of the high meadows and slides.

5 North Country Red

A mature red fox male photographed in early December near the Waskesiu River, northern Saskatchewan, going "bottoms up" as he checks a rodent hole.

"North Country Red" is from
OUTDOOR LIFE, July-August 1971
Times Mirror Magazines, Inc.
380 Madison Avenue
New York, N.Y. 10017

On the north slope of the Alaska Range the late-autumn sun had dropped behind the mountains. I stopped, and looked down at the ptarmigan tracks and fox tracks, at the feathers and blood in the snow. Less than an hour before, a master hunter had killed.

Wind from icy peaks gusted across the tundra. I stepped a few yards over to the partial shelter of willows, dropped on one knee, and rested—crouched in the snow, as I pulled a thermos from my pack and drank the last of the coffee—incredibly, still hot—with a crushed half-frozen bacon sandwich. Watching the summits to the west change from rose-gold to the cold blue of a November dusk, I thought aloud, "It'll hold clear tomorrow."

I'd just come down off a ridge overlooking the Savage River after stalking and photographing three Dall rams, and now I shouldered the pack and continued the steep descent through arctic-willow brush to the snow-drifted road. I hiked the road down to where the rolling tundra began to merge with open spruce forest. Looking ahead to the northeast, I saw a full moon just cresting the white summit ridge of Mount Healy.

Behind me were about 23 miles of cross-country and road hiking; and with something over nine miles yet to go, I was returning to the headquarters of Mount McKinley National Park. Already it had been a long day, but travel hadn't been tough for late fall in the subarctic. From scouring wind action there were both heavily drifted areas and long stretches of almost bare tundra, and over most of the terrain the snow wasn't yet deep enough to require webs or skis.

I was in Alaska then, in mid-November 1968, to study and photograph northern predatory animals. Early that morning I'd left McKinley headquarters and hiked west to check on wolf movement through the valley of the Sanctuary River. Wolf tracks traversed the closing ice of the Sanctuary, and, east of that valley, near the Savage River I checked a wolf scent station I'd discovered the week before, and found that a fresh visit had been made. Tracks, no more than a day old, indicated seven wolves, and the base of an arctic-willow bush was well sprinkled with urine.

Early in the morning, northeast of the Savage, I had noted fox and lynx tracks, and had seen and photographed two bull moose, a cow moose with a

A young red fox male in superb coat condition photographed in mid-November while hunting near the Nenana River, subarctic Alaska.

calf, and willow ptarmigan—which at that time had nearly completed their change from the mottled brown of summer to winter white. And on the return trip, capping off a great day afield, I'd sighted, stalked and photographed the white rams.

Now, walking into the wind, I drew in the cold, clean scent of fresh snow, tundra, and spruce forest. Because of the full moon rising over white, glistening peaks, visibility was excellent, and I was still watching for wildlife.

On the much easier going of the road, I didn't feel tired, and made good time, spurred by thoughts of the corned beef and cabbage supper that my old friend Charlie Ott—of the McKinley Park maintenance staff and a renowned photographer of Alaska-Yukon wildlife—had said he'd cook up for us that evening.

I was nearing the immediate area where I'd seen the cow moose and calf that morning, and was looking for them again, when I caught a dark blur of motion about 25 yards ahead and a few feet off the road under the spruces. I stopped.

Then I saw it again—arrow-swift in the broken pattern of shadows and moonlit snow. The barest instant later, I heard a shrill thin squeal that was abruptly silenced. Then, just audibly, came the crunching sound of fragile bones being chewed and eaten.

I stood very still, watching the spot where I'd lost the movement in the shadows, hoping for a chance to identify the predator before he was spooked. This nocturnal hunter had just taken small prey, likely a tundra vole. As I'd been traveling into the wind, he hadn't scented me, and apparently he'd been so intent in making his stalk and kill that he hadn't yet seen me.

Again there was a blur of motion in the shadows. Then I saw the silhouette of a fox as he crossed open snow. The bright moonlight caught his coat, picking up shadings of both very dark and light hair. At once these markings seemed familiar.

I hadn't moved, but the fox looked my way as he trotted onto the road. Instantly he stopped, a front paw raised, frozen in concentration, looking at me with that questioning intensity of a wild animal just aware of an intruder. Then, curiously, a few seconds

later, he sat down in the snow, still watching me but seemingly at ease.

I felt sure now that I knew this fox as an individual. As he sat there I made a close-up check through binoculars. No doubt about it: his facial and coat markings distinguished him definitely from the other foxes I'd seen that fall between the Savage and Nenana rivers. I'd watched him hunting quite a few times before, but what surprised me a bit now was that he was traveling several miles beyond what I'd figured was the western limit of his individual range.

"Good hunting, Smokey," I greeted the fox, which a McKinley ranger had named for his coloration.

Smokey was a cross fox—not a different species, as is sometimes believed, but merely a color phase of the red. The same litter of red fox pups can include three color phases: the typical red, the cross, and the much more rare black or silver phase.

Old friend Smokey recognized me, and it did seem that he'd stopped to say "howdy." But he was a busy hunter, and after half a minute or so he stood up, padded away a few yards to sniff at crisscrossing animal trails, then quickened his step to that tireless trot and vanished into the spruces.

A few moments later, as I continued hiking in, I heard behind me the clucking alarm of ptarmigan and the rustling whir of their wings in flight. "Smokey may have nailed his supper," I muttered.

Just a couple of hours away from a good supper myself, I hoped that my fox friend had scored, to add to that scanty first course of tundra vole. Living hadn't been easy for him that fall, and as winter progressed it would get tougher. The snowshoe hare, one of his primary diet staples, was just beginning to come back from the low point of its cycle. And though willow ptarmigan, another favorite delicacy of the fox, were then fairly abundant on the north slope of the range, they become increasingly wary when persistently harassed by predators and much more difficult to stalk.

Smokey and the other small predators of interior Alaska were facing what would be a hungry winter for many of them, a winter that would take its toll of both hunted and hunters.

Like the coyote, the red fox makes his way in a remarkable diversity of climate, terrain, and cover. But in this article I'm discussing only the northern red fox, as most of my experience with the red has been in western Canada and Alaska, and particularly in subarctic areas.

75

The fox is superbly fitted to live and thrive in bitter winter weather. Away from the Bering Sea coast, the habitat of the northern red fox—in the subarctic region of Alaska, Yukon Territory, and Northwest Territories—has some of the world's toughest winter climate.

The Canadian weather station at Snag, Yukon Territory, has recorded an official low of 81 degrees below zero F.—the North American record low at a permanently manned station (this record, of course, is in absolute degrees below zero, not a wind chill factor reading).

When trapping foxes was a profitable business, though subject to the whims of women's fashions, no ranch-raised pelts could equal the superb quality of wild furs taken in the Far North. This wonderful insulation enables the red fox to sleep above ground in subzero cold—though he prefers an underground shelter when one is handy, and near settled areas I've seen foxes using road culverts.

As shown in the photograph on the opposite page, the fox rests with his nose and the pads of all four feet tucked into the comfort of his huge tail. He breathes through the long guard hairs, in this way warming the air somewhat before it is drawn into his lungs.

Though winter cold itself is no problem to the fox, it does limit his food supply. The marmot and ground squirrel, among other rodents that are favored summer fare of the fox, hibernate in winter. When the snowshoe hare's population cycle is at its low ebb, hunting to the fox becomes a grim winter-long contest of survival or death, and sometimes he himself is stalked as prey.

In a normal wilderness cycle that is unaffected by the activities of man, the snowshoe can go from a great population high to a scarcity where even their tracks are seldom seen. The snowshoe hare, more accurately called the varying hare, is one of the keys to the animal ecology of the North. When snowshoe numbers are up, there is fat living for the fox and the other North Country predators—the lynx, coyote, marten, and wolverine—and for birds of prey such as the owl, gyrfalcon, and golden eagle. Then even the wolf often contents himself with tasty and easy hare snacks rather than expending his energy against the swift caribou or gambling for a banquet against the deadly hoofs of a moose.

The highs and lows of the hare population occur in roughly a 10-year cycle, but this period varies over the snowshoe's range, and after a time of great abundance it's sometimes many years before snowshoes near that peak again. Old-timers in the Canadian Rockies, some of whom have trapped and guided for half a century in the Brazeau, Jackpine, Smoky, Wildhay, and other river valleys, tell me that the snowshoes have never since approached the great numbers they reached before the die-off in 1937.

During the early 1960's I rarely saw a hare track in the upper Athabasca country, but during the last couple of years I've been making ever more frequent snowshoe sightings, particularly in the Snake Indian and Moosehorn valleys on the east slope of the Rockies. In northern Saskatchewan, from where—at this writing (January 1971)—I've just returned, snowshoes are either at or very near their peak.

Predators are the classic opportunists, and the wolf often competes directly with the smaller predators to take hares, ptarmigan, and rodents. And this relationship works both ways. When the wolf has good hunting for big game, the fox may get a feed on carcass remnants as the wolf moves on—or stealthily between the feedings of the wolves while the larger predators are resting. And, when the chance comes, Red further evens the score by stealing choice meat that the wolves have cached for another meal.

In the ecology of the North the lynx and the red fox sometimes become bitter antagonists. When the hare population declines, the predators must adjust their hunting or go the way of the snowshoe. The red fox, arch predator to a variety of small prey, now himself becomes one of the hunted. The Canada lynx, more dependent on the snowshoe than are any of the other northern predators, faces a precarious future, and in desperation he begins to stalk his co-predator.

On bare ground or in only a few inches of snow, the fox is much swifter than the lynx. But the lynx, in proportion to his body weight, has much larger feet than those of a cougar. And when the snow is deep and soft the lynx—with his huge feet supporting his weight—can soon overtake and kill the fox.

The fox, being one of the smaller of the northern predators, has other enemies, but generally he successfully counters them with intelligence, speed and courage. And the courage of the red fox is a courage with a special élan.

I once saw an Alaska travel movie in Seattle with a rather remarkable sequence in which a fox circled a grizzly in an obvious decoy maneuver. But this excellent footage lost impact because the cameraman didn't realize what he'd filmed. Narrating his show,

A red fox photographed in early November near Riley Creek, Mount McKinley National Park, subarctic Alaska. The fox is sleeping with his nose and the pads of all four feet tucked into the luxuriant warmth of his heavily-furred tail. As he rests, the sub-zero air is thus warmed before it is drawn into his lungs.

he told the audience that the grizzly and fox "were enjoying themselves playing a game of tag."

A grim game of tag it was. While a university student working for the U.S. Fish & Wildlife Service in Alaska's upper Susitna country, I watched two of these grizzly-fox encounters through binoculars. These encounters both occurred in early July, a year apart, above Lake Chelatna and near the upper Talachulitna River. At the den on a high bench overlooking the upper Talachulitna, only the vixen was present at the time. In the Lake Chelatna encounter, both parents were initially at the den site; the vixen remained there and the male raced out to meet the grizzly. In both situations the foxes used the same tactics against the grizzlies.

It would have been most interesting to watch these dens for several days, but I was flying every few days from one lake system to another, making surveys of sockeye salmon-spawning grounds on upper Susitna tributary rivers and lakes, and with the demands of this job there just wasn't time for continued observation of other species.

These two fox-grizzly encounters followed much the same pattern. The second encounter, on a slope above the head of Lake Chelatna, was more interesting simply because the grizzly was larger and more belligerent than the bear I'd seen in a similar situation the year before.

When the grizzly was about 75 yards from the fox den (and, with the wind behind him, he may not yet have been aware of it) the big red dashed to meet him. The fox circled the grizzly, feinting in deft rushes. Then Red suddenly saw the split-second edge he needed, shot in like a flame-red streak, nipped at the bear's heavy rump, and—as the grizzly whirled—sprang from his paw-lashing counter.

The fox circled again, bluffing and teasing in short swift rushes, then darted in for another nipping bite, retreating as the grizzly—huffing hoarsely and dripping saliva, but with astonishing speed—turned on him.

Each time the fox leaped back, he retreated **away** from the den. Finally the frustrated grizzly was drawn so far away from the den of young pups that he must have just figured "the hell with it" and started considering other food sources.

In both encounters that I witnessed, the foxes were successful. But if a grizzly can't be diverted, he'll dig out and devour fox pups with as much relish as he would ground squirrels or marmots.

During a curious encounter a few springs ago in Jasper National Park in the Alberta Rockies, I was apparently regarded as an intruder myself. It was a morning in early April, and I was prowling around on a ridge overlooking the upper Athabasca Valley.

Up there the week before, I'd glimpsed a cougar bounding off through the pines near the crest, and a couple of days later I'd chanced on a cat kill—the remnants of a bighorn ewe's carcass cached in a ledgy pocket among the lodgepole pines and covered with needles and twigs. This area called for some close watching, and that's why I was up there that morning. The ridge had a southern exposure, and though it was early spring and a cool one, the snow had melted off in the open areas and remained only in the heavier pine stands.

I found the cache site again, but it looked as if the cougar had made his last visit. Spotting no sign fresher than about three days old on the main ridge, I turned north onto a rugged spur overlooking Pyramid Lake. During a long morning I'd burned off an early breakfast, and around 10:30 I sat down on a sunny ledge above a steep slope to have a smoked-beef sandwich and a swig from my canteen.

I'd been resting and eating for only a few moments when I heard the soft crushing rustle of pine needles just behind and above me.

Wait a minute, I thought. Sit tight.

I remained very still, and the hackles on the back of my neck must have bristled. There was absolute quiet for a moment, and then a light northwest breeze began to sough through the boughs. I listened intently. Again came the footfalls. Then silence.

On impulse, I started to turn around, but an idea stopped me, this could be a terrific shot . . . don't blow it!

A very compact 35mm camera that I carry especially for quick, normal-lens "grab shot" pictures was hanging on my chest. With deliberate motions I opened the case and looked at the f: stop and shutter speed settings. Okay without adjustment. I moved the distance setting from infinity to 15 feet.

Again there was the crisp, ticking rustle of paws stepping on pine needles. Holding the camera ready, I slowly turned to look.

He was barely 10 feet away but already starting to run when I saw him—a red fox, and so light a color phase that he—or she—looked almost yellow.

I wasn't totally surprised, but that spring I was more cougar conscious than usual, and a cougar is what I'd half-expected to see there behind me. In early March of '66, in a very similar situation a few

78

miles further east near the Athabasca-Snake Indian River confluence, a cougar and I had confronted each other just as close as I'd been to the fox.

But now, hoping to get pictures of this exceptionally light-colored fox, I hiked slowly, searchingly down the ridge in the direction he'd disappeared. And three more times I sighted him as he trotted back through the boulders and pines, apparently to investigate me. But though I climbed onto that spur ridge for the next several mornings, I didn't see the fox again, and never learned whether he was trying to lure me away from the vicinity of a den of very young pups or whether this was just an interesting example of red fox curiosity.

On Kodiak Island, Alaska, I first came to know the red fox in his wild habitat. I was working my first season in Alaska, assisting on a salmon study for the U.S. Fish & Wildlife Service on the upper Karluk River-Karluk Lake system. That area was and still is great fox country. It is now part of the Kodiak National Wildlife Refuge.

I was keenly interested in all the wildlife of the area, but only the sight of a Kodiak brown bear fishing could top the thrill of watching a graceful, playful red coursing the tundra in search of prey. At that time I didn't own a camera and had never taken a picture. The magnificent potential for color photography in that country didn't immediately strike me. Indeed, for a while I looked with some puzzlement at anybody who would fool around much with cameras when he could be fishing instead.

Trout fishing in the Karluk River during the four and a half months we were there (from mid-May to early October) ranged from very good to incredible, and I suppose that if I could have gotten away with it I'd have fished 16 hours a day. But through this love of fishing I gained a greater appreciation for other aspects of the outdoors.

After rolling out of the sack two or even three hours before breakfast, I'd take care of my first job of the day, checking the salmon counting weir to detect and repair any holes the current might have washed under the pickets. Then I'd joint up my fly rod and fish for Dolly Varden and steelhead (rainbow) trout. Both the rainbows and Dolly Vardens in the Karluk system are almost exclusively anadromous, or sea-run.

In the cool, beautiful hours of early morning there was often a stiff breeze that kept the hordes of white-sox, no-see-ums, and mosquitoes down so effectively that you didn't need a head-net. I'd work the fast water and the big, deep and swirling blue-green holes with streamer patterns.

One morning just after I hooked a Dolly Varden—about a two-pounder—a prowling otter spotted the fighting char as it flashed in the current. The otter speared through the channel, closed just behind the

The amazingly effective seasonal camouflage of the ptarmigan is a great help in evading predators. The ptarmigan is a major food staple of the red fox.

In a scene bespeaking bitter winters that take toll of both hunted and hunter, a red fox traverses wind-scoured snow.

dolly; then for a few seconds held back as if playing, his sleek, brown body curving with lethal grace as he followed the darting char. Then, as the fish veered sharply in the current, the otter shot ahead and grabbed it. He surfaced a few yards away with the bleeding char gripped in his teeth. He looked directly at me a moment, as if to say, "Tough luck, buddy," and then took off downstream.

I can't say that I "played" that otter. The line just scorched off the reel until the spool was bare, and then the leader parted.

Unless I got a request for some pan-size trout for breakfast or a big one to bake for supper, I released all my fish. As I fished, I'd watch the country around me as well as my fly in the current. Crying gulls wheeled over the river, and occasionally a bald eagle would fold his wings and plummet down on a salmon as it broke the surface.

On some mornings I'd see a fox hunting on the tundra or trotting along the riverbank, and sometimes a brown bear or two would be fishing downstream. In the evenings after work and supper I'd fish again, using mostly dry patterns then. And often I'd still be at it at 11:00 P.M. in the quiet, mystic northern twilight.

Fox sightings were frequent during my work and fishing, and in late June a remarkable opportunity came to us for close and continued observation of fox nature. A red-fox pup—orphaned at about the age of six or seven weeks—was flown out to the Karluk Fish & Wildlife Service crew on the regular mail-and-supply run. A commercial fisherman, arrested by F.&W.S. agents for operating an illegal salmon trap that had been sighted from the air, had shot the vixen at her den near Uganik Bay, and then had captured the largest pup and kept it as a pet. The pup was found on his boat when it was confiscated.

It took about a week before Bobby, as we named him, began to feel somewhat at ease around us. He had a wild wariness that he never quite lost. For the first few days we kept him in the cabin, feeding him meat scraps supplemented by canned milk to cure a diet-deficiency lameness. After that, Kodiak Island was his; he was free to go wherever he wanted.

For about three weeks Bob stayed near camp; then he began to range farther and farther. In the early mornings he was my fishing companion. Bob would play on the riverbank, biting and tossing pieces of driftwood, wading in the shallows, and watching with intense interest the migrating salmon that swam close to shore.

On each of these outings I'd catch three or four Dolly Vardens for Bob. He'd devour a couple of them immediately, then carry the remaining fish or two in his jaws back to camp to bury under the cabin. That spot, he'd decided, would be his winter cache. Fortunately for us, the weather was generally cool!

My giving Bob those few fish each day in no way spoiled him.

When he first came to us he was so young that he could have had little, if any, training from his parents; yet he hunted as naturally as a duck swims, and he quickly learned from his experience.

For many hours each day he coursed the tundra, catching lemmings, birds, ground squirrels and mice. From the river he dragged up spawned-out salmon that had drifted down against gravel bars. He ate little of this collected food and prey at the time, but, rather, cached it along with the Dolly Vardens in the soft tundra earth under the cabin.

Bob grew impressively fast, even for a Kodiak Island red fox—believed to be North America's largest geographical race (I prefer this term to subspecies because geographical race implies the geographical isolation essential for a subspecific designation to be valid). By early October he was a splendid specimen—not fat, but carrying all the weight that his big-boned frame could handle and still retain the graceful lines of a wild animal.

Except on the occasional days when Bob stayed away overnight on a hunt, he'd regularly trot up to the cabin door, usually between 8:30 and 9:00 P.M., stand up on his hind legs, and scratch on the door with a front paw. When one of us opened the door and then stood well away from it, Bob would step just into the doorway, look carefully around the cabin interior—a display of that wild wariness that was always part of his nature—and then trot in, nervous but pleased.

On Saturday evenings, when the crew from the Camp Island research station would be down from the upper lake for supper and a card game, we'd have another pet in camp, Boots, a small dog of "Heinz 57" lineage but essentially a dachshund-terrier cross. The dog's initial animosity toward Bob was soon resolved, and they became a pair of rowdy friends.

During the Saturday night card games, Bob and Boots played in the cabin—this after miles of chasing each other at top speed over the tundra—tangling in animated sham combat that lasted until both pups were exhausted. There was much savage growling, and it looked like they were biting hell out of each other, but only feelings were hurt. Bob, especially, was "pulling" his bites. He had a rather remarkable set of teeth, and the jaws of a fox are far more powerful than those of a dog of comparable weight.

Watching Bob roughhousing with the dog, I thought of him as the essence of wild grace and speed. But one day I saw him tackle a weasel that, in trying to evade pursuit, dashed into the equipment shed. After a spectacular close-quarter chase, Bob seemed to have the weasel cornered. But the weasel made a lightning feint to one side and evaded a jaw-snap; then, with Bob a split second out of position, the weasel turned and shot under the fox's belly and out the door. Against that marvelously deft and swift adversary, the big fox pup was out of his class.

After the first six weeks that Bob spent on the Karluk, he was no longer really a pet—that is, not in the sense that the dog was. I thought of him more as a friend that often dropped by. One thing for sure: he was his own guy.

When Bob was playing with Boots in the cabin at night I'd sometimes take that opportunity to catch him (that was about the only time he **could** be caught) in order to check the weight he'd put on and to pet him for a few minutes. Curiously, though I couldn't lay a hand on him unless he was roughhousing with Boots, not once did he ever struggle or try to bite when I did catch him.

I'd talk to him and pet him, and he'd lie on my lap, apparently completely relaxed but panting from his rough play and the warmth of the cabin, his coat in mid-September already luxuriantly heavy.

But when Bob was ready for more scrapping with the dog, he was gone. A moment of inattention on my part, and he was out of my hands and on the floor, so swiftly and smoothly that I was hardly aware of it. And maybe the only reason I could catch him at all was that he let me—just for the fun he had by outslickering me.

We ended our season of work on the Karluk in early October and flew out by Grumman Goose, leaving Bob completely on his own to face the winter in the Kodiak Island bush. When the crew returned early the following May, Bob was there at the cabin. He'd already been a large fox the autumn before, but that spring he was exceptional.

Without benefit of training from his parents, he'd come through the winter in superb condition. Bob's intelligence and courage—and his amazing instinct to hunt and cache—had prevailed.

Of winter trips I've made—both with the Fish & Wildlife Service and on my own—into northern red fox country in Alaska and western Canada, the most memorable to me was a February-March trip into the Wood River Lakes country of western Alaska. In that country I learned some invaluable lessons about Red's unforgiving wilderness habitat in winter.

My job on that trip was to assist U.S. Fish & Wildlife Service biologist Charles R. (Dick) Weaver on a study of the winter feeding habits of the Dolly Varden and lake char of the Wood River Lakes system. The purpose of this study was to determine the predatory impact of the resident char population on the young sockeye salmon (the sockeye spends the first one to three years of its life in a lake before its outmigration to the sea, where it grows to maturity). The five magnificent lakes of the Wood River system, linked by rivers, range from about 19 to over 40 miles in length. Fed by springs and the snowmelt of the Kilbuck Mountains, they are drained by the Wood River to Bristol Bay and the Bering Sea.

Flying north from Seattle in early February, a few weeks after finishing my courses for graduation at the University of Washington, I transferred at Anchorage International Airport to a Pacific Northern Airlines DC-3 for the flight to King Salmon, located about 10 miles above the mouth of the Naknek River on the Alaska Peninsula. When we landed at King Salmon the weather was clear, with dazzling sunshine on new snow. As the few passengers deplaned, our breath smoked in the cold and you could feel the prickly sting of sub-zero air in your nose. It had been chilly, all right, in Anchorage, but out here it was real winter.

I was still dressed for the weather in Seattle, where early that morning a light rain had been falling. I cold-footed it swiftly across to the little terminal building so that I could change into winter bush clothing. Here I'd transfer from Pacific Northern to Bristol Bay Airlines for the hop to Dillingham across Bristol Bay at the mouth of the Nushagak River.

I asked the ticket agent about my flight. He pointed out to the field. "That's it out there now," he said. "Be 45 minutes yet. You'll be flying up there with Eddy. He'll be hauling a lot of freight, but looks like you're the only passenger."

For a few moments I stared at the plane. The silhouette of this ancient aircraft was somewhat familiar from my model-airplane-building days, but I couldn't quite place it.

"What the hell's **that**?" I finally asked, keenly interested and meaning no derision.

"Bellanca," the agent said, a bit defensively. "Built in '27. And don't knock it, kid. That was one helluva lot of airplane when she came out, and freightwise she's still one of the best bush planes in Alaska."

I quickly changed clothes, put on insulated pacs, dug a warm parka out of my duffel, and hurried outside to get a close look at the old red monoplane with the ski landing gear. Fascinated, I walked around the plane, studying the tapered wing tips, the hump-backed fuselage, and the wide struts that were actually airfoils themselves. There was adventure in every line of her. A 1927 Bellanca—built the year Lindbergh flew the Atlantic!

A half-hour later I was flying toward Dillingham, north over the frozen tundra and Bristol Bay, with a jovial and talented Native pilot who handled the old Bellanca as smoothly as if it was an executive Beechcraft.

Dick Weaver met us at the Dillingham airstrip. I checked in at the Opland Hotel, and we spent the next couple of days readying our research gear and buying provisions. Dick had chartered the services of Johnny Ball and his brother Albert, well-known western Alaskan bush pilots, to fly us in to Lake Aleknagik, our base of operations. During our project we'd be in touch by shortwave radio with Fish & Wildlife Service enforcement agent Bob Mahaffey, and at intervals he'd be bringing out mail and additional supplies on his patrol flights.

Bad flying weather socked us in, delaying our departure another day, and after our provisions and equipment were completely checked out we had some time to hike around the village. At Dillingham, the malamute hadn't yet been phased out by the snowmobile, and the town was full of sled-dog teams. It was a rare moment when the frigid air wasn't filled with howling.

The next morning there were gusty winds, and a high, thin overcast, but it was good enough flying weather. We loaded our gear and provisions into two ski-equipped light planes, and took off for Lake Aleknagik. I was flying with Albert Ball. As we climbed to cruising altitude the little plane bucked and shuddered in gusty crosswinds; then Al leveled off above the turbulence, and headed up the Wood River. Just ahead, a team of huskies was racing down the river ice toward the village. The driver waved, and Al acknowledged with a wag of the Piper's wings.

The scene below stretched the imagination. I was looking at it but still couldn't quite believe it. Both bleakly hostile and almost incredibly beautiful, it was an infinite landscape of snow-covered tundra, white hills studded with black spruce, and—ahead on the horizon—the rugged, tusklike peaks of the Kilbuck Range of the Kuskokwim Mountains. And except for the occasional blue glint on the river where lashing winds had swept the ice free of snow, there was no color but the endless sweep of black on white.

A few miles south of Lake Aleknagik we saw five moose yarded in willows near the river. Then, just over the Wood River outlet, Al nudged me, banked a little, and pointed down. There was the first fox of the trip, hunting along the lake shore, flame-red against the snow.

Al studied the snow-drifted lake ice below, watched the landing approach of the other plane, then banked around and eased the Piper down in a beautiful ski landing. In short, revving bursts of the throttle he worked the plane toward shore and then cut the engine. He grinned and nodded at the spruce-and-birch forest near the mouth of the Agulawok River, the connecting stream between Lake Aleknagik and Lake Nerka.

"Well, there's your home for a while, John."

Half-hidden among the spruces and partly buried in snow was the small, weathered frame cabin we'd arranged to use. It was owned by Dick Jones, at that time manager of the general store at Dillingham. I unbelted, tossed out my webs, grabbed a strut, and swung down out of the plane, immediately sinking to the butt in powder snow that was so fine and dry it was almost like granulated sugar.

We unloaded the gear and provisions and shook hands with the pilots. Then—as Johnny and Al revved up, took off, and swung back over us in a wing-wagging "so long"—Dick and I each picked up a load and webbed up the drifted bank to the cabin.

As we entered the cabin we noticed a definite temperature difference. It seemed at least 10 degrees colder inside. We got a fire going in the old wood range, put on a pan of snow to melt for coffee water, and packed in the rest of the stuff. Then, with coffee and lunch started, we checked over the cabin's interior.

Furnishings were sparse but included all that we really needed. There was a cupboard big enough to store our provisions, a small chow table, three bunks (with mattresses hanging from the ceiling to prevent pack rat damage), and a couple of old chairs, supplemented by "Alaska Chippendale"—wooden crates, each of which had once held two five-gallon tins of aviation gasoline.

We looked through the cupboard, checking the condition of supplies that had been left there. Dick opened the flour bin.

"Well, I'll be damned," he muttered softly. He reached in and lifted a frozen mouse by its tail. Sometime during the winter the unfortunate mouse had managed to get into the bin, had been unable to climb out, and had frozen as hard as flint. Winter had been tough in that country, and in mid-February it was a long way from over.

After coffee and some hot grub, we started actual project work. First a hole was spudded through the ice at what was felt to be a likely spot, about 50 yards off the mouth of the Agulawok River. We found that the thickness of the ice there was about 40 inches. It varied considerably, however, with the depth of the insulating snow cover, which in places was deeply drifted and in other sections almost swept clear by the wind. When we finally chipped our way through, the water—under great pressure from the ice—geysered up five feet. We trimmed the hole until it was about four feet square for easy net handling.

On our first net-setting try, we found there was a structural flaw in the movable arm of our Great Lakes jigger, and the jigger couldn't do its intended job of moving a net line from one point to another under the ice as the first step in setting a commercial or research fishing net. A modifying correction couldn't be made with the tools we'd brought with us, so hours of hand-blistering effort were required to make our first set (the jigger is composed of a wooden plank about 6' × 1'—usually painted a bright orange for easy visibility under the ice—with a movable wooden arm mounted in a slot in the middle of the board. A steel claw is attached to the arm's upper end, and the arm is hinged to a steel rod. In operation, a hole is spudded through the ice, and the buoyant jigger is shoved into the water and under the ice. Each tug on a rope attached to the end of the rod causes the steel claw to catch on the ice above and pull the jigger forward several feet. When the jigger has traveled the desired distance, another hole is cut through the ice and it is retrieved).

With the jigger out of commission, we cut eight holes through the ice in a straight line about 12 feet apart. Then we pushed a spruce trunk—with the set-line attached—under the ice from hole to hole. After the trunk and rope were pulled out at the last hole, a net of varying mesh size was set.

Once the project was under way, the net (later two were used) was checked and cleared of fish as the first chore after breakfast. At the temperatures in which we were working, the mesh froze the instant it cleared the water. After we removed the chars, we shoved the entire net into the water as a frozen mass, to thaw before being reset. On some mornings the fish, as they were taken from the net, would flop only two or three times on the ice before they were frozen through, sometimes freezing with their bodies almost straight and at other times as curved as a drawn bow.

The fish were then taken to the cabin, and the exacting job of stomach-content analysis was done. Then the dressed chars were bagged in burlap and stored out in the meat cache. Later they would be flown to the government fishery technology laboratory at Ketchikan for complete examination of oil content and protein food value.

Biological work was mostly taken care of in the morning, and much of the rest of the day was spent cutting and hauling firewood. Dick Jones and his pals used the cabin for summer and autumn fishing trips; it had never been intended for winter habitation, and it didn't heat efficiently. There were some bitter days when, even with the old wood range roaring, it was tough to get the cabin temperature up to 60 degrees F.

Sometimes at night there was a temperature difference that approached 125 degrees F. between the air in the cabin and the air outside. The only reason we left the cabin at night was to drain a coffee-strained bladder. And then the guy slipping through the door was instantly enveloped in a billowing cloud of condensation so dense that he was almost invisible in it.

You had to think of the northern winter as an antagonist against which you couldn't drop your guard and get away with it. And there were times when the way cold acted on living things was almost weirdly impressive.

One afternoon I was webbing down our packed trail, to cut and haul firewood, when my shoulder brushed against a heavy-boughed spruce. The bough growth I touched snapped off and actually broke again as it fell on the packed snow of the trail. Those boughs, so resilient in moderate temperatures, were now as fragile and brittle as icicles hanging from an eave.

We worked a seven-day week, but we had some free time each day, and I spent those hours tramping through the woods on snowshoes, checking animal trails—moose and wolf, and the furbearers: marten,

This fortunate Canada lynx, a major competitor with the northern red fox as a master hunter of small prey, here feeds on the carcass of a winter-killed elk near the confluence of the Snake Indian and upper Athabasca Rivers, Alberta Rockies.

mink, otter, and fox—and taking motion picture footage when I got a good chance.

I particularly wanted pictures of the beautifully-furred red foxes of the area, but though we'd seen several that were traveling along the lake shore during our research fishing operations, so far I hadn't had much luck getting pictures.

Then one evening in early March I sat at our chow table writing a letter by the big window that faced the lake, a window far larger than those usually found in a bush cabin. In a more pretentious dwelling it would have qualified as a picture window. As I wrote I could hear the wind picking up.

I sipped from a steaming mug of fresh coffee spiked with rum. We'd put in a pretty good grocery order with Dick Jones, and he'd sent along the bottle of rum "on the house." It was good with coffee at night and as part of a terrific energizer—the old trapper's favorite called "moose milk," consisting of a shot of rum added to a cup of very hot, sweetened condensed milk.

The powder snow was swirling in moaning gusts, hissing softly as it brushed against the window. I listened to the wind over the crackling of the fire in the wood range, and I wondered if a *williwaw* was blowing in—the Aleut name for a ferocious winter wind of western Alaska. I looked across the table at Dick Weaver, intently working on his records by the light of a gasoline lantern.

"Sounds like she's fixin' to blow," I said.

"Yep," Dick said, "and I'm afraid we're going to have a lot more snow on the ground before morning."

I nodded. Just digging out the outhouse after one of these storms was a major chore.

I wrote another page on my letter, and then, deep in the long thoughts of isolation, I looked out toward the lake at the dark spruces near the edge of the lantern light. And as I sat there musing, a fox walked out of the forest and into the light. He stood very still, the blowing snow settling in his deep-furred coat, a beautiful fox of the typical red color phase. He was looking directly at me.

"Dick!" I said quietly.

"Yeah?" Weaver said, still working on his notes. Then he looked up and saw the fox.

"Well," he said, grinning, "one of your buddies. Maybe he's just curious about the light, but probably he's figured out where those fish heads and guts have been coming from. That guy's nobody's fool."

For 10 or 12 seconds the fox stood as if carved, as blowing snow swirled around him. Then he took a hesitant step, belly-deep in the fresh powder. He made a short jump toward the cabin, paused a few seconds. Then—in a series of short, graceful bounds, sinking deep and springing again from the snow—he moved up within 20 feet of the window and stopped, head cocked to the side, watching us. I shifted a bit on my chair, and he dropped into a tense crouch, ready to spring away.

But he seemed fascinated by the lighted window and the two of us peering out at him. In a few seconds he continued the slow, tentative, ready-to-spook approach, finally hesitating again about eight feet from the cabin. Then, as if curiosity had suddenly and completely overcome fear, he jumped his way right on up to the window. He stood on his hind paws, put his front paws on the pane, and, with his nose touching the glass, looked in at us. I was sitting 30 inches from a wild fox.

After eight or ten seconds he dropped down from the window, and as we watched, intrigued and puzzled, he dug the new snow away to the side—but never taking his eyes off us for more than three or four seconds at a time. His digging formed a trench a few inches deep and about six feet long at a right angle to the cabin. This curious behavior baffled me.

The fox stopped his digging, took a few steps back toward the window, and sat in the snow watching us. Then I remembered the antagonistic relationship between the fox and the lynx when their prey is scarce (particularly when snowshoe hare numbers are down)—how the lynx sometimes hunts the fox and has a definite advantage over him in deep, soft snow.

Could it be, I wondered, that this fox had dug away the loose snow to insure a fast start—a quick couple of steps away from us—in case we proved hostile?

I stood up slowly, and the fox tensed to spring away but didn't. I moved cautiously over to the door and put on parka and mitts. With the cover of the heavy snow clouds, the temperature had risen.

As soon as I opened the door, the fox started to bound away, but he stopped 15 yards from me and stood looking back. I walked out around the corner of the cabin, and we watched each other in the blowing snow and the lantern light for a few seconds. Then Red, edgy but not really spooked, walked slowly off into the darkness of the spruces beyond the lantern light, stopping twice to look back at me, until he was gone in the forest.

Well, Dick must be right, I thought. This guy's a steady customer on the fish guts, and he's found where his chow comes from.

No doubt this fox and other furbearers had been picking up the char viscera that we had been leaving in the woods for them after each day's stomach-analysis work. During the next few weeks I watched this spot more closely, and it soon paid off with movie footage of foxes.

But the morning after the fox's night visit to our cabin, I forgot something that you can seldom afford to forget: that the north-country winter doesn't forgive mistakes.

The storm blew itself out well before daybreak; the weather turned clear and calm, and the temperature again dropped sharply. It was my turn to get breakfast that morning, and I rolled out early. Not yet fully awake, I put on Levis and a wool shirt over long-johns, pulled on pacs, stepped outside, and slogged away from the cabin in the deep, fresh powder snow.

I yawned sleepily, thinking as I stood there—hey, forgot your watch cap. Well . . . hell with it, be back in the cabin in a moment.

It was good daylight, but the first rose-gold tinge of sunrise was yet to touch the peaks. It was windless, and at first it just seemed a crisp, magnificent morning. I was just out of a heavy down sleeping bag, and the air didn't seem bitterly cold to me then.

For a few moments I looked around at the great sweep of frozen lake, spruce-birch forest, and mountains mantled deep in new snow. Then I felt a tingling, stinging sensation in my ears. A couple of seconds later I reached up and touched an ear, and there was no feeling in it at all.

I hurried back into the cabin and checked my ears in the shaving mirror. They were a dead, waxy white. The tip of my nose was just starting to turn white while the rest of my face was a deep red. I hadn't been out there 45 seconds, but without protective headgear my ears had frozen. I'd had frostbitten feet once while mountain climbing, and minor facial frostbite several times before, but never with such incredible swiftness.

Now I felt a mounting anger at myself for an inexcusable foul-up. I built a fire in the range and put water on to heat. When the water was a few degrees above body temperature, I dipped a cloth in it and then held the warm wet cloth against my ears. They stung sharply, but in a few moments circulation and normal skin color returned.

Warm water is the best treatment for frostbite, but, of course, heating water isn't always feasible. The old—and still, unfortunately, much used— practice of rubbing a frostbitten area with snow can severely damage frozen tissue. Applying direct body heat to frostbitten fingers—such as holding the fingers against the chest or underarm area under the clothing against the skin itself—is good treatment. Covering frostbitten facial areas with a warm, soft cloth such as a woolen scarf is also good if warm water treatment cannot be given. The modern shoe-pac or insulated boot with good wool socks gives excellent cold weather foot protection as long as the feet are kept dry. A particular danger in winter river crossings are warm springs, which create an opening in the river ice in moderately cold weather, but close over with dangerously thin ice in bitter sub-zero cold. Under a dusting of new snow this dangerous ice— sometimes just a small area of a few square feet in the midst of sound ice 20 inches or more thick—often cannot be detected. One early March ('66) I went through such ice myself in Alberta's upper Athabasca River in sub-zero cold; it was as sudden and shocking as the fall of a trap door. I went in to

my shoulders—pack, cameras and all, but, pushing with flattened hands down against the edge of the good ice, I lifted myself out, quickly gathered a pile of driftwood and built a great, crackling blaze—I had, of course, a waterproof packet of matches and tinder which I always carry when traveling the northern bush. I stayed there until I had thoroughly warmed myself and completely dried out my clothing and boots. After such a mishap, your body—and particularly your feet—must be warmed and dried as soon as possible. If your feet become wet in deep subzero cold, even with fast walking your blood circulation cannot for long keep your feet from freezing. In less drastic circumstances, such as when your feet become chilled on a winter hike because of inadequate or too-tight boots, circulation can be improved and frostbite prevented by frequent stops to remove the boots and massage your feet.

My ears, that morning in the Wood River country, had been rather badly frostbitten, and for several days they were painful. Even with proper and immediate treatment they turned, in two days, a critical looking blue-black and then gradually, over several more days, a purplish yellow in about the same progression you have with a severely blackened eye. But after nine days they cleared up in good shape.

As I started getting breakfast that morning, I was both angry at myself and somewhat worried. For a few half-awake moments I'd forgotten the hazard of the north-country winter, had forgotten the spruce boughs that had broken at the brush of my shoulder—as brittle and fragile as icicles, and the fish that could flop only twice before freezing.

I fed several more chunks of seasoned birch wood into the stove and reached for the coffeepot. As I started to fill it from the icy water bucket, the cawing of ravens caught my attention. I looked out the front window toward the lake. About 40 yards away three ravens were swooping down and teasing a fox. Apparently getting irritated by their harassment, the fox suddenly stopped, crouched his body in the snow, and looked straight up at the ravens as if ready to leap at them.

A northern red fox and some of his primary prey species and competitors. *Right, across the top* — willow ptarmigan, snowshow (varying) hare, hoary marmot and ground squirrel. These are a few of many small prey species that are diet items for the red fox. *Right, across the bottom* — the red fox faces formidable competition in his hunting from larger northern predators: Canada lynx, coyote, wolf, and grizzly. Not shown: the wolverine, fisher, and several large birds of prey. What the red fox lacks in size he makes up for with intelligence, speed, and a courage with a special élan.

Top — A mature red fox male of the typical red-orange color phase, photographed in early December near the Waskesiu River, northern Saskatchewan, hunting snowshoe hares.
Above — A red fox of the cross color phase in Mount McKinley National Park crunches a morsel of small prey; the action of capture and eating was so fast that I was unable to tell what the prey was.

But after a few moments the big red recovered his equanimity, seemed to decide to ignore his tormentors, and headed off through the spruces, making short graceful leaps in the deep snow.

I laughed at the fox. It was good to see him; he and the ravens had taken the anger and the edge of worry from my mind. I knew that for the time being I'd done all I could for the frostbitten ears. I'd just have to be doubly cautious for the next few weeks, keeping them covered while I worked outside. For if a frostbite injury is refrozen before complete healing has been accomplished, the tissue damage is much more severe the second time.

I put the coffee water on to heat. As I sometimes do when pondering something—maybe from spending too much time alone in the bush—I began to think aloud, deciding what to cook for breakfast. This old habit always amused Dick Weaver, and he seldom failed to give me the needle about it.

"Let's see," I muttered to myself as I measured the coffee grounds. "Had hotcakes and bacon yesterday . . . got a bit of sausage left. Guess I oughta use it, and scramble up some powdered eggs . . . and build some biscuits."

Dick Weaver had just come out of a deep sleep. He rolled over in his bag and propped himself up on one elbow. As I looked over he regarded me solemnly.

"Say," he said, "when you guys figure out what you're going to have for breakfast, be sure to let me know too."

The
Brown Bears
of
Pack
Creek

Pack Creek, Admiralty
photographed in early

"**The Brown Bears of Pack Creek**" is from
ALASKA® magazine, September 1977
Alaska Northwest Publishing Company
Box 4-EEE, Anchorage, Alaska 99509

he plane bucked and shuddered as we hit air turbulence. I turned from the window of the Coastal-Ellis Grumman Goose. The passengers had abruptly stopped their animated conversation about the spectacular scenery, their faces set in apprehensive lines. Much more of this, I thought, and some of these people are going to be losing their lunch. But fortunately we were soon out of it. I looked west again at a turquoise mountain tarn nestled in a high saddle, at pockets of residual snow clinging in ravines, then down the steep, densely timbered slopes of Admiralty Island mountains to the blue-green waters of Seymour Canal.

"Hey, John!" Hearing my named called over the

engine noise and passenger chatter, I looked toward the cockpit to see the copilot wagging a forefinger at me to come up. I unbelted and edged my way forward in the aisle between seats and lashed cargo— which included a crate of live, clucking chickens.

"Windfall Harbor's just ahead," the pilot said as I reached the cockpit. "Make things a bit easier for

Pack Creek, typical Southeastern Alaska brown grizzly habitat.

Top — A young Shiras brown grizzly female with a single cub of that year. The mother bear is in an attitude of defensive alertness. Very young Alaska brown bear cubs are quite dark, appearing almost black when first seen in the spring, but their coats become gradually lighter in color as the cubs grow older, and by the time they are yearlings they are close to their adult coloration — typically cinnamon or reddish brown in most areas of the Alaska brown bear's range, but often much darker on Admiralty Island.

Above — A very large Shiras brown grizzly male peers at me from the rain forest greenery bordering Pack Creek. An instant later the great bear ghosted back into the brush.

you if you can see the lay of the land before we set down."

I nodded. "Right. Thanks, Jim, it'll sure help."

The pilot radioed Juneau, reporting his position, then said to me, "We'll see Stan Price's wanigan in a moment. There's the mouth of Pack Creek. And there's Stan's cabin . . . tucked in against the bank. Nice sheltered spot. Beautiful place to live. Stan relays a lot of radio traffic, and he'll call out for you when you're ready to go. Good bet for you would be to make a deal with Ken Lokken. He flies Stan's mail and grub out from Juneau. Check with Stan on that. Don't know just how often Kenny makes the trip."

The pilot banked the Goose around, studying the water below through sunglasses, noting the depth-indicating gradations of color, watching for landing hazards such as boulders and submerged logs. As we turned back around the point from Pack Creek, the pilot pointed down toward the beach. "See where that little stream comes in? An old Forest Service trail starts there. Might be as good a place as any for you to put up your tent. Okay, belt in, John, and we'll set 'er down."

I stepped back to my seat, feeling a rising excitement about the trip. It was early August 1962, and I was bound for Windfall Harbor and Pack Creek to photograph the Shiras brown grizzly bear in the Pack Creek preserve (now designated the Pack Creek Research Natural Area by the U.S. Forest Service).

The afternoon before I'd been pleasantly surprised to learn that my trip would not require a more expensive charter hop. After inquiring at the Coastal-Ellis Airlines office in Petersburg and learning that I could be dropped off at Windfall Harbor, I had ticketed for next day's scheduled Coastal-Ellis Petersburg to Juneau flight (that was a few years ago, and since then I've flown with a good many commercial carriers, but I doubt that any airline in the world today gives passengers more for their money in superb airmanship, service and courtesy than little Coastal-Ellis did).

The pilot set the twin-engine Grumman down as softly as a snowflake and taxied shoreward, salt spray flying up on the windows in a hissing rush as he eased back on the throttle.

I released the seat belt catch, quickly rose, pulled up my fishing boots and strapped them to my belt, lifted my pack and .30-'06 from the aisle and placed them momentarily out of the way on my vacant seat. I checked the cord that secured the rifle's open bolt, then mentally reviewed the contents of the pack. No use worrying about anything now, I thought with a shrug. You either got it or you ain't! I actually had, of course, painstakingly checked off each item of food, equipment and clothing that I'd selected to take on this trip, but the apprehensive thought often comes when you're about to deplane to start one of these bush treks that you still may have left out something important.

An anxious, motherly, little old lady from Los Angeles stared out wide-eyed at the wild, rugged beach and the dark forest beyond, then looked at me. "You're going in **there**, alone? Why, you could be killed!"

I smiled. "No, I'll be okay."

The pilot cut the engines and came aft to open the hatch. " 'Bout as close as I ought to take her in at this stage of the tide," he said. "Well, you're an old hand at this, John. You've had a wet butt a time or two before. Don't think you'll go over your boots here, though."

I eased out through the cabin hatch into the chuck, and stood on the bottom with the lapping wavelets of salt water a couple of inches below my hip-length fishing boots. The pilot passed me my old Trapper Nelson, and when I'd hefted the pack to my shoulders he handed out the rifle. "Best of luck and take care, John," he said. "Don't let those bears chew on you."

"No way, Jim! Thanks for everything, and see you in town." I waved goodbye to the friendly passengers—both veteran Alaskan residents and excited cheechakos, then turned toward the beach, wading carefully, feeling the bottom ahead with each foot. Behind me I heard the engines start, roaring and then softening as the pilot worked the throttle taxiing out into the channel. I looked back and raised a hand as the plane started its takeoff run.

The Goose lifted off, climbed quickly, and the rolling edge of its wake sloshed over my boot tops. The sound of the plane's engines soon droned away into silence.

I waded on toward shore, and—as with any fly-in trip to a new area—the always rather strange first feeling of remoteness and solitude came even though I knew that Stan Price's cabin was just around the point, hardly a mile away.

The freshening breeze was scented with a tangy blend of salt air and spruce-hemlock forest. The only sounds now were the sighing rustle of wind in the boughs, the soft lap and hiss of waves on the beach and the plaintive crying *eee-yeah eee-yeah* of gulls. A

A young Shiras brown bear catches a bright fresh-run chum (or dog) salmon at Pack Creek. *Insets* — The same bear, devouring smaller pink (or humpback) salmon. This bear always caught the salmon by grabbing it with jaws and teeth, as did all the many other bears I've seen catch fish; never by batting it out on the bank with a paw swat. The paws were used only to trap or corner the fish in shallow water, and to hold the fish while eating it.

swift shadow fled across the water in front of me, and looking up I saw a bald eagle riding the wind on set wings.

I looked the country over a half-hour or so before selecting a campsite. Then I set up my mountain tent, blew up the air mattress, shook out my sleeping bag until the down was at full loft, and put the rest of my gear—except the provisions—in the tent.

Using parachute shroud line for its lightness and great strength, I suspended the tarp-wrapped box of provisions about 18 feet above the ground between two spruce. I've never had a problem with wilderness bears (I make a distinction here between **wilderness** bears and spoiled national park bears) when there was an abundance of the bears' natural food supply, such as berries or salmon—even on later trips to the Alaska Peninsula where no trees were available in which to make a high cache. Still, I felt there was no sense in inviting trouble.

With camp set up, I loaded a light day pack with a lunch, film, extra socks and sweater, emergency rations and a light tarp, then readied my camera gear and headed up the old trail to spend the remaining daylight hours on Pack Creek.

The trail led to an old observation platform-shelter built in the thirties by the Civilian Conservation Corps under the direction of the U.S. Forest Service. It was about 25 feet up, encircling the trunk of a big hemlock, and had a corrugated metal roof for shelter from rain.

I climbed the ladder to check for camera angles up and down the stream. The platform was well-situated, and I could see it would be useful in bear photography, but I'd need to cover a lot more country upstream from there to get the variety of bear pictures and habitat backgrounds that I hoped for.

I descended, then followed the creek upstream for about one and a half hours without sighting a bear, though I heard one that I spooked. He apparently had been en route to the creek to fish. I'd just come abreast of him and—judging from the sound—less than 40 yards away. Then a drift of crosswind must have carried him my scent. One moment all was tranquility, then there was a rush of violent but quickly fading sound—huffing, snorting and brush crashing.

Cloud cover had been building, and on my way back from the exploratory hike a light, intermittent rain began. Returning to the observation tree, I climbed to the platform-shelter to enjoy a couple of sandwiches and coffee. I was still eating my late lunch when the first bear appeared. It was a young sow—I judged no more than a three-year-old. Salmon were spawning in the stream directly across from me, and I photographed this bear making several catches.

Then very abruptly, the young bear stopped fishing, raised her head—sniffing the wind and listening, then turned and walked downstream, stopping at intervals to look back over her shoulder until she disappeared in the forest. Her almost casual behavior in leaving suggested a calm, prudent concern rather than fear. A few moments later, a much larger sow with a small, dark first-year cub walked down through the riffles from upstream. This bear showed great skill in fishing; she was a marvel of speed and dexterity.

I exposed the remainder of the film, though the light was marginal, changed film, and checked the light with a meter. In the rain forest the late afternoon light was no longer sufficient, so I packed my camera gear for the hike back to camp, and took the first step to descend the ladder. What happened next was a surprise to both me and the sow.

A big boar emerged from the forest across the creek. Obviously the sow had not scented the boar's approach, and now very suddenly she did. She whirled in a flurry of spray. With an explosive warning huff she scurried her little cub out of sight in the alders. Then she charged the boar. He was distinctly used to having his own way, and he stood still, watching her charge, a riffle foaming over his big paws. The sow blasted across the stream in a furious rush, and came to a spray-flying halt nose to nose with the boar; only about 18 inches separated the two.

It was too late for pictures, but even more than taking photos I wish I could have tape-recorded their conversation. It would have raised the hair on anyone's neck.

For about two minutes they argued, then suddenly the boar turned, lunged away, and took off in a splashing dash upstream with the sow a few feet behind, their driving paws throwing showers of spray as they went out of sight around a bend. About 15 minutes later the sow returned to her hidden cub, and I doubt that there had been any actual fighting.

Not wanting to further arouse this truculent sow's ire myself, I waited until she and her cub had moved well upstream and upwind from me. Then I squirreled down from the observation platform, and headed back to camp, elated at the photos and observations that the short day afield had produced.

I reached camp while it was still light enough to see to work, and fixed a quick and simple supper over a campfire. Afterward, taking a flashlight for use on the return, I hiked the beach around the point to say hello to Stan and Edna Price at their wanigan cabin.

In the comfortable cabin, fragrant with the aromas of a spruce fire and freshly brewed coffee, I enjoyed old-time Alaskan hospitality. Over delicious just-baked rhubarb pie I listened to fascinating conversation about former days in Alaska. Stan and Edna are wonderful people and, in a very real sense, pioneers. Stan talked of the old days of mining, fishing, hand logging and prospecting—he'd done them all; of the dour personality of famed hunter and guide Allen Hasselborg, who had lived for many years at Mole Harbor on Admiralty, guided the Alexander Expedition of 1907, and—on assignment from various museums—collected brown bear skulls and hides to be mounted for habitat groups; of John Holzworth, the country lawyer from New York State (and also guided by Hasselborg) who was among the first to get motion picture footage of the Alaska brown bear and the interior tundra-mountain grizzly, author of the excellent book *Wild Grizzlies of Alaska;* and of the bears—the big brownie that came up on the porch of Stan's cabin for a snooze one evening, and Stan, stepping out to get firewood with his eyes not yet adjusted to the dark from the bright light inside, almost tripping over the bear; of the experience of veteran guide Ralph Young and Ralph's client on Admiralty—when a Sitka blacktail deer pursued by a brown bear, both traveling as fast as they could run, hurtled across the trail a few heart-stopping yards from the two men . . . and as the client said after their nerves had calmed, "You know, Ralph, I just might live long enough to forget that it was you who guided me on this trip, but that deer and bear I'll **never** forget!"

I told Stan and Edna of the sow-boar encounter I'd witnessed earlier that evening. Stan shook his head. "That can be bad business," he said. He then told me of a tragic occurrence he had witnessed years before on Pack Creek.

It started much like the incident I'd seen. A young she-bear had growled a warning at an approaching male, hidden her cub in the brush, and had then charged the boar. This boar tried to leave at once with no real argument, but the sow overtook him and they closed in an incredibly swift and lethal encounter that mortally injured both combatants and was over in less than 20 seconds. The sow bit and tore at the boar's head, nearly scalping him, and, with a ripping bite low on the flank, eviscerated him. But the boar, **after being mortally injured,** still managed to bite her deeply in the back and sever her spinal column. Stan examined the carcasses and noted the injuries to both animals. To save the life of the orphaned cub, which he named "Packy" after Pack Creek, Stan tossed several spawned-out salmon a day onto a handy gravel bar. Packy survived, grew to be a large bear himself, and lived for years in the Pack Creek watershed.

On the morning of my second day at Pack Creek, Stan accompanied me upstream to formally introduce me to several regular customers among the bears. Stan's favorite was Susy, a young sow that I immediately recognized as the first bear that I'd seen the afternoon before. Susy had a special élan and, for her age and size, was as self-sufficient and confident a bear as I've ever worked with. For her limited experience away from her mother, she showed rather surprising skill in her fishing. While being in no way mean or belligerent, she seemed absolutely unafraid of me when I photographed her on the stream during the following week.

That morning Stan and I stood waiting patiently where thick, leaning alder growth pushed out over a gravel bar. "Get your Kodak ready!" Stan whispered suddenly, collectively referring to my tripod-mounted Heinz-Kilfitt lens and Edixa reflex camera. "Susy's coming up the creek now."

With the breeze blowing downstream, the young bear had certainly winded us, and now she saw us. But she acknowledged our presence only with a brief hesitation as she looked us over, then she went about her business. With deft speed and skill Susy caught a fresh-run humpback salmon in a riffle about 25 yards from us. I focused on the bear through the ground-glass viewfinder as she held the salmon in both front paws and began to eat.

"Sure like to get a head-on face shot of her," I muttered as I rotated the lens barrel until the focus was critically sharp.

"Well, let's see," Stan said. "Susy!" he called sharply to the bear. She looked our way for the briefest instant, then continued eating. "Susy!" Stan called again. This time she ignored us completely. Stan shook his head. "I don't know what the hell you can do with a bear that won't mind."

The brown bears of Admiralty Island are of the Shiras geographical race or subspecies. The Alaska brown bears, coastal and island forms of the grizzly, are represented by a number of geographical races,

Pack Creek, photographed just upstream from its mouth on Windfall Harbor, Admiralty Island, Southeastern Alaska. On the extreme right beyond the tide flat meadow Stan Price's wanigan cabin can be seen.

of which the three best known are the Kodiak bear (found on Kodiak Island, Afognak and Shuyak islands, and several adjoining smaller islands), the Alaska Peninsula brown bear, and the Shiras brown bear of Admiralty.

I'd been working at Pack Creek five days when I decided to take a long trip upstream, further than I'd been before, and as far into its upper reaches as I could go and still get back to camp before dark. Wading up the creek from the beach that morning, I spent about half-an-hour going the first few hundred yards as I watched and photographed the salmon swimming upstream through riffles and deep pools. Pleased with the favorable lighting and generally feeling lucky, I pushed up the creek, soon passing the observation platform built around the great tree. I came to a deep pool where several dozen salmon were schooled. They were spooked by my approach, and remaining deep, they cut across the pool in swift, darting runs, the sound of their rushes coming to the surface as a muted rumble like distant thunder.

As I hiked further, I saw a young sow and a dark first-year cub just as they emerged from the forest. Almost sure that I knew this bear from previous sightings, I uncased binoculars and glassed her carefully. She was the same sow that I had photographed late the afternoon of my arrival day—the sow that had vehemently scolded and then chased the big male. Her coat appeared lighter because I was viewing her in much stronger light. I had great respect for her. She was definitely not a bear to be trifled with.

I felt edgy as I moved closer in the partial cover of alders, set the tripod legs in the gravel, and focused the 400mm lens. The bear's image loomed large in the viewfinder. And almost immediately there was terrific action. She charged up and down the stream in a great storm of flying spray. The spooked salmon, which had been digging and spawning, resting from their journey, or swimming en route to spawning areas further upstream, now scattered in panic, sometimes swimming aground on gravel bars where they flopped violently until they regained the water or were among the unlucky several that were captured by the sow.

I've seen other bears catch salmon this way, particularly sows with cubs. This tactic is only effective in shallows with closely adjoining riffles and bars. The cubs—even two-year-olds are generally clumsy and ineffective as fishermen—quickly grab the grounded salmon. Before and since the trip to Pack Creek, I've seen a good many bears catch fish—black bears, Alaska brown and interior grizzlies catching salmon, large whitefish, suckers and trout. All of these bears caught the fish in their jaws. The paws were used to trap and corner the fish in shallow water and, of course, to hold them while they were being eaten. But the capture and removal of the fish from the water was always accomplished with the jaws. Never have I seen a bear bat a salmon out on the bank with a paw swat as some artists have portrayed.

Now, as I watched the sow and cub upstream there must have been a sudden wind shift, because she definitely got my scent. I'd remained almost still, moving just enough to operate the tripod-mounted camera. But she whirled, rose on her hind legs and looked in my direction, her wide black nose quiv-

ering. She dropped down with an explosive huff, *huuaaahhhh!*

"Oh-oh, here she comes!" I thought aloud. But for long seconds she stood, as if carved, in a classic stance of hostile readiness.

Very slowly and with great reluctance I raised the .30-'06 and held it at ready. I'd shoot if I really had to, but she'd have to be practically sniffing the muzzle when I did. I didn't believe that I was fully justified in bringing a rifle, for—as I've said in other bear articles—I felt that in a real sense I was a trespasser in the **bear's** country.

"It's okay, lady," I said. "It's okay," I repeated softly.

This time the cub had not been hidden at the first sign of danger. He was right beside the sow. Now the cub stood up and placed his paws on his mother's shoulder. This seemed to break the tension. With great tenderness, this formidably powerful wilderness mother raised a paw and held the cub against her. A moment later she turned, and mother and cub vanished into the rain forest.

A cub of that age is almost helpless if he loses his mother. However, the maternal instinct of the grizzly-brown bear sow is so strong that orphaned cubs are sometimes adopted. I have seen two cases of this—a brown bear sow from the Alaska Peninsula and a mountain grizzly sow from British Columbia's Selkirk Mountains. Both were caring for burly second-summer cubs, each also a tiny cub of that year. Considering the length of the grizzly female's breeding interval, there can be no other explanation.

When I visited famed hunting guide Jim Stanton at his cabin at the head of Knight Inlet, British Columbia, in 1965, Jim told me that he had observed this remarkable grizzly behavior in that area.

Though I'd been initially against taking a rifle on the trip, I reluctantly decided to on the strong advice of noted Southeastern Alaska hunting guide Ralph Young. He cautioned me that because of the proximity of the Pack Creek preserve to heavily hunted open country, there was some chance—particularly on the long treks I planned to take upstream—of running into a rogue bear that had been wounded by a hunter's bullet, had recovered, and had associated man scent with the lingering pain he had suffered.

A dramatic case of this kind was related to me by Jim Stanton. Stanton and a client were stalking a very large grizzly on the Klinaklini River, which drains into the head of Knight Inlet. There was an abrupt wind shift, and Stanton saw the grizzly react to it. Instead of spooking, the bear turned and began following the man scent directly upwind. The tables had been turned, and guide and client came to the chilling realization that the bear was hunting **them.**

But the bear was killed cleanly at close range, and as the men stepped up to the kill they immediately noticed a grotesque lump on the bear's forehead. When the head was skinned out, this lump was found to be calcification that had formed around a double charge of goose shot fired at such close range that it hadn't started to open to a pattern. Stanton speculated that the shots most likely had been fired by an Indian from a canoe. The bear had survived. One can only wonder if the man did.

I waited now, giving the sow and cub time to get well away from the creek before I continued. There were fleeting periods of sunshine, but cloud cover was closing. The fetid smell of decaying spawned-out salmon was strong. Ravens croaked from their roosts in the spruce and hemlock. Just ahead of me I spooked several salmon and they shot upstream over a shallow riffle, their snouts driving through the current, water flying up in roostertailing V's.

Your eyes adjust quickly to gloom, and in this forest it was hard to realize how much the light was screened by the trees. I hiked under the great moss-hung Sitka spruce and hemlocks, sometimes over long dead and decaying windfalls, where moss and seedlings grew from the trunks of dead giants, through berry brush and ferns, and skirting patches of devil's club with its diabolical tiny thorns.

Sometimes, perhaps enjoying the spell of wild country too much, one can lose the edge of alertness and be taken by surprise. Late that afternoon, with the wind blowing my scent downstream, and the running water muffling my footsteps, I rounded a bend of the creek and confronted a great bear. This time I was too close to even think about pictures. I stood absolutely still, tripod-mounted long lens and camera balanced in one hand, rifle slung over a shoulder. And for long, taut seconds the bear was just as still. He was like a museum mount in a habitat group. The huge Shiras brownie was incredibly wide across the head. He was one of the three or four biggest bears I've ever seen, including those on Kodiak Island and the Alaska Peninsula. He was very dark, and in the shadows he appeared to be almost black.

As I tensely watched and waited, I saw the hair on his shoulders rise up as stiff and straight as bristles on a brush. I thought, He's not going to give ground.

For a few moments the low flat rays of the late afternoon sun shafted through a break in the clouds, and glinting, coppery highlights shone briefly on the bear's dark coat. The great head moved slowly from side to side, the nostrils in the wide black nose quivering. And then he spoke from deep in his massive chest. It was not a roar, and not really a growl. It was, curiously, very much like the first low grumbling of a Hereford range bull before the rumble becomes a bellow, a low *roooooouuuhhh!*

Moments of silent, waiting tension. And then the great bear turned and was gone, almost soundlessly into the shadows of the rain forest, almost as if I had momentarily looked away.

I waited a few minutes to give the bear plenty of room, then pushed on upstream. I'd gone a quarter-mile or so further when again the sun shone briefly through a break in the clouds. I hadn't taken a watch, and was startled at how far the sun had dropped to the west. I turned downstream immediately, with rugged miles ahead of me to cover before darkness. I hiked as fast as I could against the swiftly approaching dusk, no longer trying to be quiet.

The wind carried my scent downstream, but the light was soon too dim for photos anyway. Several times, though I didn't see them, I heard spooked bears splash across the stream and go crashing, huffing and snorting off into the forest.

Stan and Edna had told me to be sure to stop by on my return, to let them know that I was okay. Edna had said they would "keep something hot on the stove" for me. Remembering her delicious venison hash and rhubarb pie, I reached the observation tree in excellent time.

From there I took the old trail to the beach. For all its humps and hollows, roots and rocks, it was like a city sidewalk compared to the country I'd traversed that day. In a few minutes I caught the good salt smell of Seymour Canal, and the drift of welcome smoke from Stan's spruce wood fire. Overhead came a whistling rush of wings, and a flight of teal swept seaward in the chill, darkening gloaming sky.

104

7 Moose Country Autumn

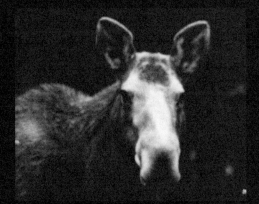

In late May, near the upper Snake Indian River of the Alberta Rockies, this big cow moose (with a new calf hidden nearby) belligerently approached me. A cow moose with a young calf can be as dangerous as a sow grizzly with cubs.

"Moose Country Autumn" is
excerpted from "Wrack and Ruin"
OUTDOOR LIFE, July 1968
Times Mirror Magazines, Inc.
380 Madison Avenue
New York, N.Y. 10017

The bull moose stopped grunting. Now in the quiet of the subarctic night I could hear only the rush of the creek running under ice. I edged carefully out on hands and knees, and filled the coffeepot in the current. Here open water had closed to four feet across, and in pockets where the current was slowed anchor-ice was freezing on submerged rocks.

I climbed the bank and walked back in the spruces toward my fire. The flashlight's probing beam picked out moose tracks in the day-old snow. A bull had come by my camp the night before and had paused a few moments within a dozen yards of the tent. His belligerent grunting had snapped me tautly awake just after I'd sacked out at 10:40.

Now, pointing the light along the moose trail, I saw other tracks cutting across it. They hadn't been there in the morning. Two wolves had gone through sometime that day. I stepped over and shone the light directly on the prints. Large adult and pup of the year, I thought.

At my campfire I set the coffeepot on a stone, built up the blaze with split spruce, tossed in a corned-beef tin, and sat down on a log. The pitchy spruce crackled, and I nodded in the drowsy warmth, feeling the day's rugged miles of hiking and climbing. Then bitter wind gusted through the spruce-aspen cover—flaring the blaze away from me, and for a moment it was as if there was no fire at all. In the second week of October on the north slope of the Alaska Range, winter stalked the subarctic autumn.

Against the black sky, the lights of the aurora borealis glowed in flickering arches and bands of crimson, yellow and green. You can't get them on film the way they really look, I thought.

Then I heard the bull moose grunt again from the far side of the creek. There was the rustle and snap of breaking brush. He was hooking and slashing at the willows with his antlers. The grunting became continuous and bellicosely louder.

I hadn't seen the previous night's tough-talking visitor, but I figured he and the moose across the creek were the same bull—one I had photographed several times in the past two weeks.

I'd first sighted him when he was battered but victorious in the company of two cows. The price he had paid for his fleeting triumph had been high. His hide had been gashed over ribs and flanks, one eye had been gouged out by an antler tine, and hide had been scraped from his face.

Two days later I'd seen him again when he was alone and still more battle-scarred. His cows had been lost to another bull. His adversary was no bigger than he was, but had two good eyes and was fresher and stronger. For over a week the defeated bull had been ranging near my camp.

I was in the heart of McKinley National Park, Alaska, for the last phase of a grizzly bear study and photo project I'd been working on for three years (1966-68) in British Columbia's Selkirk and Monashee ranges and the northern Rockies of Alberta. The grizzly work had gone better than I'd expected during September. And though October weather on the north slope of the Alaska Range is anybody's guess, I wasn't worried about it. I'd come prepared to take it rough. Even if I was stormed out, I already had good bear action and habitat photos and memorable observations.

But now beside my campfire I listened to the bull across the creek. No doubt about it, he was headed my way, fighting the brush with his antlers as he pushed through the willows.

Euu-uhhh! Euu-uhhh! Euu-uhhh! Each bitter, belligerent grunt seemed to say, "My cows are gone, and I've had the hell beaten out of me, but I'll find somebody I can whip!"

I heard his hoofs clatter on the rocks on the far side of the stream, the tinkling of breaking ice, splashing in the open channel, more ice breaking, then the hoofs striking rock again on the near bank.

Then out of the willows and into the spruces on my side of the creek, the bull moved as silently as a wolf. Suddenly I saw him—a huge dark shadow at the edge of the firelight 40 feet away.

For a few moments he didn't move. Then he took several steps closer. I stood up from the log, slowly, carefully. The bull stopped. He stood there, his battered head turning in a slow arc as he looked off into the spruces. Firelight caught the polished antler tips and the eerie reflection from his one eye. I saw the dark cavity where the other eye had been and the patch where the hide was gone, low on his face.

There was a big brushy spruce handy, just behind me. Because I was in a national park, I didn't, of course, have a rifle. But I figured I could make a quick climb if I had to. Helluva cold night to sit in a tree, I thought.

I was more concerned, though, about my camp than possible danger to myself. Would the bull vent his rage by tearing up my tent and sleeping bag?

Now the bull stood very still, the one baleful, firelight-reflecting eye fixed on me. I briefly considered shouting at the bull to try to spook him away. No, I decided quickly, that could be a very bad show.

I had to wait him out. The next move was very definitely up to him. Long, nerve-tightening seconds passed. Embers cracked in the campfire, and the bitter wind sighed softly through the spruce boughs. Otherwise there wasn't a sound.

Then slowly the bull turned and walked away into the darkness. *Euu-uhhh! Euu-uhhh!* The sad, angry grunting started again, but the sound grew fainter.

"Good luck, old-timer," I thought aloud. He'd need plenty of it to get through the winter. Gaunt, battered, and minus an eye, he was wolfbait on the hoof.

In the North Country, wolves often prey on bulls that have been severely injured in combat. Downwind, they can detect the fresh blood scent from a considerable distance. The trailing begins and moves swiftly toward the closing stalk. The bull's reactions to a few testing rushes soon tell the wolves whether he is only superficially injured or actually disabled and vulnerable. The battered, one-eyed bull near my camp was a classic candidate for wolf predation.

Near the end of October I came upon the fresh but thoroughly picked-over skeletal remains of a bull. Judging only from the antlers, I'm inclined to believe it was the one-eyed old-timer, but I couldn't be sure. It was 100% utilization of the carcass by the wolves and scavengers. Tracks in the snow indicated that the carcass had been fed on not only by the wolves, but by a wolverine, at least one fox, and a host of ravens and magpies.

From my own experience afield in good moose

A bull feeds on aquatic vegetation in the Yellowstone River, Wyoming. The long-legged body conformation of the moose makes him well adapted for both browsing and feeding on water plants.

country—in western Canada, the northern Rocky Mountain states, and Alaska, I believe you stand considerably less chance, for a given period of time spent, of witnessing bull moose combat than seeing a bull elk fight in typical Rocky Mountain elk habitat. The main reason is that the moose, unlike elk and caribou, is not essentially a herd animal. While moose do yard up during winters of heavy snowfall, for most of the year they are well spread out over suitable habitat. The fact that moose engage in much of their serious breeding season activity during late evening also contributes to the difficulty of observing them.

One of several rather curious moose combat encounters I've witnessed happened on a high willow slope above Alaska's upper Savage River in mid-October of '67. I was glassing the mountainsides two hours before dusk, searching for a large dark-coated grizzly with a silvery wash over his face and shoulders that I'd seen the day before. But the bear was nowhere in sight, and I was about to case the binoculars when I spotted two bull moose up on a high, willow-thicketed bench. They were standing still at the time, facing each other a dozen yards apart. Only their heads moved. It seems to be a part of moose philosophy that there is all the time in the world, even in the rutting season, but I had a hunch there was about to be some action.

For the time being, I forgot about the grizzly. I decided to climb to the bench, stalk these bulls, and see what developed. It was going to be a long hike up to the moose, though, and the light was fading. I considered the route to take.

If I made a direct approach through alders and willows, I'd lose sight of the bulls and not see them again until I was almost at their elevation. A just-perceptible east wind was blowing across the slope. I picked out a leaning spruce snag close enough to the bulls to serve as a landmark and started out.

As I pushed up through the willow cover, I heard low whining grunts that increased in frequency, then the cracking impact of antlers. They were going at it. I climbed faster, even in the chill air quickly breaking a sweat.

I hiked in a climbing traverse almost to the snag and then turned directly up the slope.

When I sighted the bulls again they stood almost as I'd last seen them, about 80 yards ahead of me where the slope leveled out. The bulls had heard my approach through the willows, and when I stepped out of cover they were already looking my way.

Now I just stood still and waited. In the growing anger of their encounter the bulls wouldn't be spooky, but I wanted to see how they would react to my presence.

Not surprisingly, after a few seconds the bulls looked back at each other. I checked the light with a meter. Not good, but there was still enough for 160 A.S.A. exposure index color. I untied the canvas rain-dust cover from the tripod-mounted telephoto and reflex camera, and then set lens apertures and shutter speeds on that gear and my grab shot camera. I wasn't yet close enough to get the pictures I was after, but I wanted to be ready.

I waited several minutes and then walked slowly toward the bulls in plain sight, hoping to get as close as possible to ideal picture range without stopping the show. Both bulls watched me intently.

I moved very deliberately and finally set the tripod in the snow on a small rise. The bulls hadn't taken their eyes off me. I had a feeling that I'd worked up to the very edge of their tolerance.

I eased slowly out of my day-pack, removed a couple of film rolls from it, and put them in a handy pocket of my parka. As I adjusted the tripod, low whining grunts came from the bulls. I looked up. They'd turned their attention back to each other.

Then I heard a distant barely-audible grunt from the slope above me. Searching with the naked eye I spotted another bull, then with binoculars picked up two more, all headed down the slope. The three new bulls were converging on the two combatants.

The antagonists stepped toward each other, antlers held low, whining grunts (a ridiculous sound for such a huge and formidable animal) coming in quick succession. I triggered the shutter as their antlers met in cracking impact. The sharp, polished tines clattered as the bulls tilted their racks, braced their great legs, and levered with powerful neck muscles.

Both bulls had good racks, but one moose had a definite weight advantage. The bulls strained to push each other backward. There was a violent, cracking play of antler tines, and the sliding, bracing, driving hoofs cut dark streaks in the earth under the snow.

Then the smaller bull finally began giving ground before the relentless push of his adversary. Suddenly he broke away, pivoted, and ran, but then stopped at 20 yards. The big bull didn't follow up his advantage. He just stood with his head low, waiting.

For a few moments the bulls were motionless, facing in the same direction. The bigger bull made a few whining grunts. I've always been fascinated by the vocal sounds of wild animals, and I found his curious grunt particularly interesting. Right then I couldn't resist the temptation to try it myself.

The reaction was instantaneous. Both bulls turned and faced me. For long seconds there I thought I'd said the wrong thing.

Then suddenly one of the approaching bulls pushed through the willows and came into full view between the two adversaries. This turned their attention from me to him. He was a young bull, probably a three-year-old, with little pie-plate antlers, though there wasn't much difference in body weight between him and the smaller of the two battlers. The grunting of the two other newcomers sounded very close, but they remained concealed in the brush.

While the two bulls glowered at the young stranger, I checked all three through my binoculars for injuries. They all had antler gashes and scrapes from recent fighting. The second largest bull was heavily marked on his ribs, flank, and rump. As is evident in the accompanying pictures, all the bulls had lost considerable weight during the rutting season, about 10% of their heaviest body weight attained in late August just before the rut starts.

In a moose fight, head-on antler sparring seldom results in serious injuries. A bull is sometimes gored in the eye, however (see bottom photo, page 111), and on rare occasions the antler tip pushes through the eye socket and penetrates the brain, resulting in instant death.

Fatal injuries in moose fights are not common. When death does occur from combat, however, it is more likely the result of antler tine penetration in the rib or flank area causing damage to vital organs, massive blood loss, and—in cases where immediate death does not result—infection (usually peritonitis—inflammation of the abdominal membrane). The palmate antlers of moose do sometimes lock in combat, but that hazard is more common with elk and whitetail deer.

As I watched on that high, willow-thicketed bench above the Savage River, there were five bulls in the immediate vicinity, but there wasn't a cow in sight. I hadn't seen a cow before or during the stalk, but one or more could have been bedded down in the cover nearby.

Now the young bull stepped brashly toward the largest of the fighters. The big moose didn't move out of his tracks, just lowered his head and waited. The newcomer hesitated, as though realizing he was taking on more than he could handle, but then

moved in quickly and whacked his small antlers against one big palm. He braced himself, trying to lever his weight against his huge adversary. Then what happened next surprised me.

The big bull's former opponent joined in, and each of the smaller bulls drove against a single palm, pitting their combined weight against the veteran.

For a few moments it was a shoving, grunting, antler-cracking standoff. But the big fellow's rage was growing. With a quick, violent, tine-clattering twist of his rack, he crashed it first into one bull's antlers and then the other's. Both smaller bulls backed up. As they did so, the veteran lunged forward and hooked savagely at his first opponent's ribs. But that bull "rolled with the punch," and only hair was scraped off.

October dusk had come, and the only shots that could be taken now were skylined silhouettes. But I watched the intermittent action for about half-an-hour longer before heading down to hike back to camp.

That curious whining grunt of bull moose is characteristic during the rutting season. I've never heard it at any other time of year, though they may make this sound occasionally during other seasons. Moose may have almost as varied a vocal repertoire as elk, but except during the rut, they use it much less often.

Several times, when I was hiking into a stiff wind, I've startled bedded or browsing moose that were less than 50 yards from me. Their reactions ranged from mild curiosity to challenging belligerence to alarm that spooked them quickly out of sight. But none of them, cows or bulls, uttered a vocal sound.

However, every cow **elk** that I've surprised at close range, at least the ones that I've seen, made a characteristic sharp, shrill bark. The cow elk also uses this bark to express a suspicion of danger—such as when sighting the moving but unidentified silhouette of another animal or a man in the forest. Clearly, it's a danger signal to other elk. A bull elk in the same situation often makes a squealing grunt.

Down in Wyoming's Gallatin Range one early October afternoon in 1964, I was crossing a slope through a dense stand of lodgepole pine. A strong, gusting wind carried to me a sound that I at first thought was made by a power saw. Hiking upwind toward the intermittent sound, I stopped abruptly in the pines near the edge of a small meadow. In the open, less than 40 yards from me, and unaware of my presence, was a cow moose. She raised her head and made the strange groaning call. It was a rather

A bull moose fight photographed near dusk on a slope overlooking the upper Savage River, interior Alaska, in early October:

Left and above — Two large, heavy-antlered bulls, momentarily resting during a break in the skirmishing, watch the approach of a younger bull — of comparable body weight to the older moose, but with much smaller antlers.

Below and upper right — The two younger bulls join forces to attack the huge veteran in driving, grunting, hoof-skidding, hooking, antler-crashing combat. The fighting, still unresolved, went on long after light suitable for photography was gone. As is evident in these photographs, bulls lose about one-tenth of their body weight (from their peak of condition in late August) during the course of the breeding season. On good range, however, this weight loss is quickly regained before the onset of winter.

This bull, photographed in mid-September on the north slope of the Alaska Range, lost an eye to the driving antler tine of an antagonist during the breeding season. Such a handicap probably would be fatal in a testing encounter with wolves.

111

remarkable sound, and if I hadn't been that close to her I'd have found it hard to believe that she'd made it!

Except during the rut, moose are relatively silent vocally. And when they want to be, they can also be astonishingly quiet in their movements. In the Willow Creek-Snake Indian River country of the Alberta Rockies a few years ago in early July, I saw a cow moose silently vanish into the forest ahead of me. Moments later she circled back behind me for a closer look. I didn't hear a sound from her, and wouldn't have seen her the second time if she hadn't spooked up a grouse. She was hardly 50 feet away. Very likely she had a young calf hidden nearby.

Moose are very dependent on hearing, and their own quietness helps them pick up and interpret sounds. They have superb hearing, and their sense of smell is also highly developed, but their eyesight is only fair.

Basically moose tend to be loners rather than herd animals, and their rutting season behavior differs from that of elk. Unlike the harem-gathering bull elk, the bull moose usually only has one cow with him at a time. The cow moose is receptive to breeding for only about a week or so, after which the bull searches for another cow. Gathering several cows and trying to keep them together is usually too difficult, although I've seen some interesting exceptions to the general rule.

One rather spectacular exception I observed back during the first week of September 1958. I was flying with bush pilot and master guide Jay Hammond (later to become Alaska's governor) over an upper tributary of the Alaska Peninsula's Naknek River when we saw a big bull with **eight** cows. No other bull was in sight. It was the beginning of the rutting season, and I can only speculate on the competition involved in collecting such a harem and on how that bull fared when other bulls showed up later.

Most of the breeding takes place from mid-September to mid-October, but I've seen some rutting activity from the first week of September almost to the first of November.

Some young cow moose are mature enough for breeding during their second autumn, when they are 16 to 17 months old, though most will not breed until their third autumn. Bulls are probably capable of breeding just as early as cows, but a young bull stands almost no chance to compete effectively against older, more powerful bulls until he is about five years of age. A bull is in his prime and has his best antlers when he is 6 to 10 years old. It's possible for a moose to live to be 20 or a bit older, though few ever approach that age in the wild.

The great majority of moose calves are born during the last two weeks of May and the first three weeks of June, with a few just before and just after that period. Most often, single calves are dropped, but on good range twins are common, and triplets appear occasionally.

Moose reproduction responds quickly to the quality and abundance of the food supply. The best habitat for moose is a burned-over combination of forest and tundra that has grown up to deciduous brush, particularly willow, birch, and aspen. In such areas the calf crop is heavy.*

The bush country fires that create fine moose habitat, however, can critically damage winter caribou range for many decades. The primary winter food staple for northern caribou herds is a form of lichen that grows in mature spruce stands. This continuing damage to caribou winter range by wildfire is probably at least as important a factor in the decline of the caribou as over-hunting and predation.

The antlers of a bull moose are grown for rutting season combat, and are relatively unimportant as weapons of defense. Cows and bulls both defend themselves against predators with lightning blows of their front hoofs.

Antlers are useful to the mature bull for only the short rutting season. Velvet is not shed until the last of August or early September, and moose annually lose their antlers earlier than elk. Mature bull moose drop them from late November through January. Younger bulls carry them longer, sometimes into early spring.

Prime bull elk start losing their antlers in late March and early April, and I've seen bull elk in Alberta and Wyoming still carrying their old racks during the first week of June—these were immature bulls and old-timers well past their prime.

The effectiveness of the moose's hoofs as weapons of defense is impressively borne out by an incident related to me by an old Alaskan friend who witnessed it many years ago at a section station on the Alaska Railroad. An orphaned female moose calf was brought into the station in the early summer. The calf

---

*A classic example of fine moose habitat created by fire is the Kenai Peninsula which was swept by huge fires shortly before the turn of the century, and again in the summer of 1947.

was bottle-fed by the section men's families, and became a playful but gentle children's pet.

She grew rapidly, perhaps faster than she would have in the wild, and though she was impressively large in her second year, she was still docile and gentle, and she had never shown any signs of fight. She stayed close to the station, and, as far as anyone knows, she had never faced an enemy.

Then one day when the moose was two years old, a dog musher hiked to the station to visit a friend. Unknown to him, three of his big malamutes had gotten loose, followed him, and were just catching up when he reached the station.

The young moose was bedded down in full view beside a shed, and the dogs spotted her instantly. The

Two bull moose rest and browse willows after October combat on a high tundra bench overlooking the upper Savage River, subarctic Alaska.

sight of the moose apparently triggered in the dogs an impulse to attack. Reacting as one, they raced toward her in a bounding rush. Some of the onlookers were too shocked to move. Others reacted, sprinting after the dogs and yelling to try to divert them, appalled that the gentle pet was about to be savaged in front of children that had raised her.

For what seemed critical seconds the young cow remained lying down. She may, momentarily, have been bewildered by the dogs' rush. And they were almost upon her when the protective instinct of

thousands of years took over. Then, with an almost incredible fluid swiftness, she was on her feet. As one observer said, "It was like I'd turned away, and then looked back, but I'd never taken my eyes off her!"

The young moose reared as the nearest dog leaped. Her front hoofs blurred in lightning jabs. With a piercing yelp, the big dog fell, viscera dragging and backbone severed. The other dogs turned to flee, but were also caught by the lethal hoofs.

Their stunned owner quickly ended their suffering with his rifle, and then in mounting anger raised it to shoot the moose, but before he could pull the trigger again the rifle was knocked upward and snatched from his hands.

A bull moose must be respected as a potentially dangerous animal any time of the year, but it is usually only during the rut that he will go out of his way looking for trouble. I've had some edgy moments while photographing bulls during the rut. After hooking at willows and slashing off spruce boughs, angry bull moose have stepped a few yards toward me, but I've never yet had to tree.

Several years ago in early September, I worked close to a big bull to get a portrait of him looking out from a framing of spruce boughs. It was very evident that he was angry at a smaller bull that had been following him and his cow for several hours. I took a

Moose often like to graze on meadow grass like an elk, and this is somewhat awkward because of their long legs. This bull, on his knees, was photographed in the Gallatin Range, Wyoming, in early July.

few frame-filling head and shoulder shots with a telephoto, then gingerly backed off. I had the shots I'd been after, and I also had a feeling this guy could be pure trouble. The signs were there. And seconds later it happened.

The bull exploded out of the spruce cover, charged past me on a dead run, and went for the young bull. The intruder had been caught napping, and driving antler tines came perilously close to his rump before he began to open ground on his pursuer.

You don't often see a moose at full speed. A trot usually suffices, even for a spooked moose, and I was much impressed the first time I saw a moose running wide open. I can't believe that any horse can approach that speed over the tussocks and holes in the tundra without breaking a leg.

Calves accompanying breeding cows are accepted and tolerated by the bulls. I've never yet seen a bull hook or push at a calf, no matter how irritable the bull was.

One mid-September day near the upper Savage

114

Shaking his head frequently to momentarily rid himself of flies, a young bull moose *(left)* rests in the willows and high grass of a meadow in the Gallatin Range, Wyoming. Taken in early July, this photograph is a close-up view of his growing antlers in "velvet." The antlers of mature, prime bull moose vary greatly in shape; some have especially long, vicious looking tines *(below left)*, others have broad, rather flat palms *(below right)*, and still others, such as the one pictured on the next page, have deeply dished palms. These mature bulls, photographed in September and October in different areas on the north slope of the Alaska Range, were all powerful and successful herd bulls. They all quickly discouraged challengers. As formidable as these antlers appear, they are dropped in early winter and are much less important as defense weapons against predators than for their primary purpose — breeding season combat.

Left — A cow moose, photographed in mid-September near the upper Savage River. This cow is a prime, mature animal in superb condition.
Overleaf — Autumn tundra, Mount McKinley National Park, interior Alaska.

Subarctic moose habitat on the north slope of the Alaska Range photographed in early November. A peaceful post-breeding season gathering of moose—both bulls and cows — on a slope overlooking the upper Savage River. These bulls, on good feed during an open fall, are quickly regaining the body weight lost during the breeding season.

River in the Alaska Range, I was closely watching two bull moose that had been fighting and appeared about ready to go at it again. As I waited during the lull in the action, checking the focus through the ground glass viewfinder of my tripod-mounted camera, I heard a willow branch snap just behind me. I looked up. A big, gangling moose calf was almost literally looking over my shoulder! I could have reached out and touched his nose. How he moved up so quietly I don't know.

Both astonished and startled, I growled a loud "Get outa here!" The calf turned at once and trotted toward his mother, who was peering out of high willows some 50 yards away. I immediately regretted my brusqueness. He was just a big, awkward, innocent and inquisitive youngster, and from the expression in his eyes he had certainly looked as if his feelings were hurt.

In the fall, cows with calves three and a half to four months old or older are still very protective but not as dangerously aggressive as they are in early summer. Until the cow finally runs her near-yearling calf off to face life on his own, she is always protective, but she's less belligerent about it as the calf grows older.

A cow with a newborn or very young calf is something else. Unlike the caribou calf, which can outrun most predators a week or so after birth, a moose calf is helpless and entirely dependent on its mother for protection. Then, next to the grizzly mother with

young cubs, there is no more dangerous wild animal in North America than the cow moose.

One early-July evening on a mountain slope above Lake Chelatna in Alaska's upper Susitna drainage, I stalked a cow moose with a few-week-old calf. With a brash college sophomore confidence I moved up close and shot a motion picture sequence of the cow and calf crossing a belt of high grass. Only the little fellow's head showed occasionally in the waving green as he followed his mother. Then cow and calf vanished in tall arctic willow brush, and I followed. After some tough going through the willows, I broke out onto a gently sloping alpine meadow below the ridge. As I looked around I heard a rustle of willows on my right. The cow confronted me at 30 yards.

She watched me a few moments, then turned and started trotting up the slope, but pausing at intervals to look back at me over her shoulder. As I stepped away from the willows for a better shooting angle, she stopped short, swung around, and came back at a swift, smooth trot. She ran past me to a small thicket near the meadow's edge, lowered her head into the brush, and grunted and sniffed at her calf.

Then with the hair on her neck and shoulders bristling, and her ears laid back, she walked slowly toward me while I stood happily buzzing away with my little movie camera. She stepped so close that the movie film shows my shadow across her flank. The spring-wound movie camera ran down, and I slowly lowered it. The realization hit me suddenly that I could be in very big trouble. The cow looked at me, her angry eyes speaking a warning that said it might already be too late. But after several long seconds she slowly turned, and again started up the slope.

She stopped to check on me about 20 yards away. Her eloquent warning had registered, and, certainly ready to heed it, I headed back down to the lake.

8 Wild River

Author John Crawford at Talachulitna Lake recording survey data and brewing tea after an earlier stream survey in Alaska's Susitna drainage. Photo by Gene Hull.

"Wild River" is
from *ALASKA*® magazine,
February-March 1970
Alaska Northwest Publishing Company
Box 4 EEE, Anchorage, Alaska 99509

The mist of early morning had burned away in the sun, and now the jagged summits of the Kilbuck Range tusked the sky to the west. The Grumman Goose banked over the glacial silt-tinged stream at the head of the lake, and turned back to follow the shoreline.

From the co-pilot's seat I watched through polarized sunglasses for the stippled red that marks a school of spawning-ready sockeye salmon. With each sighting I recorded the estimated number of salmon in the school, and the location, on a clip-boarded sketch map.

Over the north shore, pilot Phil Zang, who had just radioed our base at King Salmon, tapped my shoulder. "Gonna set her down, John," he spoke loudly over the engine noise. "Have to adjust that antenna."

"Okay, good," I said. It had been a long morning, and I was ready for the sandwiches and thermos of coffee stashed under the jump seat behind us.

For the past two days Phil and I had been flying an aerial survey for the Fish & Wildlife Service (for the branch now officially known as the U.S. Marine Fisheries Service) of western Alaska's Tikchik Lakes. Our objective was to get as close an estimate as possible of the number of sockeye salmon that had returned to the lakes and their feeder streams to spawn.

As Phil started the plane's descent, I spotted a cluster of tents on a point several miles ahead. On the water, I took a look with binoculars. There were several tents and a helicopter. "What's the layout ahead, Phil? Didn't know there was anyone in here."

"Let's see," Phil said. I handed him the glasses. "Yeah, sure enough. That's an oil exploration outfit. For Shell. Heard they were up here."

When Phil taxied the amphibian to the beach, it was impressive to see how abruptly the bottom dropped away. With the bow over the shoreline, the landing gear couldn't touch gravel, and back as far as the cargo hatch the bottom disappeared in cold blue

depth. We had landed on Lake Chauekuktuli (pronounced cho-ka-too-lee by the natives), about 75 air miles north of Dillingham, Alaska, important Bristol Bay salmon canning community.

Just that week (mid-August 1957), I'd made my first trip into the Tikchik country—though I'd spent several months in the Wood River Lakes system a few air miles south—and to say I was impressed would be an understatement. The rugged beauty of this region is a dramatic contrast from the bleak barrens of the Alaska Peninsula on the south side of Bristol Bay. The Tikchik Lakes shelve off rapidly to great depth, with—on a sunny day—remarkable gradations in color as the water gets deeper, shading toward the middle to an almost purple blue. The spruce-poplar forest gives way to brush and grass toward the heads of the lakes and as you go north in the system. Above high, sweeping meadowlands of short alpine vegetation, the range is crested by serrated ridges and spiring peaks with residual snow in autumn still clinging to the faces and hanging in the ravines.

There are six major lakes in the Tikchik system, and five in the Wood River group just to the south. From a casual glance at the map, they appear to be part of the same great system. The heads of Lake Kulik (Wood River) and Lake Nuyakuk (Tikchik) are only a half-dozen air miles apart. With the exceptions of Grant and Nishlik, the major lakes are quite large, ranging, roughly, from 10 to 50 miles in length. A number of smaller lakes, one-half mile to three miles in length, nestle in the foothills and drain to the larger lakes of both systems.

The Tikchik Lakes are drained by the wild Nuyakuk River, the five major lakes to the south by the Wood River, and both outlets feed the great Nushagak, which carries the snow melt of the Kilbuck and southern Taylor Ranges to Bristol Bay and the Bering Sea. The two systems comprise one of the most unique and magnificent lake regions in North America.

Game fish present in the Wood River-Tikchik Lakes region include arctic grayling, rainbow trout, northern pike, sea-run Dolly Varden, and the Dolly's

The Allen River as it spreads out in a great sweep of deep, smooth and swift water, with shallow water and rapids below. This photograph was taken immediately below the Allen Canyon.
Inset — An arctic grayling, hooked on a fly, photographed just before its release.

very close relative, the lake or arctic char. Also resident in some of the lakes are two species of whitefish and freshwater ling.

As the salmon survey demanded sharply attentive observation for closely estimating the schools of fish, there was little or no opportunity to watch for big game and other wildlife while the survey itself was being flown. But when the aerial work was completed Phil and I had seen—just while entering and leaving the area, and along the shorelines—11 moose, 5 wolves, and 9 grizzlies (I'm making no distinction here between the grizzly of interior mountain-tundra habitat and the coastal Alaska brown bear which, of course, is a grizzly himself). No black bears were sighted during our survey.

When Phil and I returned to the U.S. Fish & Wildlife Service base at King Salmon, Mark Meyer, Commercial Fishery Management Supervisor for the Bristol Bay area, reviewed the report of the aerial survey. One major question arose. A foot survey was needed to determine how far salmon ascended the Allen River connecting Lake Chauekuktuli to Lake Chikuminuk. Two waterfalls on the Allen appeared from the air to be approaching or beyond the limit of what sockeye salmon can ascend. The sockeye is not capable of the spectacular leaps of the king and coho salmon and the steelhead trout.

Mark Meyer asked Louie Wolfe and me to prepare gear and provisions for a foot survey that would cover the Allen River from Lake Chauekuktuli to Lake Chikuminuk.

Louie Wolfe is an ex-Navy Chief Warrant Officer with 21 years of active service behind him. He was a gunner on a torpedo bomber during World War II in the Pacific, and served until his retirement as a survival instructor in Alaska, at Thule, Greenland, and at Whidbey Island NAS, Washington State. He is a veteran woodsman with the stamina, fortitude and multiple skills that in Alaska are summed up simply under the "good man" heading.

The job itself, we felt, could be wrapped up in four days. But, in that country, when an assignment is supposed to last four days, you provision for a couple of weeks. Weather in the Wood River-Tikchik region is notoriously unpredictable; it can deteriorate with dramatic suddenness and remain socked in for over a week.

An abundance of good grub selected, we quickly assembled our basic gear. The outfit included a light nylon tent, down arctic sleeping bags, tarps and air mattresses, a shortwave transmitter and receiver, a

CWO Louis N. Wolfe, U.S.N. Ret., a veteran woodsman with the stamina, fortitude, and multiple skills that in Alaska are summed up simply under the "good man" heading. Photo by CPO "Mac" McGary, U.S.N.

.30-'06 rifle, a press camera, the light scientific gear needed, a 12 foot canvas-rubber boat, a three hp outboard motor, and a bit of our own equipment each of us wanted to take.

On the afternoon of August 21, Phil, Louie and I took off from King Salmon to set up our base camp at Lake Chauekuktuli. We touched down near an old trapper's cabin just west of the Allen River mouth and about two miles down the lake from the oil exploration camp. The cabin had been used recently by field biologists from the Fisheries Research Institute of the University of Washington. We unloaded and beached the gear quickly, as Phil wanted to return to King Salmon before dark.

With provisions and equipment secured in the cabin, we hiked the beach down to the river mouth, watched a milling school of salmon, and examined bear and moose tracks on the gravel bars. Getting back late to the cabin, we fixed supper, drank coffee and shot the bull till about 11:00, then hit the racks. Tomorrow would be a long day.

First chore after breakfast the next morning was to set up the shortwave set, rig an aerial, and radio the King Salmon base on our two frequencies to test the equipment. Transmission and reception were excellent.

Then provisions were sorted as to what to carry on the survey and what to leave as a reserve at the base camp. When our packboards were carefully loaded with the food and equipment for the trip upstream,

which would be started early the following morning, we hiked up the river about four miles to get a better idea of what we were in for. We observed sockeye salmon in the river up to a point about two miles above the mouth. We'd originally planned to use the canvas-rubber boat and the small outboard motor for part of the trip, but on this "shakedown" hike we could see that the current was much too powerful for that size motor and the idea was abandoned. The boat alone would have been useful on the return, but we decided that the country was too rough to justify the extra backpacking weight.

On the morning of August 23 we radioed our King Salmon base, informing the operator of our estimated date of return—the 25th, and headed upstream. We were packing heavy, as we wanted to have a grub cache at our midway camp which we would probably use both going up and on the return. It was rough terrain and a wild river, and the going was slow as we picked our way cautiously over boulders and jutting cleavers of bedrock. The deep, powerful current made it impossible to cross the river and take advantage of easier terrain, which would have been better both for travel and observation of the salmon.

But the country was as beautiful as it was rough. Wild flowers, heather, moss and alpine grasses grew among the boulders in striking natural rock gardens.

Traveling as fast as we could effectively do the job, it was late in the afternoon when we reached a low falls, split by a cleaver of bedrock, about eight miles above the mouth of the river. Beyond a point about three and a half miles above the mouth we'd seen no salmon, but this falls was no barrier to the fish. It was little more than a powerful rapids with only a few feet of vertical drop.

Just above this falls was the beginning of an almost-sheer-walled gorge. Recalling it from the aerial survey, I realized that it extended far enough upstream to preclude our finding a good campsite above it before dark. Here just below the rapids was a large gravel bar that would make a good place to camp.

But wanting to size up any immediate problem ahead, I left my pack on the bar and continued upstream, while Louie gathered firewood and fished for grayling. The rugged canyon rim varied from about 60 to 75 feet above the water.

I'd hiked about a quarter-mile along the rim when I came to a fissure in the rock. It was around 70 feet in length and met the river gorge at a right angle. In the flat rays of the evening sun I couldn't see its bottom. The fissure was about five feet wide at its junction with the gorge and tapered to a fraction of an inch at its terminal end. It reminded me of an earthquake fault or a fresh crevasse in a glacier. Short subalpine vegetation grew in a thick turf to the rim of the fissure, spreading fibrous roots in a thin layer of flaky gravel that could hardly be called soil.

I hiked a few hundred yards farther upstream, then headed back. I was concerned now that we had underestimated the time needed to survey the river up to Lake Chikuminuk and hike back to our base camp. In country that rugged, distance in air miles means little to a man on foot.

Returning to our gravel bar campsite, I talked it over with Louie. In distance, we were a little better than halfway to the lake, but the going would be tougher from here on.

We decided to start as early as we could get away, and to make a light go of it, taking only one pack with provisions, the cameras, a pocket transit—to aid in determining approximate height of falls, the rifle, and a rain jacket, extra sweater, shirt and socks for each man in the event of a siwash camp. We would try to complete the survey to the lake and return to the midway camp before dark, leaving the river on the return and taking advantage of the fast travel on the ridge crests above the heavy thickets of alder and arctic willow. The tent, sleeping bags, nonessential personal gear, and the bulk of the provisions would be cached and picked up on the return.

Our minds made up, we felt a lot better about it. With still an hour and a half of good daylight left, I jointed up my rod and had a great session of grayling fishing with Louie, though I couldn't match his finesse. Louie handles a fly rod like it was his idea in the first place.

Using a variety of dry fly and streamer patterns, Louie and I caught and released about 20 grayling between us, before keeping two nice ones apiece for supper.

I'd just lost my favorite fly, an Alaska Mary Ann streamer, on a four-pound-plus arctic char, and was reeling in my line when I heard what—for a moment—was an almost incredible sound.

A helicopter was flying down the gorge. For awhile I'd forgotten about the oil exploration camp at Lake Chauekuktuli. The chopper hovered over our campsite bar, then started to settle. I saw Louie pounce on a notebook that started to blow in the river from the wash of the blades. I picked up my two grayling—

now gilled on a willow branch—and forded the deep, icy current to meet the visitors.

The helicopter crew, pilot Dale Koponen and mechanic Sam Gregory, worked for Economy Helicopters of Yakima, Washington; and their services, along with the chopper, were on seasonal lease to Shell Oil Company. We had a good time shooting the bull for a few minutes; then, as dusk was not far off, Dale and Sam took off for their camp. They'd told us they were about ready to pull out for another area.

While I'd been up the river looking at the gorge, Louie had gathered plenty of driftwood for the night's fire. There was a growing chill in the air, and the good, subtle forest smell of summer going into autumn. I kicked off my wet boots, put on dry socks and moccasins, and began building a cooking fireplace with flat river stones.

"John," Louie said, looking up and grinning as he cleaned and scaled the fish, "I'm gonna show you how to fix grayling like you never tasted 'em before."

Well, I've eaten grayling cooked several ways, by myself and quite a few others, but nobody fixes them better than Louie. We built a driftwood fire and let it burn down to red embers. Louie split each dressed fish, and removed the backbones. Then he skillfully wove a grill from the tips of green alder branches. Holding the grill over the coals, from which there was no smoke or visible flame, Louie broiled the grayling, adding salt and pepper and basting lightly with butter. The smell of the fire, cooking grayling, and steaming coffee merged with the scent of northern forest.

When we were ready to eat, we built up the fire. The grayling were memorable. They were delicious, and would have been acclaimed as such in the finest restaurant in San Francisco.

For dessert we had bread and butter and raspberry jam with coffee. We talked and relaxed by the fire. Occasional chill gusts of wind flared the blaze away from us, making us appreciate the fire all the more. A low bank of clouds hung on the southeastern horizon, otherwise the sky was clear. The early autumn dusk darkened to full night.

We didn't talk much now. We drank the good black coffee and listened to the night—to the river and the restless soughing of the wind in the spruce and poplar forest. We felt some of the strange moodiness—a subtle pleasure in itself—that people often feel when they sit by a campfire in wilderness, confronted by the timeless and eternal.

123

Above — The first major falls above the gorge on the Allen River. This falls is not high enough to be an obstacle to the salmon.
Opposite page — An aerial view of the same falls , taken by Dale Koponen from a helicopter during the high water period of early summer.

About 10:30 we blew up the air mattresses and turned in. The weather was holding clear, and we didn't use the tent, but it was cold enough that we wore long-johns as a supplement to the sleeping bags. For a few minutes more I listened to the wind, the rush of the river, embers cracking in the fire; watched stars falling in the black sky. Next thing I knew it was morning.

Waking at sunrise, we rolled out quickly, already wishing we'd been up before dawn. We fired up last night's coals, and put on bacon, eggs and coffee. After a quick breakfast, each carefully considered

item to go up-river was loaded into one pack. The re-maining provisions and gear, including the sleeping bags, were tarp-wrapped and cached. We shoved off. I started with the pack, Louie with the rifle.

We climbed through arctic willow and spruce up the steep, ledgy slope, crested out on the rim of the gorge. In places it was a sheer chasm. The river sped through the canyon, powerful, gurgling and swirling in the confinement of the granite walls, blue-green in its depth.

From the canyon rim, we could see grayling finning in the current, at one point about a dozen at

once, not schooled—well spread out, holding posi-tion a few inches below the surface, their great dorsal fins waving gently in the current, most of them colored bronze with a subtle purplish sheen on the sides—but two were a marlin blue-black. Louie and I had both taken 23-inch grayling at Ugashik Narrows on the Alaska Peninsula, and several of these fish were in that class.

About two and a half miles above our midway camp, we reached the first of the two largest falls that I'd seen on the aerial survey. It was spectacular and beautiful, but not high enough to block the migration of the salmon. Louie determined its approximate height, and I took several photographs for the survey record.

From aerial observation I could remember in good detail major features of the river, and gauging our slow progress—though we were moving as fast as we could do the job well—I could see already that it was going to be a close squeeze to reach the lake and return to our midway camp before dark. I was especially concerned about a stream that joined the Allen River from the west about a mile and a half below Lake Chikuminuk. It was small as far as its present water volume was concerned, but from the air its canyon appeared deep and almost sheer sided near the confluence. A time-consuming detour would be required to cross it.

At 12:30 P.M. we stopped for a quick bite to eat, and to record observations in our field notebooks.

Then we pushed on, climbing over boulders, walking along shoals in the river, sometimes shoving our way through jungle-like alder thickets where the river was too deep, or the cleavers and pitches of bedrock too steep and slick.

We studied the river, watching ahead and turning to check again behind for fish breaking water. A sockeye salmon often leaps in flat, on-the-side jumps in a series. The sockeye, reaching sexual maturity after its return to fresh water, changes from its silver-sided, blue-backed (though sometimes dark-grayish, greenish or olive-brown) salt water coloration and takes on a vivid red over most of its body, with the head and tail becoming a light green or olive color. In both aerial and ground surveys, if there isn't too much sun-glare and cloud reflection on the water, this red color is easily seen in all but glacial and heavily turbid stream conditions.

But we had seen no salmon above our midway camp. Had they ever come up this far? We kept our eyes open for a jawbone or a section of vertebral column from a carcass cast up on the rocks by high water, or left in the brush by bears. If your observation is competent, negative information can be just as important as what you actually see.

To find out whether or not salmon were ascending the Allen to Lake Chikuminuk or, if not, how far they were coming up the river, was the major objective of the survey, but we also briefly recorded our observations on any factors that would affect the ecology of the stream. These included gradient and type of streambed, water temperature, the increase of water volume and velocity from confluent feeder streams, the presence of mammals and birds that prey on adult salmon (eagles, ospreys, otters, and bears), and the presence of species that prey on the one-to-three-year sockeye smolt on their outmigration to the sea, such as chars, trout, gulls, terns and jaegers.

By 2:00 P.M. it was clear to us that we wouldn't be able to continue on to Lake Chikuminuk and still get back to our midway camp before dark. We decided to climb a ridge above the gorge to look at the river and the country ahead.

As we emerged from an alder thicket into the relative open of high grass and scattered willow, there was a sudden, explosive *huaaahhhh! huhhh!* from 25 yards in front of us. Louie, still carrying the rifle, bolted a round into the chamber of the .30-'06, then stood waiting, rifle raised.

Brush rustled softly; then there was a snapping of alder limbs, and we saw a glimpse of straw-brown hide. The sound stopped abruptly. There were long seconds of stillness, with only the soft humming buzz of insects. We could see nothing. Then . . . *huaahhh! Huhhh!* Another few moments of silence. Then the grizzly crashed from the thicket.

He broke into the open, rushed in a butt-bouncing gallop up a steep meadow slope, stormed a brush-waving trail through a fringe of alder and willow, crested the hill and was gone. Louie and I looked at each other and grinned. Then I noticed Louie's wrists. They looked like they had been bathed in blood. So did mine.

Hordes of tiny flies, white sox, had been biting us savagely, but we had been so intent on the bear that we actually hadn't felt them. We washed the blood off our arms, and put on repellent.

Reaching the hilltop, we found that Lake Chikuminuk was hidden by an intervening spur ridge. But what we did see, we didn't like. A blue-black storm front was building up over the Kilbuck Range to the west.

"Doesn't look so good, Louie," I said.

"Nope, it sure doesn't. With the tarps back there wrapped around the gear, I'm afraid we're in for a wet night."

"How long do you figure it'll take to get down here?"

Louie shook his head. "Hard to say. But I don't think we'll be in it much before nine-thirty or ten. Maybe later."

We'd gambled on the weather and lost. A siwash camp, with several hours of it in a storm, was certain if we continued on to the lake. Then, the only alternatives would be to remain at the lake or start back and travel as far as possible before dark. Hiking at night in this country was, of course, out of the question. If we started back now, by keeping on the ridges above the brush, we could reach our midway camp before dark. We could then return early in the morning by the same high route, and pick up our survey at this point. But on the other hand, while it would mean a rough night, the actual survey work could be completed today, and, starting at daybreak tomorrow, we could be back for a good rest at the cabin on Chauekuktuli by late afternoon. We decided to go on.

We'd been hearing the roar of the water for some time, and it was near sunset when we reached the great pool below the upper falls. A granite cliff curved around just ahead of us, blocking our view of the falls itself. We left the rifle and pack on a boulder, then picked our way on knobs and ledges around the cliff to where we could see the falls. We hugged the rock wall—wet with mist and spray. It was no place from which to take a picture. It was hard enough just to hang on and look. Not as high as I'd thought from aerial observation, the impressive thing was not its drop, but the thundering volume and velocity of water that plunged through the narrow cut.

This, to the salmon, was the one impassable barrier on the river. Once we had a good look, we edged our way back to the secure footing of the mossy bank. Were it not for the upwelling eddies, the pool would have looked like a mountain tarn, for it had the round shape and great depth of a glacial cirque lake. The bedrock dropped out of sight a few feet from the banks. The crystal water was so deep it looked cobalt blue. The low, flat rays of the westering sun warmed the already beautiful color tones of the autumn vegetation, and reflected on the great pool that was alive with leaping grayling. It was one of the grandest wilderness sights I've ever been privileged to witness.

But there was no time to linger. Dusk was not long away. We made a climbing traverse above the falls and its funnel-like gorge. The spruce trees, few and scattered now, had given way to brush and short alpine turf. Tonight we'd need plenty of firewood. Though the objective of the survey was accomplished, we would push on to Lake Chikuminuk. The lake offered the best siwash campsite, as there would be seasoned driftwood on the shore.

Soon we reached the deep tributary canyon that joined the Allen River from the west. A small stream, fed by springs in the Kilbuck foothills, raced between 75-foot walls of sheer granite. We were forced to follow this gorge for over a mile before we found a safe place to descend and cross it. One thing was in our favor; this was the first long stretch of easy going we'd found on the trip. We made good time, alternately walking and jogging on the short turf.

The sun had dropped behind the Kilbuck Range when we descended into the canyon and crossed it. We hurried on, hiking in the twilight on the short alpine turf of heather, moss and tundra grasses. We were feeling the day's work now, but kept up the fast pace. We wanted to take advantage of every minute of light remaining. Then from the grassy top of a spur ridge we saw the 20-mile expanse of Lake Chikuminuk hardly a mile ahead.

It was full night when we picked our way down the last brushy slope to the lake shore near the outlet of the Allen River. On the beach we quickly built a fire from dead alder. There were no spruce growing in the near vicinity. Once the fire was burning well, we built a windbreak of green alder. Louie used a handmade bowie knife to cut alder—a superbly honed and heavy knife that weighed two and a half pounds. He was cutting alders thicker than a big man's wrist with one clean stroke.

The sky was darkening fast as the storm front moved east. We sat resting by the fire, intruders in a vast and silent land. For awhile the only sounds were the waves lapping on the beach, embers cracking in the fire, and the soft murmuring rush of the river as it left the lake. Then two loons began calling; next to wolves howling, the most haunting sound in the wilderness. A cold gust of wind penetrated the break, fanned the fire and scattered embers.

We ate supper very slowly—canned corned beef, pilot bread crackers, canned fruit, and coffee. We enjoyed the simple meal and the fire, our pipes and conversation. We knew that later on it was going to be a rough night, but after you've lived so long in the bush you learn not to worry too much about things that can no longer be helped.

After eating, we gathered a large supply of dead alder and what driftwood we could find. I opened the pack and dug out extra clothing. Louie tossed the few cans in the fire to burn out the scent, then crushed and buried them. He has the real woodsman's respect for country, whether he's camping in a state park or the wildest reaches of Alaska or Canada.

We each put on an extra shirt, sweater and dry socks, and lay on the sand by the fire to get what sleep we could before the rain came.

Shortly after 11:00 the rain started with a few scattered drops. We didn't bother, at first, to get up. The fire was burning well, and we were still comfortable. But shortly after midnight it opened up. We piled wood on the fire, gathering all the dead alder that was close at hand. We got the fire blazing so hot it was consuming green alder. But there was little comfort from it. By 2:30 the morning of August 25 the wind was driving the rain in lashing sheets.

We spent the hours until almost daybreak cutting alder, feeding the fire, and turning in front of it like grouse broiling on a spit. Just before dawn we had breakfast, repeating the menu of the night before, and using our remaining food.

Then, at first light, we broke camp, shouldered the rifle and pack and headed out. The job now was to get back to our midway camp, and then to the cabin at Chauekuktuli as quickly as safety would permit. We tramped over the foothills to the deep confluent canyon, crossed it and pushed downstream, keeping as much as we could to the open ridge crests, traveling in the high country parallel to the Allen River.

The night of exposure had taken its toll. We were tired, but despite our fatigue, and the frequent descending and climbing again in the jumbled topography of the Kilbuck foothills, we were making good time. Several times we stopped to rest, and, very hungry now as well as tired—we were out of grub until we reached our midway camp—we made our stops at blueberry patches. The berries were ripe and delicious, but we began to nod as we sat eating, and twice I fell asleep with my mouth full of blueberries.

About 10:30 the rain eased off to intermittent showers, and a heavy fog formed over the foothills, severely limiting visibility. We descended to the river and hiked along the bank, or in the shallows. Our time was slow now, compared to traveling the ridges, but the fog gave us no choice.

At a few minutes after noon we were nearing the first big falls, picking our way over boulders and ledges. Then, as I stepped from a boulder to a short pitch of granite bedrock, I slipped.

I shot skating down the sheet of rock, standing up but out of control. As I tried to regain balance, my left foot skidded across in front of my right and caught against a small upthrust ledge. My right shin, and behind it my whole weight and momentum, drove against the trapped lower left leg.

I heard two cracks like a thin spar breaking. Pain knifed in searing stabs as I slid into the river, riding on the broken left leg. The lower tibia had broken in a spiral and fragmented just above the ankle. The fibula had broken in an overriding fracture a couple of inches below the knee. Friends who had broken a leg in football or skiing had told me you could hear a bone when it goes. I'd always found it hard to believe that in the moment of fast action you really could. But I believe it now.

I heard Louie call behind me. "You okay, John?"

Both of us had slipped a couple of times the day before, and had come out of it with nothing worse than a bruised butt.

"No, Louie, I've done it. I've broken a leg."

"Oh, no! Are you sure?"

"Yeah, no doubt about it." The pain had eased off, and rage and disgust at myself were boiling up in me. I'd dropped my guard a moment and put a grim complexity on a trip that, except for the uncomfortable night, had been little more than a routine survey assignment.

Louie stepped cautiously down behind me, and lifted the pack off my back. With him pulling and lifting under my shoulders, and me pushing at the same time with my hands, I was out of the water in a few seconds. "Look at that foot!" I said.

While the right foot was pointing almost straight up in a normal position, the left was turned in, lying on its edge on the rock.

Louie nodded. "Yep, it's broken bad." He crouched down to examine the leg. I'd left my fishing boots at the midway camp, and had worn an old pair of German mountain climbing boots for the trip up-river. I'd worn them for better traction and all-around utility, but the lug soles no longer had the crisp bite they once had.

"It just about opened up on you," Louie said. "I'm afraid it still could if it's not handled right."

Neither of us said anything for a few moments. We were thinking hard. It was 12:20 now. Less than eight hours of daylight remained. We thought immediately of the oil exploration camp and the helicopter. Two days before the crew had been almost ready to leave, and perhaps by now they were gone. But it was our best chance.

Louie looked at me intently. "Your color's good yet. How do you feel, now? I'm thinkin' of shock."

"I feel like the south end of a northbound horse. I don't know about shock."

"No use being sore at yourself," Louie said.

"Could have happened to me. Could have happened to anybody. You feelin' sick at all?"

"No, only the leg. And it's not bad. Just for the first few seconds."

"Look," Louie said. "I think I'd better straighten your leg and pull it out a bit. Some traction will ease the pain."

"Go ahead."

We heard a soft, grating crackle as bone fragments moved. Pain stabbed hot for an instant, then almost disappeared. "That's a lot better," I said.

The rain was falling heavier. "I'd better get started," Louie said. "That chopper is the one chance we have of getting you out tonight." He turned away. "In the meantime, you're gonna need a fire bad."

"Just get me a few pieces of drift, Louie. I can work on a fire while you're gone."

"Okay, it'd save time. Now, we'll see if we can get you up under that spruce against the cliff."

I looked around at it. There was some shelter there, all right, and I could move myself up. I worked backwards using my hands and good leg and pushed up the granite sheet until I was under the spruce boughs. Dragging the broken leg worked as traction, and relieved the pain rather than causing more of it.

Louie carried over some good pieces of driftwood and dead spruce boughs for kindling, then brought up the pack. Until I was moved, we felt it would be better for circulation in the torn tissue if the leg was left unsplinted.

"When you see the helicopter," Louie said, now ready to leave, "give us a wave with the flashlight. I'll radio King Salmon and ask them to stand by. If the Shell crew has pulled out, or if it's too dark for Dale to get in with the chopper I'll hike up by flashlight tonight with the sleeping bags and tent. Well, see you later, Buddy."

He was dead tired, but he would have done just that. Louie climbed out of the gorge and was gone.

In the pocket of the pack there was a .50 caliber cartridge case full of matches. Under the partial shelter of the spruce boughs, I carved shavings off the driftwood, broke up some dead spruce twigs, tucked crumpled scraps of paper under the pyramid and attempted to light it. Trying repeatedly, I couldn't protect the feeble flame against the wind and lashing rain. Then the dry paper was gone. I reached for my wallet to see what expendable identification cards I could use to help kindle a fire. As soon as I touched the wallet, I knew there was no use

looking at the cards. I was as wet as a drowned wharf rat from the waist down. I decided not to try to build a fire again until the storm let up.

I dug down in the pack to find the flashlight. It was wrapped in a woolen shirt with Louie's .38 Smith & Wesson. I checked the light and put it back just under the flap.

I sat under the partial shelter of the spruce boughs, thinking, watching the river and the storm. The wind was whipping veils of mist up the canyon. The storm was dramatic and swiftly changing, like watching a time-lapse weather sequence in a motion picture. The wind and rain were picking up, and I knew the weather could get much worse before it got better.

I felt depressed and heavy-hearted about the spot I'd put Louie in. I felt I'd let him down. To myself, I couldn't excuse my carelessness. Louie was tired, too tired, and he had over 11 grueling miles to go in dangerous terrain. Several prospectors had vanished in this country without a trace.

But after a while I just acknowledged the futility of worrying about the situation, and, to an extent, relaxed. Louie was tired, but he was also an exceptional outdoorsman. And he'd been in more than a few tough spots before, both as a flier in the Pacific and as a survival instructor in Alaska and Greenland. When the chips were in the pot, Louie could do the job.

Most of the pain was gone from the leg, but I began to feel a deep chill. The cold caused a muscular spasm in the sound right leg. For a few moments, the limb shook violently on the rock.

Then, after about half an hour, I seemed to feel warmer—at least used to the cold. This was the effect, probably, of the blood being charged with adrenaline, and heart and lungs working harder than normal.

I began to watch the storm with a kind of detachment, watched the way you sometimes listen to good music—hearing it without thinking about it, but, instead, letting it drift your mind back through memories. And so it was with the storm. With an oddly unusual clarity I recalled past experiences, some from back in childhood that I hadn't thought of in years; and other, more recent, happenings—mountain climbing, fishing and hunting trips, other river surveys, experiences in military service and as a university student; back through foul-ups and things done well, through the sobering and the laughable—and several times, sitting there cold and wet under the spruce boughs, I found myself laughing.

My mind came back to the present finally, and I wondered about the situation at hand, and what was just ahead—how far down the river Louie was now, if the oil exploration crew had pulled out already . . . and how the devil I'd get out of there if they had, if my leg would have to have surgery, how soon I could walk on it again, and what the nurses would be like when I got to the hospital.

During the hours of thinking and watching the storm I often started to nod, but I caught myself just before dropping off to sleep, shook my head—trying to clear away the tiredness. Finally I just went out like a light, falling asleep sitting there on the rock in the rain. The cold soon woke me up, but the great drowsiness was still there. I didn't feel any pain in the broken leg now, and, had it not been for the strange position of my left foot, I'd have doubted that the accident had really happened. The whole experience of the afternoon seemed, somehow, unreal.

The gray light of the stormy afternoon was darkening to dusk. The wind and rain hadn't let up much, but I decided to try the fire again. I looked around, spotted a knob of pitch and some dry moss on a densely boughed spruce several yards away. I pushed my way over there, got the pitch, some moss and a few dead bough tips, then crawled back. I built the material into a little pyramid, started to reach for the matches in a side pocket of the pack, but stopped and lay back a moment on the rock. Bone fragments had shifted around the break and were causing stabbing pain. I sat up, and took the cartridge case of matches from the pack. Suddenly, almost incredibly, I heard the sound of the helicopter.

I pushed out from under the boughs. Sure enough! I pulled the flashlight from the pack, waved it in a tracering arc. The chopper came flying up over the far side of the canyon, made a sweeping turn across the river, the craft shuddering in buffeting gusts of wind. It swung downstream, and as it passed I saw Louie wave from the bubble. Then out of sight, I heard the chopper landing, seeming 150 or 200 yards downriver.

I waited. It seemed like a long time had passed, and I hadn't heard them coming through the brush. I yelled, "Hey Louie!"

"Yeah!" came the welcome answer. A couple of minutes later Louie and Dale Koponen came picking their way along the rocky bank, carrying blankets and a Stokes litter. Dale had flown in his Bell G-2 helicopter in weather that would have made any chopper pilot wonder.

"Well," I said, "you're the best two men I've ever met."

Dale Koponen grinned. "No sweat," he said. "How're you doing? Just about ready to tuck yourself in for the night, huh?"

I laughed. "Yeah, I just about was."

Louie uncapped a thermos and poured a steaming cup of coffee, sugared and creamed and not quite scalding. I'd pay 50 bucks for a cup of coffee that would taste that good again.

Dale and Louie went to work. They could hardly have been more efficient if they had practiced together for two weeks. While Louie splinted the leg, Dale gave me a shot with a morphine syrette in the upper arm. Pushing down with my hands, I edged into the litter with one man supporting the leg. They folded the military blankets over, tightened the straps, and we were on our way. But how sorry I felt for those guys! I weighed about 210, and the litter and blankets added a few pounds more.

It was tough, anxious work for them, packing a few yards, then stopping to rest, stepping along slippery boulders and bedrock, walking in the river where the water was shallow enough. Then Dale noticed a small bar of rock ahead that was just big enough to set the chopper on.

"By golly, I think I can move it up. It'll cut the packing distance in half."

While Dale was gone, Louie told me about his trip down. He'd tried to radio out to King Salmon when he reached the cabin at Chauekuktuli, but was unable to get through. He had hiked and run along the beach to the oil exploration camp and arrived there while the crew was eating supper. The entire camp jumped into action, readying the helicopter and the first aid equipment. For over an hour the ceiling had hung so dangerously low that the trip could not be attempted. It had lifted in just marginal time, and Dale and Louie had sighted me, waving the flashlight on the rock, barely 25 minutes before darkness.

We heard Dale start the helicopter. He brought it up, the chopper shuddering a bit in the turbulent gusts. Dale hovered a moment over the bar, then eased the chopper gently down. Louie and I watched with admiration the superb skill of a pro doing his job under hazardous conditions when the pressure is on and seconds count. The litter packing distance had been cut more than half.

When we reached the helicopter the litter was lashed over the landing skid on the right side. "Is there time for me to pick up the pack?" Louie asked

Dale. Besides other gear in the pack, including Louie's .38, there were three cameras with a total value of well over a thousand dollars. But the sky was darkening fast.

"No, we'll have to leave it, Louie," Dale said. "This is going to be tight. We'll need every minute of light we've got left. We'll pick up the pack tomorrow."

The helicopter rose from the bar with Dale and Louie crowded against the left side of the bubble to balance my weight over the right landing skid.

Just to see the chopper flying up the canyon had given me a sense of vast relief and well-being, and during the flight that feeling of euphoria was heightened by the morphine injection Dale had given me. Unmindful of the rain and the violent flapping of a loose blanket corner, I raised my head over the

Pilot Dale Koponen and the Bell G-2 helicopter he flew in stormy darkness to rescue me. Photo was taken on Lake Chauekuktuli by Sam Gregory.

edge of the litter and happily watched the darkening wilderness below.

Full darkness had come when we reached the oil exploration camp at Lake Chauekuktuli, but flares had been set out to mark the landing site. Dale settled the chopper gently to the ground.

"Good show, boys!" I heard someone call as the crew hurried over to untie the litter.

In the big dome-ceiling mess tent, I was sacked out and the leg was resplinted. Outside rain pelted the fabric, and the tent trembled in whipping gusts of wind. But inside it was as warm and cheerfully comfortable as a ski lodge, and roast beef sandwiches and coffee tasted better than prime ribs at Solly's. For the job Louie and Dale had done I was more grateful than I could say.

The following morning the weather opened enough to allow Phil Zang, with Mark Meyer, to fly in with the Grumman Goose. When I was packed aboard, we took off for Dillingham.

At the Kanakanak Alaska Native Service Hospital a few miles out of Dillingham, Dr. Waggoner x-rayed, diagnosed the fractures, and put the leg in a traveling cast for the commercial airline flight to Anchorage. "That leg is a job for Bill Mills," he said.

At Providence Hospital in Anchorage, the leg—now colored like a black eye—was put under ice packs for three days to bring the swelling down prior to surgery. Then Dr. William J. Mills Jr., the great orthopedic surgeon and frostbite expert, performed open-reduction surgery and secured the bone with steel screws. Early the following spring I went on a 40-mile snowshoe trip, and found the leg as good as ever.

Louie and I can look back on working and exploring in one of the most magnificent wilderness areas remaining on the North American Continent. But through fatigue and carelessness, rushing to complete a job, I made a blunder that—had it not been for my great good fortune in having Louie and Dale to get me to shelter and medical attention—could have cost me a leg. The North Country is the land of the calculated risk, but this experience points up the fact that—like the prospectors who sought for the gold of the Kilbuck Range and were never seen again—if you get careless the bush will take its toll. The eternal mountains and rivers of Alaska are not concerned with the plans of men.

9 A Challenge at Kamishak

An Alaska Peninsula brown bear mother with her three second-summer cubs at the McNeil River falls.

"A Challenge at Kamishak" is from
ALASKA® magazine,
January-February 1973
Alaska Northwest Publishing Company
Box 4-EEE, Anchorage, Alaska 99509

To the north the mist was rising on the mountains. In the chill of early morning I pushed through a belt of rain-beaded alders and stepped out onto open tundra. Warming under the parka shell, and starting to break a sweat, I stopped a few moments. From here it wasn't far to the falls. I'd traveled fast coming up from the bay, probably too fast for good observation and caution. Standing resting at the edge of the brush, I looked at the country around me, feeling the wind on my face. The wind carried the cold, clean, good scent of rain and tundra and the sea. Weather's changing, I thought. Might be a storm coming up. Well, no matter. You've already had more than one guy's share of good luck on this trip.

A dozen yards away, a cock ptarmigan walked out of the alders into the sunshine that had just broken through the wind-shifting clouds. Sunlight caught the dash of red above his eye, in vivid contrast to the subdued mottled brown of his summer plumage.

From this point to where I'd hit the river, the going would be easier, mostly on short, tundra turf, but with a traverse through waist high grass bordered by thickets of arctic willow and alder. Keep on your toes, I thought. And thinking back, I smiled, recalling a story a friend had told me of his experience on Kodiak Island—walking in high grass against a stiff wind he had almost literally stepped on a sleeping old boar brownie. We'd both had a good laugh when he told it, but right now it wasn't as funny.

As I hiked on toward the falls I was keying up—with the tingle of anticipation, the wondering about what would happen today. I was alone and unarmed in Alaska's greatest brown bear country and, appropriately enough, was "all ears and eyeballs."

Without thinking of it that way, I was, as I neared the river, putting on my psychological armor. When I look at a big wilderness bear that I've decided I'm going to stalk and photograph at the closest range I

feel I can get away with, I know something of that same adrenalin-charged edginess that I used to get just before a match when I boxed in college. It's easier to do it than to think about it.

In a few more minutes of hiking I arrived at the falls on the McNeil River, where Alaska Peninsula brown bears converge from many miles around to fish for salmon during the spawning runs. But now, as I looked upstream and down, there was no bear in sight—the first morning in a week that there hadn't been at least one bear on the river fishing when I reached the falls. From my vantage point, however, I could see hundreds of chum salmon resting in the pools below the falls, their dorsal fins, heads and backs continually breaking the surface. There were both bright silver fresh-run fish and salmon that had come in earlier that were now vividly marked with the red-purple barring of their spawning coloration.

Every few seconds one or more salmon would try to fight their way above the falls, often leaping, but mostly with tremendous swimming efforts, staying just below the surface—dorsal fins visible above the water, knifing through the foam—and with driving tail strokes powering their way up and over.

Among the salmon were Dolly Varden chars, sleek and gleaming from the sea, waiting to feed on the eggs of the salmon. The chars, too, were surmounting the falls, lashing their caudal fins in surges of power, arrowing beautifully up from the pools— not arching like the salmon, but almost in flat trajectories—hitting the falls below its crest, for a moment just seeming to hang in the foam, then powering upward, spray flying from their wakes, and swimming over the top. You'll never get a better chance for jumping fish shots, I thought.

I slipped off my pack and tripod-mounted a Linhof press camera. Walking carefully into the river, I picked my way out near the base of the falls, placed the tripod legs securely in the current on the rock bottom, studied the framing through the big 4x5 inch ground glass viewfinder, memorized the area the

My driftwood beach fire at Kamishak Bay where — with all my film supply exposed, and living off the country for food — I read while waiting for an aircraft pickup.

lens covered, snapped in a film holder and set the camera for an exposure.

Concentrating to react the instant the right picture appeared—the split-second that the salmon peaked in its arch above the foam—I put almost enough thumb-pressure on the cable release to trip the shutter, "taking up the slack" as a rifleman does in his trigger. A big male chum salmon leaped, for an instant was silhouetted beautifully against the falls, then plunged back into the foam and was swept down. I'd triggered the cable release, but I thought my reaction had been a bit slow for the most dramatic picture.

I reversed the film holder, recocked the shutter. Tautly alert now, captivated by the picture potential of this situation, I took up the slack in the cable release and waited. I could hear nothing but the rush of water, and my eyes were held to the few square feet that were the target area for my picture. And then I **felt** a presence.

I looked up . . . and into the face of a great brown bear sow. Not a dozen feet away, she stood on the brink of the falls, flanked by three second-year cubs, and for a few moments all four bears stood as still as if they were museum mounts in a habitat group.

My eyes swept briefly over the family, and then I just looked at the huge mother. The river foamed over her paws, and the wind rippled the still-dry hair on her massive shoulders, but for that time she was motionless. As my first pulse-leaping shock faded, the thought came, What a shot!

I almost reached for the bulky press camera—for a moment thinking of raising it, tripod and all, and taking the picture—but in the next instant I thought, no, I better not move at all!

I realized then that any motion on my part could break a precarious truce. So I just stood still and looked into the face of the brown bear mother. And I was close enough to see the pupils of her eyes.

Then abruptly the sow turned on the foaming ledge, and without a huff, grunt or growl she started walking away along the brink of the falls with the cubs bunched behind her. In a few moments she was across the river, her bulk poised on the rocky bank, waiting for a good chance to catch a salmon. Our eye-to-eye encounter probably lasted between 20 and 30 seconds.

Had this powerful, dominant, wilderness mother sensed that I meant no harm to her and her family? I felt certain that she had, and that a moment of almost mystic understanding had passed between us. She was, I'm sure, absolutely unafraid of me, and one swipe of her great paw could have knocked me into eternity as easily as she would give a misbehaving cub a disciplinary cuff on the rump. But she had only stopped and looked at me and then had gone her way.

I didn't have a rifle with me, and hadn't brought one along on the trip, although legally persons entering the McNeil River area are permitted to take firearms for their protection. But the McNeil area was set aside as a reserve area for the **protection of the bears,** and I personally feel that there should be the same firearm restrictions there as there are in national parks. In wilderness areas man is an intruder, and I believe that persons entering a wildlife reserve to photograph bears or any other animal should be willing to take their own chances or they should stay out. Anyone using common sense, and who respects the bears not just for their formidable power, but also respects and appreciates them as wonderfully interesting animal personalities is very unlikely to get into trouble with them.

With the bear family across the river, I stood a few moments at the foot of the falls just relaxing from the tension of the close encounter. Then for about half-an-hour I took pictures of the salmon. Finally satisfied that I had the shots I wanted, I sloshed my way back to the bank of conglomerate rock, removed the bulky press camera from the tripod, and mounted a telephoto lens with a reflex camera.

During the rest of that day I shot all my remaining film on bears. As well as the family I'd met on the falls, my subjects included two other sows with younger cubs, a young male bear about three years old, and a huge old boar—the biggest bear I'd seen in the area, and the biggest I'd seen anywhere with the exception of one old male in the Karluk Lake area of Kodiak Island.

The young male was very much afraid of the big old-timer. The youngster arrived at the falls about 20 minutes before the old boar showed up. As the young bear sat at the river's edge, waiting for a vulnerable salmon, he suddenly whirled. He had scented the approach of the big boar. He instantly started to flee, but, confused by tricky wind currents, he took off on the same trail on which the giant was coming to the river. The ancient, deep-worn trail dropped down the

bank through high grass and arctic willow. With the big bear hungry and hurrying, and the small bear thoroughly spooked, they were on a collision course. Then at about 15 yards they saw each other. As the old boar momentarily hesitated—apparently in some surprise—the young bear stood up on his hind paws in a moment of desperate indecision, then whirled and dropped to all fours, galloped back down to the river, fled along the rocky edge until he was a few yards upstream from the falls, then cut up the bank through the brush.

During six great days of generally fine weather and cooperative bears, what I had thought was a far more than ample supply of film was entirely exposed.

I'd arrived from Anchorage a week before at King Salmon on the Alaska Peninsula. Because my departure date from Seattle was contingent on several factors beyond my control, I couldn't prearrange a charter flight weeks in advance. This had to be worked out when I got to Alaska. Upon my arrival at King Salmon I quickly sought out an old friend, master guide, bush pilot, state senator Jay Hammond (later to become Alaska's governor) to see about a charter with him. During previous years I'd flown with Jay on a successful moose hunting trip and on a number of charters with him for the Fish & Wildlife Service. But now, as it happened, he was booked up with scheduled charters for the next several weeks, mostly for oil exploration crews.

"Weather permitting, John," Jay said, "I could get you in there tomorrow. But with the schedule I've got now it would be about three weeks before I could pick you up. And in there, with any luck at all, there's a good chance that a week of shooting would get you all the pictures you want."

I could, of course, have chartered another bush pilot with open time and arranged an earlier pick-up date—again depending on weather. But I decided on the plan to have Jay fly me in, and, if I hadn't contacted him to let him know that I'd come out earlier, he would fly back in to pick me up in about three weeks. There is usually enough air traffic into the Kamishak Bay area in July and August that I felt there would be no problem in getting a hop out with another pilot if I did want to leave earlier.

The details of the charter worked out, I went to the little general store at King Salmon to buy grub to supplement the light, survival-type provisions I'd flown up from Seattle. At the general store I was rather taken aback at the steep prices, but considering freight costs they probably weren't unreasonable.

At McNeil River falls a mother brown bear and cubs play for a few moments in the rapids before getting down to the serious business of fishing.

At that time—the summer of 1965—I was just getting well started in the tough endeavor of free-lance nature writing/wildlife photography. And working out penny-pinching logistics and learning just how far a buck will stretch were a basic part of the game. When I'd flown up from Seattle I had several Alaska areas in mind for picture work, with the Kamishak Bay trip getting first priority. Just how much other ground I could cover depended on how the boodle held out.

I had to consider the possibility of staying at Kamishak for three weeks—or somewhat longer in the event of bad flying weather. But at the King Salmon general store I went a bit light on grub, figuring that the chances were actually quite good that I'd be out of there within 10 or 12 days, and, if not—having already spent considerable time on the Alaska Peninsula working for the Fish & Wildlife Service, I was confident that I could get along very well living off the country.

Leaving early the following morning from the float plane dock at King Salmon, we took off in Jay's Piper Super Cub, and in a spectacular flight over a majestic sweep of mountains and tundra we crossed the Alaska Peninsula to Kamishak Bay.

There I'd pitched my mountain tent on the tundra a few yards above the beach. There were no trees within miles of my camp, so there was no way—with the materials at hand—that I could rig a bear-proof grub cache. All I did was wrap my food box in a tarp and place it on the ground well away from the tent. If a bear wanted the food, he was obviously going to get it, and there was no sense in having my sleeping bag and mountain tent torn up as well. But it has been my experience with wilderness bears—including the black bear and the mountain grizzly of the interior ranges of Alaska and western Canada as well as with the Alaska brown—that when there is an abundance of a favored natural food, such as a good salmon run or a heavy berry crop, it's rare for them to break into your grub cache.

There at Kamishak Bay, I often heard bears at night—less than 40 yards from my tent—walking along the beach toward the head of the bay. But my food was never touched on this trip, even though it included butter, cheese, salami sausage, and even honey. However, if trees had been available within a reasonable distance of my camp, as a common sense precaution I would have hung the box between two trees at a height of 18 to 20 feet above the ground.

During my bear photography work on the McNeil I made the hike up-river early each morning—the trip varying in difficulty due to different stages of the tide, fording two feeder streams, traversing through and around arctic willow and alder thickets, through belts of nearly waist-high grass, and over lovely stretches of short tundra vegetation—primarily composed of varieties of lichens and heather with a scattering of vivid, multi-hued iris. This diversity of tundra plants is woven into a short, springy turf that creates near sea level a floral association comparable to the alpine meadows of the Rockies.

Facing seaward from the head of the bay there are spectacular cliffs of a soft conglomerate rock, worn back many feet by the thundering surf of thousands of years. My overall impression of Kamishak Bay, the McNeil River, and the surrounding mountains and tundra is—abetted by dramatic weather changes—how much the country resembles northern Scotland. I feel that Kamishak Bay and the watershed of the McNeil should be considered for inclusion in the national park system—simply as an addition to the almost adjoining Katmai National Monument. This would give more definitive protection to the bears and other wildlife of the area.

The bear photography on this trip was mostly a waiting game, and not much hiking was needed. But I was out from the first good shooting light of morning till after sunset, and I carried plenty of ready-to-eat food in my pack. During the long days afield I had a bite whenever I was hungry. It was soon evident that I'd cut it too close when I'd purchased the grub and, at this rate of consumption, I'd be out of food in about a week. But I'd figured from the start that when and if it got down to living off the country I wouldn't have much trouble. And, while I was making the most of the good weather, working long days getting bear pictures, I felt it wasn't the time to cut down on rations.

At that, the way I was going through the rolls of Kodachrome and High Speed Ektachrome, it looked like the grub would outlast the film.

As it turned out, my provisions lasted just a day longer than my film supply. On the morning of my eighth day at Kamishak all that was left of my food was salt and pepper and an eight ounce jar of instant coffee. So now that my wolverine appetite had disposed of the grub, and with the film gone in a week of fine weather and cooperative bears, all my attention was directed toward living off the country.

With the commitments that Jay already had, it would still be about two more weeks before he could

A timid young male bear (the lowest in the hierarchy of dominance of the bears fishing at McNeil falls at that time) sniffed the breeze and caught the scent of a swiftly approaching much larger male bear. Tricked by deceptive air currents, the frightened youngster dashed up the same trail the big bear was descending. Then realizing his mistake, he stopped, stood erect an instant *(inset)*, saw the big hungry male hurrying down the trail, dropped down and raced upstream through the brush. The big male brownie picked up speed near the foot of the trail, rushed down the bank scattering frightened sea gulls, then, hardly breaking stride, lunged into the river and scooped up a salmon.

fly in. A photographic party had left the day of my arrival, and a three-man Alaska Department of Fish & Game bear study crew had worked on the McNeil a few days during the first week before their pick-up by an ADF&G Grumman Goose. After that I'd seen no one and no passing aircraft.

Each day now I hiked along the beach at low tide, hunting mussels that grew in large grape-like clusters on the rocks. Steaming them in a kettle—as you would butter clams—I found them delicious, and for a couple of days they were all that I ate.

Then in mid-morning on my tenth day at Kamishak, I sighted a big boar brownie prowling along the beach a hundred yards or so seaward from my camp, walking lazily toward the head of the bay and the river mouth. As he padded along, head low and great shoulders rolling, he sometimes took a bite from a watercress-like plant that grew near the high-water line. I watched him through binoculars a few minutes, then went down to the beach and picked some of the plant. Sampling it, I found that it had a crisp and surprisingly pleasant taste. I gathered a large handful, and that evening I boiled it—eating it like spinach and drinking the broth as a tea.

Ptarmigan were abundant on the tundra, and—though, of course, I had no gun—they were so unwary that I probably could have killed some with rocks had I really needed this potential food source. But I would have killed ptarmigan only in a real emergency. And, too, I was reluctant to go far out on the tundra, for if a plane did show up it would be much more difficult to signal the pilot. With all film exposed and grub gone, I wanted to get out as soon as possible, but, even if another plane didn't fly in, I had no worries about getting along until Jay's return.

While I always felt a bit hungry subsisting just on the greens and mussel fare, it was no hardship. But after the third day on this diet I decided to go after something more substantial. Since it was poor flying weather with a low cloud ceiling, and I felt it very unlikely that I'd see a plane that day, I took my fishing gear and went upstream to the falls.

It was just after 10 A.M. when I got there, and it happened to be another brief slack period between bear visits. I jointed up my fly rod, waded into the river below a deep, beautiful, glacier-blue pool, and began casting a fly I'd tied from fluorescent red yarn. On the fly's second drift over the hole, a silver flash

stabbed across the current. The strike telegraphed down the rod as a quick-pulsing jolt. The split-bamboo curved sharply down, its tip pumping with the quick, hard tugs on the line. The big fish had hit the fly with fierce predatory speed—as he would a herring or a salmon smolt at sea—and he had hooked himself well. I didn't know what he was; had it been late fall I would have guessed a small coho salmon.

He powered into the current, fighting the sting of the hook with shakes of his head. He started a run across the pool, and as the line sped through the guides I palmed the single-action reel, catching the handle on my fingers to brake. The taut line sliced through the current, and at the far edge of the pool the fish broke the surface, leaping in a mist of spray. He was a beautiful, olive-backed, silver-sided, sea-run Dolly Varden that may well have gone seven or eight pounds. After the big char plunged back, he swerved sharply from the diagonal of his run, powering upstream, and for a few seconds I took in line.

But as I put pressure on him he turned again suddenly, and speared through the water across and downstream, running out line against my braking right hand. My numbed fingers were taking a beating. I was hoping he wouldn't get into the surging force of the main channel, but he did. Now he was in big water, and there was no holding him with that tackle. Besides his own weight and power, he had the force of the river going for him, and I couldn't stop his run. I made him work for it, but in seconds he had run the line out until the reel spool was bare. My rod tip curved sharply down. This rod can't take any more, I thought. I'll just have to let him break the leader.

In the instant that I started to lower the rod, to take the strain off it and transfer it to the leader, the tension suddenly went out of the line. The rod whipped upward. As I reeled in, I shook my head. I'd put on a heavy six-pound test leader, selected for holding fish, not for finesse. And it hadn't broken. But the hook on my yarn fly had almost straightened. Some fish!

For a few minutes I'd forgotten about bears and the fact that I wasn't fishing for sport, but because I was hungry. I knew very keenly then the old thrill of the trout fisherman on wild new water. I knotted on another yarn fly, stripped some line off the reel, sent

A mother bear shares a salmon catch with her cub, then truculently eyes me as I move to a closer vantage point.

it back over my shoulder in the rolling S curve of a back-cast, then whipped it forward, dropping the fly several yards beyond where I'd hooked the big char. But as the fly started its drift, I saw a bear—a small one, appearing to be a cub recently sent out on his own by his mother—walking down one of the trails to the river.

He padded warily down to the far bank, stopping every few yards to look over his shoulder. He was edgily alert. I recognized him now as the youngster that had suffered the traumatic experience of almost running into the huge old boar. He saw me immediately—as I stood on a rocky bar a third of the way across the river—and he stood up on his hind paws, his head moving from side to side as he sniffed the wind. Then he dropped to all fours, still watching me. An instant later I felt a solid strike, and I was busy with another fighting fish.

This, too, was a Dolly Varden, not as big as the one before, but even more lively. He wasn't hooked as well, though, and with two jumps and a powering run through rapids the hook was thrown. As I reeled in to check the yarn fly, I looked across at the young bear. He had moved downstream a few yards, and seemed no longer interested in me, but was dividing his time between watching for salmon and watching for other bears.

He sat alertly on the rough conglomerate rock at the river's edge. For a young bear, he was quite a good fisherman. A number of times on other days I'd seen him plunge into the river and grab a struggling salmon in his jaws. But he was missing vulnerable fish now because of his frequent looks upstream, down, and behind him. Evidently, he was low bear in the swatting order, and he wasn't about to be caught napping.

I reeled in the last few yards of line, caught the leader in my hand, and checked the fly. The hook was okay. Then I looked again across at the young bear, and saw him standing up on his hind paws intently watching something downstream. In the next instant he dropped to all fours, pivoting as he came down, ran 20 yards upstream, then stopped to look back over his shoulder. I looked down-river. The huge, dominant old sow with the three second-year cubs—the family that had startled me on the brink of the waterfall—was walking up on my side of the river.

Already the sow must have seen me, and not hesitating she came on, fluidly graceful despite her bulk, great muscles bunching and rolling under the cinnamon-brown coat. I stood still to await developments. It looked like a showdown was shaping up. Maybe my fishing here just won't work out, I thought.

Almost opposite me, and a bit under 60 feet away, she stopped. I stood still, holding my fishing rod, and watching her. *Huuuaahhh! huhh!* she said. That translates as "Beat it!" Maybe I was standing where she wanted to fish. But where could I go? Any movement toward shore could be misunderstood by her, and a few yards farther out in the river I'd be swimming. The next move, I decided, was up to her.

The sow and I looked at each other. This wasn't like the still, almost hypnotic encounter of the first close meeting at the falls. The cubs, strung out, moved up together just behind their mother. Her great head was moving slowly back and forth. If she charged me, I decided I'd just have to drop my gear, dive for the deep, swift water a few yards out from me and swim downstream. But I was only going to do this if I had to. Then I thought, Well, why not just call her bluff? . . . if she is bluffing.

"I think I'm hungrier than you are, old lady," I thought aloud. Then I turned my back on her, and, though I wasn't feeling entirely confident, I worked some line out in a back-cast and whipped the yarn fly out across the pool. I watched the fly a moment as it started its drift, sinking gradually in the current. But I couldn't resist the impulse to look behind me!

The sow and cubs were walking on upstream, and a few minutes later the family was across the river, the cubs playing and the great mother diligently fishing.

Concentrating on fishing myself, and feeling pretty well at ease now, I didn't see all the new arrivals come down, but within half an hour there were nine bears on the river, all of them within 120 yards of me. One bear, a younger sow, was fishing only 25 yards away, sometimes closer, and didn't seem to mind my presence at all—at least no more than if I was just another bear. And, after a few minutes, I was able to relax to the extent that I considered the young sow just another fisherman.

I hooked and lost two more big chars before I landed a pair, which I kept, each weighing two pounds or a bit more and—no question about it—the smallest that I'd tied into. These were all I'd need for an excellent meal.

I picked up my two Dolly Vardens off the bar of rock, threaded a length of twine through their gills, and carrying rod and fish I walked carefully through the current, trying not to startle the closer bears by an awkward, too sudden movement—like the splashing motion of trying to regain your balance when your foot slips on a rock. Reaching the west bank of the river, I turned and looked at the fishing brownies in grateful wonder. I'd done my fishing among nine Alaska brown bears, as close to them as they were to each other. I'd caught a nice pair of Dolly Vardens, and the bears had made good catches of chum salmon. After the first few minutes, I hadn't felt uneasy at their presence, and I doubted that they had at mine. Feeling strangely and deeply moved, I raised a hand to them. "Good fishing," I thought aloud. Then I climbed the steep, grassy slope above the river and headed for camp.

Back on the beach, I dressed the chars, built a driftwood fire, cut the fish up so they would fit into the small kettle, added an inch of water and a sprinkling of salt and pepper, then set a rock of about four pounds on top of the lid, making, in effect, a crude pressure cooker. In a few minutes the fish were done, and as I probed them with a fork the meat fell away from the bone. I added a bit more salt and pepper, then fell to it. The chars had been caught little more than an hour before, and—quite aside from my hunger—I doubted that fish could have tasted better at a great restaurant in New York or San Francisco. Later, I also found Dolly Varden delicious when grilled over coals of dead, seasoned alder—with the fillets laid on a grill woven of green alder.

So almost overnight, I'd become what anthropologists call "a primitive hunter and gatherer." I prowled the beaches, collecting the watercress-like plant, picking mussels off the rocks at low tide, and, when the weather was overcast, I went up the river to fish for char. When there was a feasible ceiling for flying, I remained close to the beach to signal in case a plane showed up.

Often I'd hike the beach not to gather food, but simply to think. I walked under the towering, fortress-like cliffs undercut many feet by the battering storm seas of centuries, and looked seaward at the great wave-eroded pedestals of rock—resting and nesting places for tens of thousands of sea birds.

As I hiked, I pondered different possibilities. I felt certain that I'd taken some spectacular pictures, and was anxious to get out to have the film processed, but I had no worries about getting enough to eat. The only really frustrating aspect of the situation was being out of film to record the unforgettable daily sights—dramas of wildlife action, the changing weather, and stormy sunsets at sea.

142

The weather chilled off with intermittent rain and fog that second week at Kamishak. When the food I needed for the day had been caught and gathered, and I'd walked off my restlessness with a "thinking hike," I would build a fire on the beach and read. There was a massive supply of driftwood on the beach—much of it probably from hundreds of miles away, deposited by ages of pounding surf.

In the misty rain, wearing a wool shirt and an old ski parka I sat on a drift log by a crackling fire of salt-seasoned wood and read—the most absorbing of several beat-up paperbacks were A.B. Guthrie's *The Way West* and the old Jack London adventure classic, *The Sea Wolf*. And maybe—with the crackling warmth of the driftwood fire in the light rain, the soft, plaintive *eeeeyeah, eeeeyeah* of gulls riding wind currents on set wings, and the pounding and rolling hiss of the surf—I read with greater concentration than I would have in the comfort of home.

The reading by the fire was good, and the long hikes under the cliffs at low tide were good, and when the late dusk came I'd return to the fire, build it up, then just sit there and watch it, thinking, and sometimes I'd sing for awhile, mostly older western folk songs and a bit of Italian opera — I don't know what the bears thought of that.*

My fifteenth day at Kamishak dawned clear with just a few wisps of high cirrus across a lovely August morning sky. I rolled out of the sack hungry, restless, and feeling a hunch.

That afternoon, kneeling on the wet sand, picking mussels off the rocks, I looked up quickly to the east. "Hey!" I whispered. There was a barely audible drone of an aircraft engine.

Moments later I spotted it coming in low over the sea from the east, the first plane I'd seen since the ADF&G Grumman Goose had come and gone 11 days earlier. As the plane banked to the north over the far side of the bay, I held it in the field of my binoculars. A Cessna floatplane with three aboard. The plane flew upriver, banked several times over the falls, and headed back. Grabbing the bag of mussels, I sprinted up the beach.

With rising excitement I waded out into the bay until I was nearly butt-deep in the chuck. Repeatedly I raised my right arm and brought it down in a swift arc. The Cessna banked overhead, swung back

toward the head of the bay, turned again, and descended for a landing.

The pilot taxied the plane around facing the head of the bay, cut the engine, and stepped out on a pontoon. "Howdy," he said, smiling. "I'm Bob Barnett. Need some help?"

The two passengers with Barnett were oil geologists that he was flying out to a field camp. Taking off from Homer, Bob had swung over the McNeil to give his passengers a look at the brownies fishing.

A pick-up for me, for a flight out to Homer, was arranged for the following day.

About 6:30 next morning, with the good weather holding, I "rolled out and rolled up" a couple of hours before Bob's arrival, packed my gear into a Trapper Nelson and a Marine Corps sea bag, and toted it to the beach.

Shortly before nine o'clock the Cessna arrived with Bob and Mrs. Barnett. "Mornin', John," Bob said, tossing me a securing line. "We've got a change of plans I think you'll like better. We'll be taking you right on in to Anchorage. Won't cost you any more than for the hop to Homer. My wife and I decided to take a business trip to Anchorage to check on a house we're selling up there. We've got lunch aboard for the three of us, and we'll stop a couple of hours at Lake Clark for some grayling fishing. Then we'll head on in through Lake Clark Pass."

"Great!" I said. "And if we're going to Lake Clark, I'd like to leave word for Jay at his place that I got out okay."

"You bet," Bob said. "We'll stop by there."

The flight through awesomely spectacular Lake Clark Pass I'd made several times before, and it was something to look forward to. Seemingly just off your wing tips are tusking black spires as sharp as the Needles of Chamonix in the French Alps, with tortured, savagely crevassed glaciers hanging as steep as frozen waterfalls in color shades of incredible blues and blue-greens. It's a beautiful, twisting pass; and going through it you experience the kind of intimate, visually stunning Alaskan mountain flying that the high-passing jet travelers miss.

I hefted my gear to Bob standing on a pontoon, and we shot the bull a few moments as he arranged my stuff in the luggage space behind the seats. While we chatted, I pulled out my wallet and paid him in soiled and water-worn bills, feeling pleased with the charter. It had already been a bargain, and this flight to Anchorage through Lake Clark Pass was a real bonus.

---

*I remembered singing—while sitting thoughtfully alone by winter campfires in the Canadian Rockies—when I'd be enthusiastically joined by several mountain coyotes who were much better.

The McNeil River, Alaska Peninsula, photographed in late July on one of the rather rare occasions when there were no bears fishing. The terrain and vegetation pictured here are typical of the surrounding Alaska Peninsula landscape.

Below — Fresh-run chum salmon working their way up the rapids at the base of the falls on McNeil River.

Right — An Alaska Peninsula brown bear mother with three second-summer cubs has just padded down one of the remarkably direct, well-worn bear trails to fish at McNeil River falls. This great sow was the bear to which all other bears fishing that stretch of the river — both male and female — deferred. She was a totally confident bear, moving with majesty, coming to the river when she wanted to and leaving when she was ready, not stopping at times like the other bears, to apprehensively sniff the wind.

Bottom — Despite her great bulk, the sow moves with the graceful speed of a jaguar and, with a lunge into the foam, clamps her jaws over a struggling salmon, and then shares her catch with her cubs *(inset)*.

A classic Rocky Mountain bighorn ram duel. These photos were taken in the Alberta Rockies in mid-December. High on a mountain bench overlooking the valley of the Athabasca two big, heavy-boned bighorn rams in superb condition — each weighing about 275 pounds — faced each other. The crashing echoes had stilled, and the rams stood stunned and motionless, one of them bleeding from the base of the horns. A dozen long seconds passed, and the cold, pine-scented wind shifted a bit and I was close enough to smell the rams themselves — oily, musky-sweet and as unforgettable as a blend of strong pipe tobacco. Then one ram raised a hoof and sharply jabbed the chest of his antagonist *(above)*, at the same time making a series of curious growling grunts — a sound so eloquently expressive you could readily translate it to English (and it wouldn't go in a family magazine!). Suddenly the rams turned away from each other and walked away in opposite directions. Then, as if responding to an audible signal, both rams turned *(right)*, stood almost erect on their hind hoofs, facing each other on what could well be the most dramatic "line of scratch" in nature, and started their charge *(lower right)*. At the onset, both rams took several quick steps toward each other on their hind hoofs *(opposite page)* before dropping down in the final driving lunge. Each chunky body was streamlined and driving straight as a javelin toward his opponent.

Just before collision — at a combined speed of 40-45 miles per hour, rams turn their heads slightly on the side, usually taking the impact of a clean hit squarely on the boss of the horns (below). But the ram on the left here absorbed a tremendous blow low on his face (right). This frequently results in upper jaw fractures. Obviously, these fractures make it difficult — and sometimes impossible for a few days — for the injured rams to feed. But with the rams' tremendous vitality the healing process is rapid. Well over half of the mature rams I've seen over many autumn-winter seasons spent in bighorn country, showed definite evidence — in their humped nose-jaw profiles — of upper jaw fractures sustained in combat. In the instant following the rams' impact, a shock wave rippled down the muscular back of each antagonist, and their hind hoofs left the ground, driving out straight and stiff behind them. This ram duel lasted from 10:45 A.M. to 2:30 P.M. and covered about two and a half miles of icy slopes and mountain bench country! Five other rams, hearing the crashing impact of their horns, bounded up from lower slopes and followed along as both "observers" and trade-off participants.

The golden eagle was soaring in widening spirals. In majestic solitude, his great wings set, he rode the chill wind of April above the northern Rockies. From his altitude he could see the entire Cascade Valley, the headwaters of the Panther, and eastward to the valley of the Ghost. It was too early in the spring for his succulent staples, the Columbian ground squirrel and the hoary marmot, to be out of hibernation. Perhaps, with the marvelous resolution of his vision, he was searching for a snowshoe hare— just beginning to change from winter white to the brown of summer—crouched nibbling in the willows; or, a mile or so up a confluent valley, for the telltale ravens and magpies near the carcass of a winter- killed caribou or elk.

But then as I watched from the rugged slope below, the eagle, seemingly without a wing beat, dropped in a beautiful, gliding sweep toward a band of bighorn sheep on the ridge.

I was puzzled, for only the occasional very young of mountain sheep fall prey to eagles. And these bighorns made up a mixed herd of adult rams and ewes and younger sheep down to sturdy yearlings. But I was about to find out that the golden is a fun-loving sportsman as well as something of an egotist.

Now the golden braked with flaring wings a few feet over the sheep, hovered momentarily, then climbed and banked around for another pass. Again he dropped, and, as he hovered, the bighorns looked up unperturbed, barely interrupting their grazing. But four more times the eagle planed down in wind-hissing dives, each time a bit lower. And then on the seventh pass, just as the golden flared his wings to hover, a young ram stood up on his hind hoofs like a rearing stallion. The ram's front hoofs blurred in jabbing thrusts. Brown plumage drifted away on the wind. The eagle staggered, side-slipped, nearly brushed the ridge crest, then flapped powerfully, recovered and climbed, apparently uninjured. Buoyed in a rising current, he set his wings and rode the wind out over the valley of the Ghost.

Since that memorable April morning over a dozen years ago, above the Ghost River in the Palliser Range of the Canadian Rockies, I've seen golden eagles in sporting play with other bighorns, the Rocky Mountain goat and even the high-ranging grizzly. These encounters tell something of the proud and spirited nature of the high-dwellers—of both the eagles and the earthbound, and, to me, they are all among the most fascinating of the world's wild animals.

This article relates some of my experiences in studying the Rocky Mountain goat, the bighorn and Dall sheep and other wildlife linked in their mountain ecology. Every time that I've gone into mountain sheep or goat country I've learned something new about them, and there have been individuals among these mountaineers that I've been proud to call my friends.

As far as trophy and meat hunting is concerned, I hung up my rifle to carry only cameras over a decade ago. Still, I have no argument with those who find an honest challenge in pitting their stamina against mountain storms and dangerous terrain to take a ram or billy. I don't begrudge the taking of any legal species as long as it is done within the rules of **fair chase** as defined by the Boone & Crockett Club, and as long as meat and hide are properly cared for and fully utilized. While I've met some slobs and certified S.O.B.'s among hunters afield, other big game hunters are among my best and most respected pals.

Many seasons afield have taught me that few wild animals die as painless a death as from a well-placed hunter's bullet. I recall an incident several autumns ago on Alberta's Big Smoky River. A young cow elk, attempting to ford at a bad place, had become mired up to her belly and brisket in quicksand-like muck a few yards out from the riverbank. She couldn't raise a hoof, but didn't drown, as she could keep her head, neck and upper shoulder area above the water. During the night a sharp freeze hit, forming about two inches of ice around the helpless elk. While the cow still had the energy to heave futiley against the

Above the still partly icebound Snake Indian River in the Alberta Rockies, two bighorn sheep hesitate an instant before leaping to a higher ledge on the shoulder of rock. Another bighorn, far down the slope, can be seen in the right-center of the photograph. Taken in mid-April.
Top inset — Three mountain goats, just beginning to shed their winter pelage in early May, visit a mineral lick on the upper Athabasca River in the Alberta Rockies.
Bottom inset — Dall sheep rams rest on an October afternoon on the rugged slopes of the Tattler Creek canyon, north slope of the Alaska Range.

entrapping mud, coyotes walked out on the ice and ate the head off her shoulders. There are many sides to Nature besides the bursting of buds in the spring, and that is one of them. And to condemn the hungry coyotes for helping themselves makes as much sense as condemning yourself for driving down to the market to purchase bacon and eggs.

Among outdoorsmen there has been much argument concerning the rarity of Rocky Mountain goats and mountain sheep mingling where they share the same range. I know quite a few veteran Canadian and Alaskan woodsmen who actually doubt that it ever happens. A couple of old-timers in Alaska once told me that goats and sheep aren't found on the same mountainside because they "don't like the smell of each other." This I can't believe. Once either species gets used to my presence on their range they don't even seem to mind how I smell after three rugged weeks in the bush. Many times near mineral licks in the Canadian Rockies I've seen mountain goats and bighorn sheep within a few yards of each other. A friend who has made several trips into northern British Columbia's Cassiar district tells me of seeing the Stone sheep, *Ovis dalli stonei,* grazing as close as 50 yards from mountain goats. In September of 1977 I observed Stone sheep and mountain goats within 200 yards of each other in the Cassiar Mountains west of the Klappan River.

I've never yet seen Dall sheep and mountain goats on the same mountainside, and haven't met anyone else who has; yet there are authentic reports of goat observations made within the boundaries of Mount McKinley National Park and in other interior Alaska mountain areas that had been considered strictly sheep range (In biological relationship, the wild mountain sheep of the world, though different in appearance—largely because of the short tail, and the stiff, hollow hair like that of the deer family, rather than wool fleece—and vastly different in temperament from their domestic relatives, are, nevertheless, true sheep. The Rocky Mountain goat, however, is misnamed; he is not a true goat as such, but an animal with characteristics of both the true goats and the Old World antelopes. He is a close relative to the chamois of the Alps and to the tahr, serow and goral of the Himalayas and other ranges of Asia).

I doubt that either mountain sheep or mountain goats object to the presence of any other large ungulate species on their range. Though the two share much in common, ideal habitat requirements for mountain sheep and goats differ, and because of this the two species aren't too often found on the same slope, even in watersheds where there are large numbers of both, such as in the Brazeau and Big Smoky drainages of Alberta and in the Cassiar district of northern British Columbia.

In any mountain region of northwestern North America there is competition for the available grass and browse among several different big game species. In the Cascade Range of British Columbia and Washington, I've watched mountain goats feeding on alpine meadows within 40 yards of blacktail deer and elk. Above the south fork of the Ashnola River, 25 miles or so from Keremeos, British Columbia, I have glassed large herds of mule deer and Rimrock bighorn sheep, *Ovis canadensis californiana,* grazing together on the open south slopes—already bare in April while the snow lay heavy in the timbered canyons. In some areas of the Canadian Rockies the encroachment of elk on the ancestral spring range of the Rocky Mountain bighorn is becoming a serious wildlife management problem. A classic example of this can be found on the slopes overlooking the Cascade River north of Banff, Alberta.

In the often close association between different species, it's interesting to observe how big game animals can get along, even, curiously, in situations of potential conflict.

One late November day in the Rockies of western Alberta, I was sitting with my back against a boulder, eating lunch on an Ice Age glacial moraine overlooking the valley of the Athabasca. The weather had moderated that morning to a comparatively pleasant eight degrees above (F.), after three days of sub-zero cold. Around 45 head of bighorns were also on the moraine, some within 15 yards of me.

I'd watched and studied this particular band for about a month. Approaching mountain sheep for close-up pictures is a completely different problem than stalking a ram with a rifle. To get good shots, even using telephoto lenses, you have to be much closer than the usual rifle range—and here there is

A bighorn ram climbs into rugged escape terrain (a biologists' term for ridges, ledgy slopes and faces to which mountain sheep flee when threatened by predators) overlooking the upper Athabasca Valley, Alberta Rockies. A mid-November photograph.
Inset — Rocky Mountain bighorn ewe and young lamb (about 3½ to 4 months old) photographed in mid-October at the edge of a steep pitch overlooking a mountain lake in the Palliser Range, Alberta Rockies.

just no substitute for time and patience. The eyesight of mountain sheep, vastly excelling that of man, is among the most highly developed in the animal kingdom, and there is little chance of your getting close enough for good pictures without their knowledge and acceptance of your presence.

Over a period of weeks this band of bighorns had become quite used to me, though any sudden or clumsy movement on my part would still spook them. I had a special interest in these sheep, because I was hoping to photograph a breeding season ram duel, and in this bunch there were five large mature rams of nearly equal body weight and horn growth.

Now on the moraine, most of the sheep were bedded down, while a few others were feeding on the tufts of grass that grew between the round, glacier-scoured rocks. One big full-curl ram was just standing still, looking off across the valley, classically posed and motionless. Presently there was a clattering of rolling rock from over the edge of the moraine.

The sheep that I could see all turned their heads toward the sound, watching with interest, but with no indication of alarm. Those that were bedded down didn't stop chewing their cuds. Then up over the edge of the moraine walked a mule deer buck. Just moments before, he'd crossed over the ice of the Athabasca and had swum the still open main channel. Icicles hung on his hide from neck to tail. On the muley's flank there was a red slash where another buck's antler tine had gouged a long, ugly furrow. Both the mule deer and bighorn rutting seasons were approaching their peaks, but this old boy appeared already too battle-weary to be looking for trouble.

The big four-pointer was apparently headed across the moraine to bed down in a stand of lodgepole pines. But he was walking slowly, head low, almost directly toward the ram.

I sat dead still, waiting, my back against the boulder, and if the buck noticed me at any time he gave no indication of it. Of the sheep that I could see without turning, some kept watching the deer, others ignored him, and he paid no attention to them, just continued his slow walk across the moraine as though he knew the most direct route to his destination and was taking it, oblivious of the sheep. The big ram hadn't moved, and now it seemed certain that one or the other was going to have to give ground.

But neither did! The tines of the buck's left antler passed the ram's head hardly two feet away. The bighorn didn't move out of his tracks, just turned his head and, apparently with only mild interest, watched this bedraggled looking stranger walk by.

Country rugged enough for protection against predators is a basic habitat requirement for both mountain sheep and goats. Given this terrain, the choice of range in a particular watershed is determined by the feeding habits of each species. The mountain goat is both a grazer and a browser during the summer and early fall; in the winter he's primarily a browser. Mountain sheep—and on this point the Dall and the Stone to a larger extent than the bighorn—are essentially grazing animals the year-around. But there are some interesting geographical variations—from what might be considered most normal or typical—in the seasonal feeding habits of both mountain sheep and goats.

During the winter in areas of heavy, wet snow—such as in the coastal mountains of Southeastern Alaska and British Columbia, the British Columbia and Washington Cascades, and in a number of interior British Columbia ranges including the Kootenay Rockies, the Monashee Range and the Selkirks—goats descend into steep, cliffy areas, usually well below timberline, and subsist almost entirely on browse. In areas of the goat's range where there is dry powdery snow, as on the east slope of the Canadian Rockies, goats winter on high ridges and slopes and feed on grasses and other alpine and subalpine plants exposed by the wind. They are found at elevations as high and sometimes higher than their usual summer range. The mountain goat's winter pelage is impressive anywhere you find him, but the coats of the animals that winter in the heights of the northern Rockies are magnificent. They are an environmental adaptation that protects the goats from lashing winds and temperatures that may drop lower than 60 below zero.

The Dall sheep—including the Stone subspecies—like the mountain goat in the northern Rockies, winters on windswept slopes and ridges. The Dall, unlike the bighorn, is rarely seen in valleys except when crossing over from summer range to winter range, and back again. When crossing a river valley, the Dalls tend to be very nervous, sensing their danger from predators; once a crossing is started—perhaps after hours of carefully watching the route they will take, searching for any lurking hazard such as wolves or a grizzly—it is made swiftly, and the sheep do little, if any, feeding en route.

While some bighorns also winter in high country and forage on wind-exposed vegetation, most of them descend to lower slopes overlooking river valleys, but, even at low elevation, are rarely seen more than a few hundred yards from rugged terrain. In Alberta, during late November and December, I've frequently seen bighorns—young sheep and adults of both sexes—standing on the ice of frozen rivers browsing on muskeg willow along the banks.

Besides their diet staple of grasses, mountain sheep (here I'm including both the bighorn and Dall and their various subspecies) feed on sedges, mosses, heather, willow and the buds of various trees and shrubs. All of these items are found, too, in the mountain goat's fare, and the goat can do very well on coarser vegetation than mountain sheep prefer. Quite often I've observed goats browsing on the bough-tip growth of timberline firs.

Mountain sheep and goats will travel miles, if need be, for salt, and the availability of mineral licks is a basic habitat requirement for both. Goats in the rugged coastal mountains of British Columbia, and in Southeastern Alaska goat country like the Boca de Quadra and Tracy Arm-Fords Terror areas, descend to salt water and lick ocean spray off the rocks.

Above the valley of Blue Creek, an upper confluent of Alberta's Snake Indian River (itself a tributary of the great Athabasca) rises an incredibly rugged and serrated mountain range known as The Ancient Wall. Spanning a watercourse on a lower slope of the range is a huge and majestic arch of limestone, carved by thousands of years of erosion. Around the base of this arch is a mineral lick where I've observed bighorns and mountain goats licking the clay-like soil within a few yards of each other. Imprinted in the moist earth there, I've seen the tracks of grizzly, cougar and wolf. For me, it is one of the most fascinating areas in the northern Rockies.

The most important predator in the ecology of the far northern sheep is the wolf. The Canadian bighorn faces the same predators the Dall and Stone do, plus the cougar. During some winters, particularly from early February into April, unusually deep snow and severe weather conditions tend to favor the hunters over the hunted. During such times there is some predation on mountain sheep by the coyote, wolverine and lynx, as well as by the larger predators.

I don't feel it is appropriate, when considering the ecology of the North Country, to call one animal an "enemy" of another. Predators are the classic opportunists; and, over the centuries, predation has been generally selective to the good of both predator and prey.

Healthy mountain sheep, except under unusual circumstances, would leave any predator behind when fleeing toward rugged escape terrain. The sheep with a leg sprained while crossing a scree slide or with a heavy infestation of lungworms would be the one taken. Even when cut off from escape terrain—such as during a valley crossing from summer range to winter range—a healthy adult ram or ewe, if forced to make a stand, can be dangerous to an attacking predator.

Both predator and prey species are magnificent animals, thrilling to see in their habitat, and invaluable aesthetic assets to the North Country scene.

I've seen coyotes, wolves and—on one memorable occasion—a cougar stalking bighorns, but I haven't yet seen any of these predators actually take a mountain sheep or goat, though I have observed wolves making kills on both moose and elk.

In early March of '73 I was watching a band of bighorns on a steep slope overlooking the lower Snake Indian River in Alberta's Jasper National Park. Suddenly I noticed that several old ewes were standing taut and still, all looking toward an area of scattered pines upstream from them and slightly lower in elevation. Swiftly, through some way of communication, the attention of the entire band was drawn to that area. This could be it, I thought, as I focused a tripod-mounted 400 mm lens on the slope.

I figured I might be about to have another chance at photographing a cougar stalking bighorns. Raising binoculars and glassing the slope, I could see nothing moving among the trees. But as I lowered the glasses, I saw the sheep—reacting almost as a single individual—turn and race across a scree slide, bound up over ledges and stop on a rugged point overlooking the river. Then I spotted the predator that had spooked them; not a cougar, but an exceptionally large and heavy lynx that was suddenly skylined on the ridge. The cat stood still for a long moment, watching the sheep with evident great interest and, perhaps, disappointment. Then he turned back toward the river, and, with stubby tail twitching and huge paws padding along the rocks, he faded almost magically back into the sparse cover of the upper slopes.

A curious experience happened several years ago to a friend of mine on another upper Athabasca tributary. He was hiking one early November afternoon, accompanied by his big German shepherd dog, when he rounded a bend in the old trail and saw a band of bighorns near the riverbank just ahead of them.

There were about two-dozen head, mostly ewes and lambs, with several young rams, and one powerful, heavy-horned, full-curl ram. The sheep had been grazing by digging and raking the snow away from the grass with their front hooves, and nibbling at willow buds. Now at the sight of the dog, they stood alert and still.

Suddenly the dog broke from the man—in his excitement ignoring the shouted orders of his master to come back—and raced toward the sheep. Immediately, at the rush of this wolf-like animal, the bighorns retreated, bounding up to the ledges of a high, steep scarp. All except the big ram.

For a few seconds the ram waited. Then he catapulted in a mighty lunge, and with an incredible burst of speed he charged the onrushing dog. The startled shepherd braked with stiff front legs, whirled and fled back toward his master. The chase lasted about 120 yards. The ram was closing fast, and a scant few yards from my friend he finally broke off the chase. The great bighorn turned slowly and reluctantly, walked a few steps up the slope, turned to eye them again belligerently, then continued climbing up to join his band. It was a wiser and thoroughly spooked German shepherd. And the dog wasn't the only one nervous. "Man!" my friend said, shaking his head as he told me about it, "I thought that guy was going to knock **me** into the river."

After years of observing both, I don't believe that any of the North American mountain sheep—not even the desert bighorn—can climb in as severe terrain as the Rocky Mountain goat. But in less difficult

Above — A Rocky Mountain goat drinks from a small mountain lake in the Alberta Rockies. In early May, this mountain goat still has a beautiful winter coat.
Right — With an early October snowstorm rapidly enveloping the peaks behind them, a Rocky Mountain goat mother and kid top a ridge crest in the northern Cascade Range of British Columbia.

country the sheep are much faster than the goat—and faster, I'm sure, than deer. When really spooked they can cover the slopes with a graceful speed that is hard to believe even when you see it. The goat is a deliberate climber. I've watched goats carefully test rock points and ledges before putting their entire weight on them, in much the same way that an expert human rock climber does.

During the breeding season of the mountain goat, in late fall, the billy doesn't gather large harems. Four females with a billy is the largest number I've observed, and even this may be exceptional, with two or three the more usual number. The goat breeding season runs from early November into December, and the young, usually singles but quite often twins, are born about six months later from about the last week in April through the first week or 10 days of June.

While serious rutting season combat between mountain goat males is much less spectacular than the duels between mountain sheep rams, it is far more dangerous to the antagonists. I've seen old nannies, and on a couple of occasions billies, resolve sudden arguments by charging each other and merely

158

butting heads together. But billies in a serious fight circle each other, feinting and hooking with their black dagger horns, and these exchanges are sometimes lethal. The deadly effectiveness of the mountain goat's horns in defensive combat against predators is discussed later in this article. I watch the ritualistic spectacle of a classic bighorn ram duel with pretty much the same feeling that I have witnessing a great sporting event—say, the heavyweight boxing champion of the world against a top-rated challenger. But there is nothing to suggest sport in a grimly serious fight between two mountain billies, and it gives you a feeling of apprehension to watch it.

During a dozen autumns of observing bighorn breeding season behavior, the earliest I've seen the first restless aggressiveness of the rams has been late October, and in some years I've seen rutting activity extend into early January.

The bighorn's breeding season behavior is more complex than that of most of the other ungulates, especially regarding the fighting among males. Early ram duels—during the last couple weeks of October through the first week or so of November—will quite often establish a hierarchy of dominance among the rams of a particular band. In such cases, the dominant ram will sire most of the next spring's lamb crop. Unlike the bull moose and—to an even greater extent—the bull elk, which strive to maintain control over harems of cows by intimidating and fighting off challenger bulls, the mountain ram is interested in a ewe only when she is actually in season and receptive to breeding.

During several bighorn rutting seasons, I've made continuous observations of interesting situations where in one band of sheep there were three to five or more mature rams of almost equal body weight and horn growth. I've seen rams in such cases battle intermittently throughout the entire breeding season without any one of them emerging as a clear cut victor. And, curiously, while the issue remains unresolved by fighting, often I've seen young rams—down to three and a half years, the minimum breeding age of mountain sheep males—among the ewes, breeding, while several mature rams were battering heads less than 50 yards away! By the time he reaches his fourth autumn, the young ram is as interested in the rutting season activity as the mature rams, but at this age, of course, he is a competitor for the ewes only through stealth, not combat.

Several mature rams will often duel together, hitting each other in alternate charges. Younger rams

Rocky Mountain goat mother and young rest on the steep slope of a mineral lick above the upper Athabasca River in the Alberta Rockies. This early July photo shows the swift current behind them gray-white from glacier melt.

frequently watch on the fringe of the action, but give ground quickly if challenged. Usually, in an active combat situation the young rams are largely ignored by the veterans.

Before real fighting gets under way, I've often observed rams bunched together, as if in conference. Then another ram, standing off several yards, may suddenly charge one of the group, driving a thudding blow into his ribs or flank, or, just as frequently, charging from behind, slamming and then levering up with his horns, and lifting the rump of his surprised and outraged colleague at a near 40-degree angle.

Such unsportsmanlike conduct may or may not precede a classic duel. But grunting and hoof-jabbing, with the two rams standing head to head, is the usual actual beginning of the drama. Following this preliminary ritual, the two rams abruptly turn from each other and walk away in opposite directions. Then, as if responding to an audible signal, both rams turn, stand up almost erect on their hind hoofs, facing each other on what could well be the most dramatic "line of scratch" in nature, and start their charge. At the onset, both rams take several quick steps toward each other on their hind hoofs before each battler drops down in the final driving lunge toward his opponent. Just before collision—at a combined speed of 40-45 mph—the rams turn their heads on the side, thus taking the impact of a clean hit squarely on the boss of the horns. But if it isn't a clean hit, one or both rams can suffer an upper-jaw fracture. This is a fairly frequent occurrence, and more than half of the mature rams that I've seen showed definite evidence—in their humped nose-jaw profiles—of upper-jaw fractures sustained in combat.

Obviously, these fractures make it difficult—and sometimes for a few days impossible—for the injured rams to feed. But with the rams' tremendous vitality, the healing process is rapid.

In cliff and canyon country where there is considerable echo effect, the sound of the rams' impact is somewhat like a rifle shot, but it still has a distinctively different tonal quality. For readers that engage

in the good winter sport of curling, the closest approximation I've ever heard of the crashing impact of two mountain rams is to hold a pair of curling stones three or four feet apart and slam them together. Amplify the sound several times, and that's about it!

In the instant following the rams' impact, a shock wave ripples down the muscular back of each antagonist, and their hind hoofs leave the ground, driving out straight and stiff behind them.

Rams **do not** crash heads in swift exchanges. The overly cute editing of some motion pictures showing ram fights (timing the action to fit a musical background) has given this false impression. The force of the head-on collision is terrific, and following impact the combatants stand in front of each other for often 10 or 12 seconds, heads raised, stunned and motionless. At such times while photographing bighorn duels I've moved so close to the rams that I could smell them—musky, oily-sweet and as unforgettable as a blend of strong pipe tobacco.

A duel between two mountain rams is one of nature's classic dramas, but though horns are chipped and broken, noses frequently bloodied and upper jaws sometimes broken—it still lacks the sustained savagery of a well-matched bull elk fight.

Oddly enough, following bighorn duels, I've often seen the antagonists graze or bed down within a few feet of each other. Then, after a temporary truce to graze or rest, when a ram wishes to resume further combat, he approaches his feeding or bedded adver-

sary and jabs or rakes his groin, belly or back with a front hoof, all the while cussing him out with the highly expressive growling grunts.

As with the mountain goat, the gestation period of both species of North American mountain sheep (there are several geographical races of both the bighorn and Dall species) is approximately six months. The lambs, singles or fairly often twins, are born in May and June. When the ewe nears her time to give birth, she climbs to a high, rugged, secluded area where she and the lamb have maximum protection from predators.

Following the rutting season, the mature rams, to a large extent, mingle with the ewes and young sheep on winter and spring range. During the summer and early fall, however, the rams keep to themselves, banding in groups of four or five up to herds numbering 30 head or more. I've seen the occasional old ram apparently ranging as a "loner."

Unless killed by predators, a fatal fall, an avalanche, pneumonia (mostly occurring in sheep already badly weakened with a lungworm infestation) or a hunter's bullet, a mountain sheep will live as long as his teeth last, rarely longer than 12 or 14 years. In the balanced ecology of a true wilderness situation, when the sheep's teeth become so worn he can't cut and chew the grasses that are his primary feed, it is highly unlikely that his death will result from actual starvation. In his gradually weakening condition, he will tip the scales of natural selection and fall easy prey to one of his hunters.

The skull of a Rocky Mountain bighorn ram photographed on a mountain slope overlooking the confluence of Moosehorn Creek and the Athabasca River, Alberta Rockies. An early May photograph.

Though Dall sheep numbers have declined in some of the hunting areas more accessible to population centers in Alaska, they still occupy most of their original range. The less fortunate bighorn has been eliminated entirely from vast areas of his ancestral range in the United States. Overhunting in the early days, diseases carried by domestic sheep and competition on winter and spring range from domestic stock and from other wildlife—most seriously from elk—are all contributing factors.

There have been a number of attempts to restock the bighorn on areas of his former range from which he has been eliminated entirely or is in danger of extirpation. These restocking efforts have been made with the mutual cooperation of U.S. and Canadian federal, provincial and state wildlife agencies. The restocking attempts have been made with the Rocky Mountain bighorn, the desert bighorn, and the California bighorn subspecies (mostly trapped in the Williams Lake area of British Columbia). Some of these transplants have been definite successes, others have apparently failed and with still others it's just too early to tell. I had the satisfaction several years ago of assisting in the spring capture and transfer of two-dozen head of Rocky Mountain bighorns from the Alberta Rockies to the Lostine River watershed in the Wallowa Mountains of northeastern Oregon.

On the Rocky Mountain goat, civilization has had relatively little impact. Today, through restricted hunting and comparatively inaccessible habitat, the mountain goat remains in geographical range and population probably very nearly the same as when he was first seen by white men. On no other large North American animal has human settlement had less effect.

The mountain goat is considerably less vulnerable to predators than the mountain sheep. This is partly due to his more precipitous habitat, but also because no animal lives that is more courageous in defensive combat. The goat is heavier than is generally believed, with some of the larger billies going well over 300 pounds. When attacked by predators, the goat's size, sinewy stamina, agility and lethal horns make him a formidable antagonist. The horns of adult goats of either sex average between 8 and 10 inches in length, with the record being a fraction over 12. As weapons, there is ample evidence of their effective use.

Old-time western Canadian bushmen—big game hunting guides, trappers and retired wardens—have told me of two cases where evidence in the form of remains indicated that grizzlies had been killed by goats. Both were in the Alberta Rockies (I've heard of other similar cases in Southeastern Alaska and British Columbia, but the evidence was not as well established). In one Alberta case, the goat also was killed. He had suffered a broken back from a paw blow after he had inflicted mortal wounds with his horns. The goat carcass with the broken back and the dead grizzly with the stab wounds through his vitals were found a few yards apart. In the other case, a slain bear was found with two obvious horn wounds, but the goat had either escaped injury or had at least been able to leave the immediate area.

A dozen miles north of the confluence of Alberta's Snake Indian and Athabasca rivers, a steep, black scarp rises some 300 feet from the west bank of the Snake Indian. This area is known as Shale Banks, and its bare, blackish soil is rich in various mineral compounds. This is one of the largest mineral licks in the northern Rockies. It is used primarily by mountain goats and bighorns, and to some extent by mule deer, elk, moose and mountain caribou. In mid-June of '67 I witnessed there a dramatic example of a mountain goat's courage in a showdown with a predator.

On that particular afternoon, seven mountain goats—a young billy and three nannies with new kids—were in sight, scattered on the steep slope and licking the soil. As I looked at the upper reaches of the scarp, where it dropped away from a heavily timbered bench, a huge old billy walked out of the pines and began to work his way slowly along the top of the pitch. Then he stopped, and for a few moments licked at the rocky soil. Suddenly, he raised his head, looked behind him, and whirled in his tracks. His head went down, and his shoulder hump jutted like a bison's. He stamped hard with a front hoof and pivoted slightly to the right so that he was facing away from me and toward the timber. Then in the pines a few yards from him, I saw a flash of tawny hide.

Standing on the east bank of the Snake Indian, I drew binoculars from their case, quickly focused and caught in full profile the sinewy, lethal grace of a cougar. Tail flicking, the great cat moved back and forth, seeming no more than six feet from the billy. The billy pivoted as the cat moved, always facing the cougar, head low, front hoof stamping in anger, black horns ready.

Again and again the cougar moved back just out of sight in the pines, only to reappear in a few moments as the drama went on.

For 25 minutes a formidable and determined predator and his powerful and courageous prey held each other to a standoff.

Finally the cougar faded back into the pines, and minutes passed without his return. The great shaggy billy turned, traversed a few yards to his chosen route and picked his way unhurriedly down the long pitch to the river. At the time the Snake Indian was high, near the peak of snow-melt and glacier runoff. Placing his hooves in precarious niches in the rock, the billy was almost standing on his head, waves slapping him in the face, as he drank deeply from the wild, frigid torrent of the Snake Indian.

Mountain goats, in contrast to the rather high-strung mountain sheep, are calm by nature and often display remarkable composure when encountered in their rugged uplands. But when they descend out of their usual habitat, goats—and particularly females with young—tend to be spooky when they drop down to visit mineral licks or to cross valleys to another range.

In early July of '67, I was camped on a glacier moraine flat, just north of the Scott Glacier in the upper Whirlpool Valley in the wilderness back-country of Jasper National Park. This remote area is a few miles east of the Continental Divide and the Alberta-British Columbia boundary. At the time, I was studying the mountain grizzly and investigating reported wolf denning sites in the upper Whirlpool

Valley. I hiked many miles in the watershed from the Whirlpool-Athabasca confluence westward up the Whirlpool Valley over Athabasca Pass and across the Divide into British Columbia. One morning I woke just before sunrise to a clatter of rolling rock, loud splashing in the river, then more clattering of rock just outside my tent.

My first drowsy thought was, maybe one of Don's horses threw his hobbles and lit out (at the time Warden Don Rose was building a log footbridge over a lower fork of the Whirlpool). I rolled out of the sleeping bag and pulled up the entrance flap of the mountain tent. A thoroughly wet nanny and kid had just forded the river and were now running across the round, glacier-smoothed rocks just in front of my tent. When I first saw them they were less than 20 feet from me. The goats had been running hard, and they paused but momentarily to look at me, then took off again, the nanny running in a bobbing, shoulder-heaving, bison-like gait, the kid right at her side. I hurried out of the tent to watch.

There is a great moraine flat across from the Scott Glacier, and the goats had fully a mile to go before they were in what, for them, would be safe terrain. With almost incredible stamina the goats never let up their pace, running until they were out of sight in the cover of the steep, timbered slope on the north side of the valley. If there's even a coyote ranging that slope right now, she's in trouble, I thought. She might get just too bushed to fight.

The Rocky Mountain goat is essentially a herd animal. They band together in from small groups of three or four goats up to herds of several dozen. In the northern Cascade Range near the British Columbia-Washington boundary I once counted 64 goats in a band. I've heard of still larger bands in reports from Canadian and U.S. forestry agencies and national park services. The large herds of goats I've observed were composed of adults and younger goats of both sexes, and kids born that spring.

In every part of the mountain goat's range that I've worked in—including goat country in Montana, Idaho, British Columbia, Washington, Alberta and Alaska—I've observed lone goats. With few exceptions these were large old males.

Late one August afternoon, on a flank of Bis-marck Peak in the Washington Cascade Range, a lone billy and I saw each other at the same time less than 30 yards apart. Instead of showing the usual curiosity and composure, he whirled and raced across a scree slide, not stopping once to look behind him,

until he disappeared behind a granite shoulder 300 yards away. I wondered if he might have taken a hunter's bullet a season or two before, recovered and associated the sight and scent of man with the lingering pain of his injury. Judging from most of my experience with goats, his totally spooked reaction was highly unusual.

Curiosity is a basic ingredient of the mountain goat's personality. On a frosty September morning in the upper Skagit country near the Washington-British Columbia border, I suddenly woke—not drowsily, but, curiously, totally alert—at the first gray of daybreak in the east. I wasn't using a tent, and, lying warm in the good down sleeping bag, listening to the chill wind in the alpine firs and the distant fall of water in a chasm, I thought how odd it was that I had awakened so early, for the previous day had been long and tough. But a moment later I felt several soft nudges against my feet and lower legs. For a few seconds I lay completely still, then very slowly raised my head. There was a blur of white coats in the dusky light, and the clacking of hooves

Above — Four yearling Rocky Mountain bighorn lambs photographed in mid-May in the DeSmet Range of the Alberta Rockies.
Opposite page — Two bighorn rams climbing a rugged slope in the Alberta Rockies pause at the crashing descent of a dislodged stone, then watch other bighorns bound up in a climbing traverse toward them.

on rock. Then a mother goat and two kids stopped about 20 yards away and stood looking back at me. For some time they had been sniffing me as I lay asleep!

A few moments later the mother grunted what seemed to be an order, and the family began climbing away. As they turned, one of the kids, perhaps in answer to his mother, made a curious, plaintive sound that I'd heard many times before. Its tonal quality was something between the bleat of a lamb and the mew of a kitten, but sustained without much rise and fall in inflection. The kids use a long version of this call to indicate distress; though, like the complaints of youngsters of any species, it's not neces-

sarily of great importance. If you're near a band of goats when the kids are being weaned, you'll hear it almost constantly. A kid will make this sound when momentarily stopped while traveling, when he thinks he can't make the next big step to a higher ledge. If a band of goats is in timberline cover, this call of the kids may be your first indication of their presence, for if the wind is right the sound will carry several hundred yards.

Goats are almost incredibly sure-footed, but they do occasionally fall. The kids, born with the courage and coordination of their parents, must learn their own limitations. I've seen four kids fall, but not far, and none seemed more than badly bruised. They just stood up from the ledge or rock slide, made the curious, mewing bleat, looked things over again and then climbed on up, sometimes taking a different route. In the Selkirk Range of British Columbia I found one adult carcass that was clearly a fall casualty, not an avalanche victim.

That goats don't fall more often is still a marvel to me. In the British Columbia Monashee Range I

watched a billy moving across a granite pitch so steep that it seemed a fantastic feat for him just to be on it. He stopped frequently to nibble at what appeared to be lichen growth, sometimes reaching for meager tidbits several feet above him by standing up on his hind hoofs. Once, with appalling nonchalance, 300 sheer feet above a jumble of shattered slabs, he raised a hind hoof and thoroughly scratched his back!

Anywhere in the mountain goat's range, he can be seen with more predictable success than any other big game animal—with perhaps the exception of bears on a major salmon spawning stream. For persons physically incapable of foot travel in rugged terrain, an easy and enjoyable way of seeing mountain goats is by boat trip into one of the mainland inlets of coastal British Columbia and Southeastern Alaska. In Southeastern Alaska, the Tracy Arm-Fords Terror area, Endicott Arm, Cleveland Peninsula and Boca de Quadra south of Behm Canal are recommended as particularly good goat observation areas.

For seeing goats at close range during the summer and early fall, you should generally figure on hiking

A young mountain goat follows his mother — just out of the frame — down a steep series of ledges on a ridge overlooking the White River drainage, northern Cascade Range, Washington, in mid-July.

up to snow line. Goats love to play and rest on glaciers and snowfields for relief from summer heat.

Late in July in the northern Cascade Range, I once climbed up to a band of 27 mountain goats lying on a shrinking snowbank in a saddle between two peaks. Just about all the available space on the snow was occupied. As I eased cautiously up toward them to try for still closer photos, the goats stood up and moved off leisurely in a single-file climbing traverse up a rugged slope bordering the saddle. Closely inspecting their bedding area, I found that the lanolin from the goat's hair gave the snow a slick, oily feeling to the touch. The snowbank was also marked by a very definite—but not unpleasant—odor, a scent no more "gamey" than that of elk.

Only the eagle can follow the mountain goat in his toughest terrain, and on rather rare occasions the eagle does manage to catch a young kid far enough away from his fiercely defensive mother. But snow avalanches in the spring and late fall, rather than any predator, are the greatest single hazard the goat faces. Often the first meat the mountain grizzly feeds on after coming out of his semi-hibernation is an avalanche-killed goat, and he will excavate tons of rock and snow to get at a carcass.

Back in '61 I made an early April trip into the British Columbia Selkirks to photograph the mountain goat, the grizzly and the spectacular and deadly spring avalanches. I was working out of the Glacier Station area about midway between Revelstoke and Golden, British Columbia. One memorable day, I was making a snowshoe traverse, climbing toward Rogers Pass, above the snowbound grade of the last unfinished link of the Trans-Canada Highway. It was a pleasant morning, about 60 degrees, sunny, but with a misty overcast shrouding the great peaks overlooking the Rogers summit.

Nearing the pass, I sighted eight mountain goats browsing on willow tips high on a rugged slope above me. Several stopped feeding a few moments to watch me. Without thinking about it, I raised a hand in

A stone sheep ewe looks down from the crest of a spectacularly rugged ridge (excellent escape terrain) in the Cassiar Mountains of the Stikine Plateau, northern British Columbia, in mid-October.

greeting, just deeply feeling the warmth of meeting again an old and respected friend.

Minutes later I dropped down to the grade at the summit of the pass. The snow was more settled and fairly firm here, so I unstrapped and kicked out of the webs. I felt a slight wind against my face, and I looked up at the overcast that was beginning to move across the upper slopes. Then, as I watched the clouds, I heard a sound from far above me. It was a muted rumble like distant thunder, or a flight of jet fighters at high altitude.

Lost in the spooky, wreathing clouds of the heights, the sound was building. It was the start of an avalanche. The late morning sun had broken the delicate balance between friction and gravity; now thousands of tons of snow and timber debris were gathering speed on the face of the mountain. It now sounded almost directly above me, but I wasn't ready with the cameras and there wasn't going to be time to get ready.

Moments later through the shifting mist, I saw it, coming in a crashing swath like storm breakers on a beach. Then, well below my direct line of vision, I just caught another movement. It was the goats. Uncasing binoculars, I picked them up in the field. They were in a traversing climb, going as fast as I've ever seen goats move, but **toward** the apparent route of the slide. Then I saw the great quartzite buttress that jutted from the slope, and realized where they were headed.

A cross wind was pushing the mist, and in a few seconds the goats were lost from view. The sound of the avalanche had grown to a roar. The slide hit a pocket, geysered up like an explosion, poured over the rim, and funneled into a steep ravine. Beside this gorge, partially obscured in mist, stood the great shoulder of rock.

The overcast thinned and swirled in the wind, briefly parted, and there were the goats. Eight of them stood on successive ledges, safe but scant feet from the slide. In a tableau of timeless drama and beauty they stood still, calmly watching the roaring, plunging maelstrom of snow.

Gripped by the impact of the scene, I stood fascinated. But the thought finally came, **get going, she's coming all the way!**

I grabbed up the snowshoes. Maybe a guy can't sprint with webs under his arm, pack on his back and binoculars flopping on his chest, but I did the best I could.

The avalanche boomed across the road grade, plunged into the Stony Creek gorge, billowed into clouds as it hit the creek bed and thundered up the opposite slope on its momentum.

Moments later, when the last rumbling echoes were stilled, I walked back and looked at the great ridge of snow and debris across the grade —snow compacted by the velocity of the avalanche, laced with boughs, bark and shards of splintered fir trunks. I looked up at the great stone buttress. The goats were moving off their ledges and calmly starting to browse again. For a few moments, two young billies butted each other in playful sham combat. Perhaps man, with his neuroses from this dangerous age can learn something from mountain goats!

In late afternoon after photographing several smaller slides, I tightened my web bindings, and headed back down toward the valley of the Illecillewaet River and Glacier Station. I was still thinking about the goats. From the sound in the high overcast, they couldn't have known just where the slide was coming. But they did know one safe place on that face of the mountain. They had known where to go, and, with the composed courage of their kind, they had watched as the greatest danger of their lives passed within a few feet of them.

I stopped a few moments and looked up at them browsing on the slope, big and shaggy in their full winter coats.

Take care of yourselves, I thought.

Afterword: The Unpredictables, Then and Now

For about a mile now we'd trailed him, through the shadows of the pine-spruce forest, over crusted, shrinking drifts of residual snow, over drying needle duff, grass and kinnikinnick, and the rounded, scoured boulders of an ancient glacial moraine. Now the grizzly stopped again; the great head turned to look over the shaggy shoulder. We stood still. The bear sat ponderously down, facing us, in good light now in the more-open pine stand only 20 yards from the river bank. We stepped a few yards closer. The grizzly's head began to move slowly back and forth. A 60-degree mid-April breeze ruffled the deep fur of his coat. His jaws opened slightly. He was panting like a great dog. Through the ground glass viewfinder of my camera I could see his teeth and the grayish gums, the bits of bark clinging to his face from rotting logs he had searched under. From the point from where we'd first seen him — crossing the river ice downstream, he had traveled slowly up-valley as we followed him, neither spooked by us nor seemingly angry. . . . but from the first he had clearly registered his awareness.

I looked up from the tripod-mounted camera and over at my companion, 16-year-old Tom Bell, who had asked to come along on this one-day trip to "do something different" after finishing, a few days before, a season of downhill and slalom competition in the Alberta Junior Ski Racing Program. I'd just returned from three weeks of wolf survey work in the wilderness valley of the upper Snake Indian River to rest a couple of days and reprovision. The main objective of this little jaunt had been to check out an old wolf denning area in the upper Tekarra Valley.

Tom, grinning with excitement, was shooting pictures hand-holding a 135mm telephoto. I looked back at the grizzly through my viewfinder, triggered the shutter, levered the film advance, framed for another shot . . . then saw something that completely caught my attention. The grizzly suddenly reached forward with both front paws, grasped the trunk of a young Douglas fir — about a nine-footer, pulled it to him, took the tree in his jaws, shook it violently, then

crunched off the crown. Something about the action bothered me. Displaced aggression? Had I missed a sign before, some more subtle warning? It appeared that we'd stalked too close to this bear, and that we'd trailed him too long. The element of calculated risk is part of my job, but I felt concerned now that I may have let Tom get into a bad spot.

"You see that, John?" Tom said softly.

"Yeah, and I don't like it. Didn't think we were really pushing him, Tom, but that guy's beginning to get owly. He's just about had it with us. What we better do now is just stroll slow and easy over to the bank, and then downriver on the ice."

"Okay, you bet."

Without looking back at the resting grizzly we walked with prickly deliberation over to the river bank, edged carefully down a short, steep pitch, walked out on the river ice, and headed downstream.

Then. . . . *huuaahhh!* came a huffing snort, and we looked back to see the bear coming down the bank in two heavy bounds, then hesitating momentarily as he hit the ice.

"What th' hell . . . ?!" Tom said. "Should we go for a tree?"

"No, no! Just keep walkin' . . . best thing to do now. Probably a bluff and won't be any trouble." But I wasn't so sure.

From the time we'd stepped out on the ice we hadn't slowed or quickened the deliberate pace of our walk.

Then, in an incredible instant, the grizzly caught up to us in a bounding rush, stopped within a dozen feet . . . then fell into step just behind, walking paw for boot with us on the ice, moving up as close as seven or eight feet, sometimes dropping back to 20. Curiously, neither Tom nor I felt during those moments what most people probably think of as tension or fear. There just wasn't time. Things were **happening now**. It was, rather, a kind of wild, adrenalin-surging excitement.

I'd half-expected to meet a grizzly on this brief wolf den-survey trip, and I'd gone over with Tom the

169

protective procedure to use if a grizzly did close in a charge and actual contact and possible mauling appeared likely — the best thing to do is drop to the ground, draw your body into a tight ball, and interlace your hands over the back of your neck, thus giving maximum protection under the circumstances to the most vulnerable portion of your spine and to your abdominal area (see Chapter Four, *Getting Along With Grizzlies*). I don't carry firearms unless I've been advised of a special situation (see Chapter Six, *The Brown Bears of Pack Creek*) and here Tom and I were in the back-country of Jasper National Park where, of course, firearms are prohibited.

Our wildly improbable trio had walked down the Athabasca River ice about 250 yards. And now, strangely, through some unconscious mental process — talking about it later Tom and I came to the conclusion that our feelings during the experience were very much the same — whatever apprehension we may have felt became a kind of exhilaration. The situation, while precarious, was certainly not out of control. We were both beginning to breathe easier (Tom and I, that is, . . . I have an idea the grizzly was breathing pretty easy all the time!), and I felt that we were doing exactly the right thing in those particular circumstances.

I'd been surprised — though I certainly shouldn't have been — when the grizzly had bounded down the bank after us. I'd felt that any aggressive action the bear might take against us would occur within the first few steps after we turned away from him and walked toward the river. But I felt now that if the grizzly had really wanted to injure us, he would have taken us on as soon as he came down the bank onto the river ice. I believed, too, that just so we kept walking down the ice at this steady, easy pace — as long as we didn't abruptly quicken our steps, or one of us didn't slip on the ice — that there was no real problem, and we'd be okay.

It had been a fair hike through the forest following the grizzly — we'd first seen him as he crossed on the ice downstream while we were talking to two fishermen who were successfully working a swift, open run in the eroding ice for Dolly Varden, rainbow trout and whitefish. We'd trailed the bear for about a mile up-valley, and I wondered now how far we were by the river route from the two fishermen. I didn't think we needed any help, but was hoping they had cameras and would get pictures of this incredible threesome — these two gypsies and their pet bear! Strange as it may seem, we were getting used to him walking behind us.

Not another sound had come from the grizzly since the huffing snort he'd made as he bounded ponderously down the river bank. With the easing of the emotional impact of the situation, I was now starting to reflect on the experience and to wonder just what the hell was actually going on. It was much too simplistic, I felt, to believe that the bear was just giving it back to us, that he was doing to us exactly what he may have felt we'd done to him. Or was it?

"How you doin'?" I asked Tom.

"Hey, no sweat," he said quietly, but actually smiling, some of the downhill racer's cockiness beginning to come out again. "You know, this is really sort of cool — just hiking along on the ice with that bear right on our butts."

I laughed softly. "Yeah, it's cool, all right."

Another 150 yards down the river ice with the bear — as the saying goes — nearly stepping in our hip pockets. Then, almost as surprising as his bounding descent of the river bank, the bear turned abruptly away from us toward mid-river. Relieved and very puzzled, I wondered, why right here? Suddenly wanting to play a hunch, I waited until he was about 50 yards from us, then started walking across **behind him.** The grizzly heard my steps. He stopped. The great head looked over the shaggy shoulder.

Then the bear turned back toward me in swift, shoulder-rolling strides. Easy, easy, I thought. My pulse was thumping, but I turned with carefully casual slowness, and walked again downstream after Tom. A few moments and a hundred feet or so later I looked back. The grizzly had again turned away and was headed back across the river. I spoke aloud in wonder. "Well, looks like that guy's made his point."

Then near mid-channel the rotting, honeycombed ice over the main current gave way. The grizzly fell through with a great, geysering splash, for a moment powerfully treaded the current, quickly climbed out on stronger ice, stood there a few moments shaking his coat in a mist of spray, then padded on across the ice and gravel bars until he disappeared in the forest beyond.

As I usually work alone and unarmed, I've often pondered the psychological aspects of dealing day by day with potentially dangerous wild animals. **Psychological** conditioning for such encounters is, I feel, at least as important as hard physical conditioning for wilderness travel. Many factors favorably or adversely affect one's mental attitude in the wilderness as elsewhere. For example, the anxiety a person experiences when lost or injured while alone temporarily changes his attitude toward the wilderness and its wildlife, and this I believe is sensed by wild animals. A more subtle, but perhaps still discernable — to a grizzly, say — change in attitude occurs with the half-aggressive-half fearful feeling of an armed individual projecting the thought 'if he tries to get tough with me I'll bust him.'

There have been times on my field projects when meeting the same grizzly that I'd worked with before at close range — and would again a day or two later — that I would let him or her alone on **that** particular day. Why? Sometimes there's a definite behavior sign that I read — such as the mauling by the grizzly of the young fir tree. And other times it's just a vague apprehension or intuition that I really can't tie to any particular action on the bear's part.

While, in the field of parapsychology, there are university studies concerning extrasensory communication between persons, conducted at such renowned institutions as Duke University and Stanford, there is no serious research going on — as far as I've been able to determine — concerning communication of this nature between humans and other species. There doesn't seem to be enough "hard" — i.e., scientifically acceptable — evidence to support it.

Nevertheless, I'm convinced myself that there **is** a form of extrasensory communication between humans and certain other species, and that animals, in varying degree, perceive our attitudes toward them. I also believe that wild animals — particularly grizzlies — somehow sense that though I'm an intruder in their country I'm still not a threat to them. And I believe that the fact that when afield I unconsciously project an attitude that is neither fearful nor threatening is a major reason I'm still alive.

If I may digress for a moment from the wilderness bush to Suburbia, there is considerable evidence that dogs have powers of extrasensory perception. As a breed, this would appear to be most true of the Alsatian (German shepherd), though the most remarkable individual dog I've ever known for this capability was an Australian shepherd. Some of these dogs have demonstrated this faculty — particularly in incidents involving grave danger to persons they were deeply attached to, hundreds of miles away — in ways that even the most doubting cynics would find hard to dismiss.

A curious related incident, both humorous and baffling — that I'll say at the outset is only an example to ponder, and proves absolutely nothing — was an experience of my long-time friend, Clifford B. Gooby, now an engineer-sales executive for Cole Industrials of Lynnwood, Washington. At that time, April 1964, Cliff was managing a camera store in Seattle's Northgate Shopping Center. Cliff, an avid pheasant hunter in the autumn, had brought his dog — a Springer spaniel — to work that day, thinking that a lunch hour walk in a nearby wooded area would help keep the dog's nose tuned, as well as being relaxing exercise for them both.

While Cliff worked on inventory records in his office at the rear of the store, the dog dozed in a chair beside him. Suddenly Cliff's concentration was broken by a rumbling growl from his dog. Looking up, Cliff saw the Springer with head raised, tautly alert. In the next instant the dog leaped from the chair, shot out of the office, and dashed around two corners into the main — or customer service — store area. Perplexed and startled, Cliff sprinted after his dog and arrived in the sales room to witness his pet with her jaws gripping a customer's leg just above the ankle. The man was standing absolutely still. The dog's teeth hadn't broken the skin nor torn the man's slacks. She released instantly at Cliff's angry command.

Acutely embarrassed, apologizing for his dog's behavior, Cliff handed the customer his insurance cards, telling him that if he wanted to bring legal suit — on grounds of "emotional trauma" — to go ahead. This gentleman, a most reasonable sort and not one to overreact, declined.

Cliff shook his head. "This is sure a strange one," he remarked to the customer. "Where she was in my office she couldn't see you. . . . she had to run around two blind corners to get out here! You know, the only other person she's ever bitten or even tried to bite was our mailman. Had a helluva time breaking her, though, and the mailman just refused to make deliveries for a while — we had to pick up our mail at the post office. But I finally got her to leave him alone."

The customer, visibly shaken, stared for a long moment. "I live quite a way from here," he said finally. "Your dog and I have never seen each other before. But you know something? **I'm a mailman.**"

If this mailman-customer had been wearing his working uniform, it would be reasonable to assume that the dog was reacting to a scent stimulus — the olfactory equipment of canines is vastly more sensitive and discerning than that of humans — to the subtle but discernible scent of packaged mail or other residual odor of post office material clinging to his clothing. But, as the man was wearing leisure street clothes, the case becomes intriguing and baffling.

On several occasions during my recently concluded 11-winter wolf study and photo project — in the Canadian Rockies, interior Alaska, northern Saskatchewan, and the Cassiar Mountains of northern British Columbia — I've encountered wolves that seemed unafraid of me, that looked at me with what seemed a curious interest and a bold, almost regal confidence — though with no evidence whatever of hostility — before walking or trotting off on their way.

Before starting my wolf project in the Canadian Rockies in 1968 I'd seen wolves in Southeastern Alaska and in Alaska's subarctic interior, but never more than four or five together. My first sighting of a large pack (and at close quarters!) — in this case 11 wolves that I saw, and there may have been one or more others screened by the timber — was in early March in the upper valley of Alberta's Snake Indian River when snowshoeing, traveling up-river against a light wind, I crested a rise in the trail to see a big grizzled-black wolf trotting toward me on the crusted snow. Both of us stopped instantly and stared at each other, while more wolves of both light and dark color phases trotted up behind him. For long seconds the wolves and I stood still, the pack posed dramatically against a backdrop of snow-laden spruces, while we looked at each other in mutual surprise and, in my case, utter fascination. I first realized then that a healthy wolf in winter coat condition is one of the world's most beautiful animals — far more so, in my opinion, than the largest and most impressive of domestic dogs.

Then, definitely not spooked, the wolves simply continued their travel downriver, just moving off the trail a few yards into the timber, six wolves passing me on one side and five on the other. I've seen larger packs since then — up to 17 wolves, but that first pack encounter was one of the greatest thrills I've ever experienced in the bush.

Whether non-rabid wolves have ever really attacked human beings in North America is still a question on which I've found wide speculation among bush residents of western Canada and Alaska. It is a question that likely may never have a definitive answer. In my opinion, however, no really valid conclusions can be drawn from the observations of continuing wolf-human encounters in such wildlife reserves as Algonquin Provincial Park, Ontario, and Mount McKinley National Park, Alaska. Things have changed too much for both wolves and men during the centuries since the early colonization of North America by European settlers.

There can be no question that the many decades of persecution of the wolf at the hands of man — by means of firearms, traps and poison — have in some degree altered the wolf's behavior. The writings of Francis Parkman, George Catlin, Lewis & Clark, and George Frederick Ruxton among others all strongly suggest that the wolf didn't have the fear of man in the early decades of the 19th century that he generally does today.

While there are exceptions — most notably Canada's Wood Buffalo National Park in northern Alberta and Northwest Territories — our national parks are generally too small to truly represent the wildlife ecology of 200 or so years ago on this continent. Not all wildlife refuges contain sufficient winter range habitat for all mammal species that are late spring through autumn residents, and some animals have to leave the sanctuaries to find winter food — the north Yellowstone elk herd is a classic example. A chronic problem of several northern wildlife sanctuaries is lack of funds for winter air and ground patrols to combat poaching. It was little publicized at the time, but when wolves were bountied in Alaska's subarctic interior, airborne hunters in winter shot wolves in McKinley National Park and landed with ski-equipped aircraft to recover the hides for sale and bounty. Greater numbers of people as recreational visitors penetrating even the most remote areas of national parks tend to produce stress in certain species — particularly, among ungulates, caribou, and, among carnivores, wolves — which are greatly disturbed by human intrusion into their denning and rendezvous site areas during the early life of the pups. Wildlife researchers themselves, to a degree, harass species of wildlife they are studying with their continuous and sometimes intrusive observation, and by their tranquilizing of animals with drugged darts to measure, weigh, lip-tattoo, ear-tag, and, perhaps, radio-collar them. In short, even within their supposed sanctuaries wild animals are today harassed and manipulated by humans.

Before the westward migration of white settlers, aboriginal hunting — aside from that directed against small isolated animal populations in higher mountain pockets and in desert areas — probably had a very minimal effect. It can be reasonably assumed that wildlife populations of both ungulates and predators tended, relatively, to be much more stable on the vast sweep of North American prairie (or Great Plains) than in mountain, forest and desert habitat to the north and west. But if there ever is an actual "balance of nature" in any ecosystem it is of short duration. The dynamics of predator-prey inter-action are shifting constantly.

During primitive times in years of drought, undoubtedly vast lightning-strike forest fires raged unchecked to be finally put out by the rains of autumn. On the excellent feed of fire succession plant growth, large populations of ungulates and — quickly building following prey population abundance — predators rose and, just as inevitably, fell when this food supply disappeared. This would, rather briefly, result in a comparatively large population of predators with insufficient available prey animals to sustain them. Moving out of the area, perhaps desperately hungry, wolves quite likely would attack and kill each other for food — as they have been known to do after killing off blacktail deer populations on islands off the British Columbia coast — and might well attack other species that are not normally their prey, such as bears.

In normal circumstances, I believe that the upright walking silhouette of a man suggests to the wolf — and always has suggested — another and superior predator. I'm convinced that the only reason a non-rabid wolf would ever attack a human would be extreme hunger — the total absence of available prey animals in an area, definitely **not** for any of the classic reasons the grizzly attacks humans — anger generated by surprise in a confrontation, territorial intrusion (particularly concerning the intruder's approach of the grizzly's food, such as a winter-killed moose or elk carcass), and the intruder posing an apparent threat to the grizzly's young. Curiously, however, wolves have actually been known to attack grizzlies for these very reasons.

As far as my personal feeling goes, I believe that the only danger to me in wolf country is from its weather and terrain-hypothermia and the ever present chance of a broken leg. But I know old-timers, both Indian and white, who have lived their entire lives in the bush of western Canada and Alaska who firmly believe that non-rabid wolves have attacked humans in recent times.

I think it is fair to say that we cannot entirely discount the statements of early pioneers and explorers of this possible aspect of the wolf's total behavior range. There is no doubt whatever that non-rabid sled dogs have attacked and killed humans, and wolves did, as a matter of recorded historical fact, feed on the bodies of smallpox victims and casualties of the Indian wars. I believe that while non-rabid wolves attacking humans was likely a very rare occurrence even in the early years of North American exploration and settlement two-and-a-half centuries ago, I feel that it is a quite reasonable assumption that it did on occasion happen.

Working in even the most remote regions of North America it is difficult now to mentally project oneself back to the time of the European explorers, the mountain men-fur trappers, and of the settlers trying to wrest a living from the land when most of this continent was wilderness — back to an unforgiving reality of lean provisions and overpowering loneliness of snowbound isolation during bitter winters. During my years of wilderness work with grizzlies, wolves and other northern wildlife, I've known minor hardship, frostbite and bone fractures in unforgiving country. And there have been times when I've gotten pretty hungry. But always somebody — outfitter, ranger, warden, Mountie or bush pilot — knew where I had gone and when I was due out. And I knew that on a particular day — weather and other circumstances permitting — that Beaver, Super Cub or Cessna would be picking me up.

To the early explorer, trapper, or frontier settler it was generally very much up to him to try to get himself out of trouble when bad luck hit. Nowadays when an aircraft goes down in the bush, a massive aerial search is launched. When an injured climber is trapped on a precarious ledge, a team of mountain rescue experts — aided when necessary by the latest in sophisticated equipment, such as a helicopter with a steel-cabled winch — brings the climber down. When a small boy, on a fishing trip with his parents, becomes lost in the dense forest surrounding a mountain lake, a sherrif's posse, search and rescue personnel from various organizations, individual volunteers, and an expert professional tracker with bloodhounds all work in a coordinated effort to find him. The point I'm getting to here is that today we enter wild backcountry with a psychological armor that the early North American explorers, mountain men, and settlers didn't have (besides, of course, topographical maps of the area showing terrain features, drainage patterns, access trails, etc.!).

We have the knowledge today that if we do get in trouble the chances are very good that we'll be bailed out, or — at the grim very least! — that there will be people trying to find out what happened to us. And this knowledge in a person of reasonable courage and confidence, gives the individual an attitude that **in itself** promotes a considerable degree of safety in a confrontation with a potentially dangerous wild animal.

A strange encounter from my own experience

might help to illustrate this point. At the time in mid-April 1970, I was studying and photographing wolves in the wilderness valley of the upper Snake Indian River in the Alberta Rockies. Late one afternoon I was hiking through lodgepole pine and spruce forest headed up the valley toward a large muskeg meadow that I wanted to watch that evening — from an hour or so before sunset through dusk. On that muskeg, the week before over several evenings, I'd seen a cow moose with a calf, five wolves, and a grizzly at different times.

Now I was walking fast through the forest in the dappled patterns of sunlight and shadow over the needle-carpeted earth and the shrinking drifts of residual snow. To the west the low, flat rays of the late afternoon sun shone through broken cloud cover. Suddenly, just audible at two split-second intervals, I heard the cushioned impact of springing weight striking moss and pine needles. I whirled. Almost magically, right beside me, was a cougar.

He was less than 10 feet away, tail switching, big front paws flexing, pushing against the mossy earth. His jaws opened in a single hiss. Then not a sound.

Stunned with surprise, I stood motionless for a long, disbelieving moment. Then, recovering composure, I looked at this beautiful animal in delighted wonder. Over years and hundreds of rugged hiking miles I'd bruised my shins and blistered my feet searching the mountain bush of British Columbia, Alberta and five western states for just such a chance as this! And I'd seen just 11 in the wild. I spoke quietly to the cougar and immediately gave him the name of a favorite pet cat at home. "It's okay, Snuffy," I said. "It's okay."

Then apparently bewildered, the cougar sat down in front of me and regarded me with the same intense interest with which I was looking at him. Even in the taut circumstances I almost laughed. The young cougar was baffled. In all probability he was looking for the first time at a man — at a strange big animal the likes of which he'd never before seen. I was wearing an originally tan-colored parka and pack, both of which had weathered over the years to a light buff color. My broken silhouette moving through the timber had, quite likely, suggested a deer or an elk.

"It's okay, Snuffy," I said again, and slowly I leaned over, not taking my eyes off the cougar, and set my tripod-mounted lens and reflex camera against a mossy boulder. The cat was so close that this telephoto lens could not have been focused on him.

Slowly, as smoothly as I could, I reached for the small "grab-shot" camera hanging on my chest, unsnapped the leather case — always watching the cougar. But now he turned. He'd finally become spooked. He moved as gracefully as drifting smoke back into the forest, swiftly, but not quite breaking into a trot. And I followed him for about 50 yards, talking to him constantly — trying to keep him in sight a few moments longer, shooting what pictures I could of his retreating backside and tail. But then, with one great floating leap over a tangle of windfalls he vanished in the shadowed timber.

What could have happened if someone psychologically unconditioned for travel alone in the wilderness bush had encountered the cat and had panicked and run at the cougar's rush? Well, he's one of "the unpredictables," and what could have happened is open to some speculation.

However slight, there is an element of hazard involved in meeting "the unpredictables" on their terms, in their home — the northern wilderness. But to put things in perspective, I believe that with common sense, reasonable courage and confidence, and respect and love for wilderness country and its inhabitants, that one is far safer working for months at a time in the wildest remaining areas of North America than he would be dealing day by day with urban traffic — either as a motorist or a pedestrian.

Epilogue

I'm sitting at my Royal Portable — which looks, after years of traveling with me to unlikely northern places, like it hadn't quite survived an air drop — hopefully for the last time for a few weeks. Before I started on this project I couldn't realistically imagine the work involved in preparing a book for publication, nor, I suppose, could anyone else who hasn't been through the process.

I'm leaving shortly to work on a grizzly bear photo assignment in British Columbia I've taken on at the request of a New York publisher, and after that I want to pack it in for awhile and think things over. And somewhere, not too far from wilderness, perhaps coastal British Columbia or Southeastern Alaska, I want to get my own little place and put down some roots.

It is cool and raining lightly today in this small pleasant town — just north of Seattle on Puget Sound, and perhaps helped by the rain itself, and the fact that the preparation of the book is indeed done — after seemingly interminable weeks, the memories of what it was like living in wilderness are coming back strong today. . . .

. . . The distant fall of water in a chasm that, as you lie in the sleeping bag just before dropping off, you sometimes can't quite tell from the soughing of the night wind through the firs. . . . after days of sub-zero cold in the Rockies, the smell and feel of a chinook wind in the morning . . . the first sight of a mountain crocus by a snowbank in early April . . . the taste of water from the moss and pebbles of an alpine meadow pool . . . the whispering hiss of powder snow driven by fitful winds against the cabin windows on a February night . . . the good, resiny smell of a pine forest as dusk falls on a warm day . . . the tunking drop of spruce cones on your tent . . . from 40 yards the incredible challenge bugle of a bull elk on a frosty September dawn in the British Columbia Rockies. . . . on a star-lit 30-below January night on the Chaba, the wild singing of the wolf pack rising chord on chord. . . . and that small lake on an upper Susitna tributary in the chill of early evening in the hauntingly lovely, much-too-brief sub-arctic autumn, with the gold of aspen against the dark green of spruces, the peaks of the Alaska Range — stark white in new snow — looming beyond, and over the lake the call of a loon carries softly through rising mist.

Edmonds, Washington
August 1980

John S. Crawford, author of *Wolves, Bears and Bighorns,* grew up near Sunnyside, Washington. A graduate of the University of Washington, he formerly worked for the U.S. Fish & Wildlife Service; he served in the U.S. Marine Corps, and later as a U.S. Army survival instructor. Crawford is now a free lance outdoor author, nature cameraman and wildlife researcher. Since 1966 his field work has been directed primarily toward the study of northern predator animals in western Canada and Alaska.

Among other magazines and newspapers, his wildlife articles and/or photographs have appeared in *ALASKA*® magazine, *Outdoor Life, Sunset, True, Field & Stream, National Geographic, ALASKA GEOGRAPHIC*®, *National Wildlife, The American Rifleman, The American Hunter, The Seattle Post-Intelligencer* and *The Seattle Times.* Crawford has contributed wildlife photos to nature books published by *Reader's Digest, National Geographic Society, Time, Inc., McGraw-Hill, Little-Brown, National Wildlife Federation, Lane Magazine and Book Company, Hurtig Publishing Company, Hancock House* and other publishers in North America and Europe. The text of his portfolio book *At Home With The High Ones* (Alaska Northwest Publishing Company, 1974), including some of its photographs, is one of the ten articles republished in *Wolves, Bears and Bighorns.*

His photos of northern wildlife have been used by the U.S. Forest Service, the Canadian Wildlife Service, the U.S. National Park Service, the National Museum of Canada, and, also in Canada, by the National and Historic Parks Branch of the Department of Indian Affairs and Northern Development.

John S. Crawford's photographic work on the wildlife of the northern Rockies was represented in *The Athapaskan Peoples: Strangers of the North,* an exhibition produced jointly by the National Museum of Canada and the Royal Scottish Museum, and shown in North America and Europe following its opening in the summer of 1974 in Edinburgh, Scotland.